T0279400

Named in remembrance of

the onetime *Antioch Review* editor

and longtime Bay Area resident,

the Lawrence Grauman, Jr. Fund

supports books that address

a wide range of human rights,

free speech, and social justice issues.

The publisher and the University of California Press Foundation gratefully acknowledge the generous support of the Lawrence Grauman, Jr. Fund.

The publisher and the University of California Press Foundation also gratefully acknowledge the generous support of the Anne G. Lipow Endowment Fund in Social Justice and Human Rights.

Why SNAP Works

Why SNAP Works

A POLITICAL HISTORY—AND DEFENSE—OF THE FOOD STAMP PROGRAM

Christopher Bosso

UNIVERSITY OF CALIFORNIA PRESS

University of California Press
Oakland, California

© 2023 by Christopher Bosso

Library of Congress Cataloging-in-Publication Data

Names: Bosso, Christopher J. (Christopher John), 1956- author.
Title: Why SNAP works : a political history-and defense-of the Food Stamp
    Program / Christopher Bosso.
Description: Oakland, California : University of California Press, [2023] |
    Includes bibliographical references and index.
Identifiers: LCCN 2023000939 (print) | LCCN 2023000940 (ebook) |
    ISBN 9780520392816 (cloth) | ISBN 9780520392823 (ebook)
Subjects: LCSH: Supplemental Nutrition Assistance Program
    (U.S.)—History. | Food stamps—Political aspects—United States—
    History. | Poverty—Political aspects—United States—History.
Classification: LCC HV696.F6 B68 2023 (print) | LCC HV696.F6 (ebook)
    | DDC 362.50973—dc23/eng/20230510
LC record available at https://lccn.loc.gov/2023000939
LC ebook record available at https://lccn.loc.gov/2023000940

Manufactured in the United States of America

32 31 30 29 28 27 26 25 24 23
10 9 8 7 6 5 4 3 2 1

To those who close that gap between want and plenty

Contents

Figures

Acknowledgments

Books are funny things. Ideas for them sometimes seem to come out of thin air, maybe inspired by a passage in a news article or a moment in time dimly recalled years later. While the proximate inspiration for this book was a Trump administration proposal for a box of food (as per chapter 1), the kernel of the idea for it goes back to a previous book, *Framing the Farm Bill* (University Press of Kansas, 2017), in which I detailed the surprising centrality of the Supplemental Nutrition Assistance Program in holding together—and almost blowing up—the nation's most important agriculture and food legislation. That book in turn was prompted by a talk I was asked to give in 2014 on farm-bill politics to a group of nutrition students. Researching that talk piqued my interest in the Farm Bill as a lens into US politics writ large—so much so that I dumped another project midstream. So there you go.

Having established what a book is about, then there is the question of how to go about it. Do I write for fellow scholars or the more general reader? Here I try to do a bit of both, although my scholarly colleagues will note that I devote my time trying to explain what happened, not proving any particular hypothesis. Nor is the book based on original scholarship in the strict sense. I did not spend weeks rifling through boxes in presidential libraries (even taking into account limits to what could be done during COVID); did not gather, clean, and analyze my own data; and did not hold extensive interviews with key stakeholders. On the other hand, I did scour every publicly available book, government document, scholarly study, and any other material that might help me to understand the origins, evolution, and current status of the nation's largest food-assistance program. Anyone wanting to "replicate" my findings can read those same materials. Whether they come to the same conclusions is another matter. After all, we approach the same facts through differing disciplinary lenses and personal values. While I try to be dispassionate in laying out the facts, I'm not dispassionate about what was or what should be.

I also stand, figuratively, on the shoulders of those whose scholarship on the history and politics of food stamps/SNAP and of food-assistance policy generally made this book possible, in particular political scientists Jeffrey Berry, Ronald King, and the late Ardeth Maney and sociologist Janet Poppendieck, whose foundational work on New Deal–era food relief stands apart. I also acknowledge the scholars of agricultural and food politics and policy, in particular fellow political scientists John Mark Hansen, Kenneth Finegold, John Ferejohn, Adam Sheingate, and the late William Browne, along with economists Diane Whitmore Schanzenbach, Parke Wilde, and James Ziliak, without whose work I could never understand the economics of food assistance. I likely left out more than a few others, for which (and to whom) I apologize, so check the bibliography. I send another shout-out to the journalists who cover food and agriculture, starting with Chuck Abbott, Helena Bottemiller Evich, Catherine Boudreau, Ximena Bustillo, Jason DeParle, and Jerry Hagstrom. That some of our most astute observers of food and agriculture now put out their own subscription-only newsletters or work for specialized outlets says much about the state of contemporary journalism, so please support them when you can.

I give special thanks to the several anonymous reviewers, whose feedback helped make this book better, even when I opted not to follow specific suggestions. Oh, and the usual disclaimer: while I relied heavily on the work of others, any errors or misinterpretations are entirely on me. There, I said it.

Thanks go to colleagues at Northeastern University, in particular Alicia Sasser Modestino, David Rochefort, and especially John Portz, whose keen eye for details saved me more than once. Don't tell anyone, but being a university professor is a great gig, in no small part because we get to be in a community of smart and interesting people on whom we can try out ideas. I'm also grateful for the feedback provided by Jeffrey Marshall of the University of Vermont, longtime friend and resident bibliophile, who would tell me when my writing was dreck. Also, thanks go to the research assistants and budding scholars who supported parts of this project, notably Giuliano Espino and Xena Itzkowitz.

I send a note of appreciation to the professionals at the University of California Press, starting with acquisitions editor Kate Marshall and extending to editorial assistant Chad Attenborough, production editor Francisco Reinking, and associate director of publicity Emily Grandstaff. I had targeted UC Press as my first choice because of its deep list on food policy and politics. I am so pleased that this book joins its ranks, one hopes without diminishing it. Any joy you get from this book benefited immeasurably from the labors of copyeditor Susan Silver and indexer Jen Burton, exemplars of the professionals who so often save authors from themselves.

And, finally, my special gratitude is for Marcia Goetsch, life partner and resident photographer, who understands more than most that academics and book writers (but I repeat myself) are temperamental sots on the best of days. To say I couldn't do it without you is cliché and inadequate.

1   *Tales at the Intersection of Want and Plenty*

There's a feeling that in a nation of abundance, where there is surplus food and, indeed, wasted food, that no one should go hungry.

—REP. BILL EMERSON, Republican from Missouri, 1990[1]

Not Just a Box of Food

Our tale begins with The Box. Okay, to be precise, it begins with a February 2018 proposal by the US Department of Agriculture (USDA) for an "America's Harvest Box" of "100 percent U.S. grown and produced food" to be delivered each month to eligible "food-insecure" US households as part of benefits obtained from the Supplemental Nutrition Assistance Program (SNAP)—formerly known as food stamps.[2] In this plan, said to be the brainchild of Secretary of Agriculture Sonny Perdue, the USDA would purchase at bulk discount shelf-stable products such as peanut butter, pasta, and canned vegetables and ship a prescribed mix to enrolled households in some yet unspecified manner. The cost of what was in The Box would be deducted from SNAP enrollees' monthly allotments, which otherwise come in the form of a dollar amount loaded onto an Electronic Benefits Transfer (EBT) debit card. Not coincidentally,

[1]

the idea for the Harvest Box was floated at the same time that the Trump administration proposed a set of program rules designed to cut the roughly $60 billion in annual SNAP spending by one-third over the next decade. White House Office of Management and Budget director Michael Mulvaney enthused about The Box: "What we do is propose that for folks who are on food stamps, part—not all, part—of their benefits come in the actual sort of, and I don't want to steal somebody's copyright, but a Blue Apron–type program where you actually receive the food instead of receive the cash. It lowers the cost to us because we can buy [at wholesale prices] whereas they have to buy it at retail. It also makes sure they're getting nutritious food. So we're pretty excited about that."[3]

A side note: other than conflating a box of dried and canned goods with a pricy fresh-food meal-kit service like Blue Apron, Mulvaney was imprecise—perhaps intentionally so—insofar that SNAP households do not get "cash" in the strict sense. Instead, as noted, they get a specified dollar amount deposited each month into their EBT debit cards to be used to purchase food—and, despite urban legends, *only* food—at over 250,000 participating retailers. In this regard, SNAP benefits technically are "in-kind," not cash.

Another side note: Mulvaney's reference to "food stamps" rather than the Supplemental Nutrition Assistance Program is telling. The federal government stopped using paper coupons after switching to debit cards two decades ago, and program advocates tend to avoid the term "food stamps" even as critics tend to stick to it. Both are aware of the political baggage of the old term, so their choice of labels is not incidental.

All right, one last side note: Mulvaney's statement that a prescribed mix of foods offered in The Box will ensure that SNAP

FIGURE 1. Farmers to Families food boxes. Source: US Department of Agriculture, as contained in US Government Accountability Office, *USDA Food Box Program: Key Information and Opportunities to Better Assess Performance*, GAO-21-353, September 2021, www.gao.gov/assets/gao-21-353.pdf, 7.

households are "getting nutritious food" presupposes that current program enrollees don't eat nutritionally adequate diets or that they have different diets than other Americans or that they simply don't know enough to purchase and prepare "good" foods. We'll unpack these assumptions later in this book.

In any case, Perdue's Harvest Box idea was denounced by nutritionists, hunger relief organizations, and, tellingly, food retailers as impractical, expensive, nutritionally deficient, and misguided. Critics equated The Box with Great Depression–era breadlines in which the needy stood for handouts of surplus agricultural commodities purchased by the federal government and distributed as charity through local relief agencies. A typical response came from Jim Weill, president of the Food Research and Action Center, a leading antihunger advocacy organization: "The president's budget proposes to replace in significant part the very successful current system of having SNAP enrollees use EBT cards to purchase food through grocery stores, supermarkets, farmers markets, and other normal commercial channels with a Rube-Goldberg designed system of commodity distribution via food boxes that will be administratively costly, inefficient, stigmatizing, and prone to failure, and that will return the country to Depression-era anti-hunger approaches."[4] (For any reader under the age of, say, sixty-five, a "Rube-Goldberg designed system," named after a mid-twentieth-century US editorial cartoonist and inventor, is one that seeks to perform a seemingly straightforward task—in this instance getting food to those who need it—in the most convoluted and impractical manner possible. Weill's depiction of The Box was intentional, but generationally anchored.)

At the same time, the Trump administration and most House Republicans were pushing an array of SNAP rules changes as Congress went through reauthorizing the Farm Bill, an omnibus (or "catch-all") legislative vehicle within which most federal agricultural *and* nutrition programs are nested—for reasons we'll get to soon enough.[5] In particular, they sought to restrict flexibility in applying program "workfare" rules and to require most able-bodied adults without dependents (ABAWDs, in bureaucrat-speak) to work at least twenty hours a week or be enrolled in state-authorized job-training programs to get any benefits. Proponents of the proposed rule argued that SNAP, or any social-welfare program for that matter, should not reduce incentives to work. Critics of the rule pointed out that many SNAP enrollees already worked but made too little money, lacked access to affordable day care, or lived in areas with few good employment opportunities and that the practical effect of inflexible work requirements would take food away from nearly a million needy people.[6]

A Land of (Too Much) Plenty

Meanwhile, the Trump administration was locked in disputes with major US trading partners, the effects of which were beginning to pinch the nation's export-dependent agricultural sector.[7] Soybeans piled up all over the Midwest grain belt as China reacted to new US tariffs on their manufactured goods—taxes that raise the price of imports and whose costs ultimately are borne by consumers—by imposing tariffs on US agricultural commodities, particularly soy and corn used to feed animals. China also boosted soybean purchases from nations like Brazil, underscoring the interchangeability of such basic foodstuffs.[8] Mexico, stung by Trump's abrupt decision to scuttle the 1992 North American Free Trade Agreement, already had slapped new tariffs on US pork. Similar retaliations came from India against US apples and out of the European Union, which targeted products from areas represented by top congressional Republicans—symbolically, Kentucky bourbon, from the home state of Senate majority leader Mitch McConnell.[9] Taken together, these retaliatory actions hurt exports of US food products.

All the while, US farmers just kept on producing. Given the perverse logic of agricultural economics, most had little choice. A crop of Iowa corn planted in April *will* be harvested in October and eventually *will* be sold at whatever price can be obtained on global commodity markets, potentially at a loss, unless other ways can be found to use it up at a favorable price. To offer but one example, when the Energy Policy Act of 2005 mandated the blending of plant-based ethanol in gasoline, it was obvious that Congress meant as much to use up more corn and support corn growers as to lessen the nation's dependence on imported petroleum—likely more.[10] The dilemma is worse for perishable commodities like fruits, meat, dairy, and eggs, which, unless properly processed and stored, go bad rather quickly. Farmers need to keep producing to offset their sunk costs, if nothing else, so *someone* needs to buy all that food.

The combined results of largely unrestrained production and the effects of Trump's trade wars worsened already problematic surpluses on a range of commodities, from soy and pork to apples and milk—and even bourbon—that further depressed bulk prices, shrank producer revenues, and threatened to hurt a key part of Trump's electoral base. In response the administration sent to farmers some $16 billion in "trade mitigation payments"—which critics called little more than outright handouts to already well-off producers. It also more than doubled spending, from $758 million to $1.95 billion, on The Emergency Food Assistance Program (TEFAP), through which the USDA uses taxpayer dollars to purchase and distribute surplus agricultural commodities (except bourbon) to the nation's network of food banks, which in turn supply a vast array of food pantries and other agencies serving millions who need food.[11] (TEFAP, first authorized by Congress in 1983, once stood for the *Temporary* Emergency Food Assistance Program but is now essentially permanent. We'll talk more about that in chapter 5.)

All of this was *before* COVID-19 swept the country in March 2020 and closed tens of thousands of schools, hotels, restaurants, and businesses and with them long-established markets for agricultural commodities even as everyone rushed to their grocery stores to stock up for the unknown—only to find threadbare shelves. There *was* plenty of food around, but it wasn't always in the right place. The pandemic's economic havoc also pushed millions into sudden food insecurity, even actual hunger. Families living paycheck to paycheck suddenly found themselves out of jobs and in their cars at pop-up food-distribution centers. The sharp surge in need soon led the federal government to ramp up spending on its various food-assistance programs, from SNAP to TEFAP to, yes, a "Farmers to Families" food box, the pandemic version of Sonny Perdue's Harvest Box containing food that might otherwise go to waste for the lack of a market.[12]

At the Intersection of Want and Plenty

Okay, you must be asking by now, *What do these tales have in common?*

Glad you asked. At one level they all relate to an agricultural production system often awash in soy, corn, dairy, and pork—even cranberries.[13] Those in China, India, and Mexico who buy US agricultural commodities usually can get them elsewhere—Canadian cranberries, anyone?—and decisions they make to reduce imports from the United States means more unsold commodities at home. And, despite our renowned portion sizes and all-you-can-eat buffets, even we Americans can only eat so much. Unsold food, unlike unsold oil or steel, eventually goes to waste. Hence, The Box, and the boost in TEFAP distributions during the pandemic. Both were designed to use up unsold farm output and prop up commodity prices as much as to help Americans who needed food.

More precisely, these episodes individually and together speak to a tension that has marked US agricultural and food policies— *they are not the same*—for a century: how to minimize or reduce seemingly endless surpluses generated by immensely productive

US farmers, keep commodity prices high enough to allow those farmers to get a "fair" price for their goods without making food *too* expensive for consumers, and, finally, ensure that no American goes hungry. We need food to be affordable even for those with low incomes, but not so cheap that farmers cannot make a decent living. In short, and even with a robust export market, we need to figure out ways for every American to be able to buy as much food as possible, one way or another.

Out of these tensions emerged the nation's largest, most expensive, least understood, most controversial and widely critiqued, and yet most consequential and resilient food-assistance program: food stamps, now the Supplemental Nutrition Assistance Program. A coupon-based scheme first devised in the Great Depression to enable the needy to "purchase" surplus farm commodities and revived in the early 1960s as a way to leverage the private marketplace to address pockets of hunger and malnutrition has since evolved into the nation's foundational food-assistance program, one that continues to be based on and defended within that nexus between abundance and need.[14] Or, as it was put in the 1930s, to address the "paradox of want amidst plenty."[15]

How did it get this way? And is this the best way to help those who need food? That's why we're here.

Tell Me a Story about Food Stamps

This book tells the story of the Supplemental Nutrition Assistance Program. In a larger sense it tells a story about the tension between how best to shield US farmers from price-depressing agricultural surpluses and how best to help Americans who need food, two conundrums typically, but not necessarily, linked together. Sonny

Perdue's much-mocked Harvest Box reflected a solution with a long pedigree in US food-assistance policy, one in which the federal government purchases otherwise unsold agricultural commodities and distributes them free to those in need through local governmental and charitable institutions.[16] *The Box.* Another solution, typical in most other affluent nations, is to supplement the incomes of the poor through direct cash assistance—"welfare"—so that they can buy more food in the retail marketplace.

As we will see, SNAP is neither direct food donation nor direct cash assistance. Instead, it is an ungainly—and ingenious—compromise. It also is a uniquely American policy response; no other nation anchors its food-assistance system in a similar manner.[17] How SNAP came to be in the first place, how it evolved over time, and how it continues to serve as the bedrock of US domestic food-assistance policy over six decades—more, if you go back to the program's Depression-era origins—is a story worth unspooling. Such an account would tell us a lot about the surprising interconnections between US agricultural and social-welfare policies and why our food-assistance system—from commodity donation to food stamps to subsidized school meals—is the way it is. Social scientists employ the term "path dependence" to describe how today's policies bear the imprints of past decisions.[18] US food-assistance policy, with its roots in the Great Depression of the 1930s, most certainly displays such imprints. While history may not repeat itself, as the saying goes, it sure does rhyme, and a recounting of the past helps us to understand why we do what we do in the here and now.

This being said, the story to come is not an exhaustive account of every action on or debate about the Food Stamp Program over its many decades. Such a detailed narrative would take many more

FIGURE 2. SNAP logo. Source: US Department of Agriculture, accessed February 18, 2023, www .myplate.gov/myplate-kitchen.

pages than I propose to write and—much as it pains me to say this—more than most of you likely care to read. Instead, I focus on key moments over time, vignettes that speak to a story of policy origins and evolution, all the while focused on a central question: How do we explain the survival and continued centrality of what is essentially a "welfare" program serving millions of low-income Americans? The answers may surprise some of you.

Nor is the analysis I offer in the final chapter an exhaustive evaluation of the program's workings and impacts, on which there is a vast scholarly literature. Instead, I draw insights from the many studies that speak to SNAP's impacts on nutrition and overall economic well-being. I readily cite those works in the notes and bibliography if you wish to go down any particular rabbit hole. There are many of them, I promise.

Enough throat clearing. Let's talk a bit about SNAP.

SNAP: A Primer

The Supplemental Nutrition Assistance Program—known officially as the Food Stamp Program until 2008—is by far the nation's largest government-funded food-assistance program, whether measured by annual budget or by numbers of people served.[19] Before the

COVID-19 pandemic hit in March 2020, federal spending on SNAP hovered around $60 billion annually, supplementing the food-purchasing power of around forty million Americans, or about 12 percent of the total population. In all, SNAP accounts for nearly two-thirds of all federal spending on nutrition, more than double the National School Lunch and Breakfast Programs combined.[20]

Like all federal food-assistance programs, SNAP is administered by the US Department of Agriculture, whose primary mission is to promote food production—and to get us to consume more of what is produced. As we will see, responsibility for food production *and* food assistance does not always coexist easily within the USDA's hallways or with agriculture's patrons in Congress. That the various federal food-assistance programs largely remain under the auspices of the agricultural establishment and not, say, the social-welfare community is more about agricultural politics than anything else. Whether that's good or bad for nutrition policy is something we'll consider later.

Those enrolled in SNAP typically are categorized as being "food insecure," a condition defined by the USDA as existing "whenever the availability of nutritionally adequate and safe foods or the ability to acquire acceptable foods in socially acceptable ways is limited or uncertain."[21] While conditions of food insecurity are most closely linked to income, they also can result from physical and mental impairment, limited access to adequate food-retail stores, and other individual or household factors.[22] Prior to the COVID-19 pandemic, this category encompassed roughly 13.8 million US households (about 10.5 percent of all), one-third of which experienced *very low* food security or a disruption in normal eating patterns due to limited resources at some time of the year.[23] Such conditions rapidly worsened with the dislocations generated by the pandemic, propelling SNAP spending to $80 billion in fiscal year 2020 and to nearly $114 billion in fiscal year 2021, in part due to temporary increases in maximum benefits levels for families with children (which expired in February 2023).[24] Historical data on SNAP enrollment and spending are in table 1 in the appendix, which also offers a timeline of key moments in program history.

SNAP is a means-tested entitlement program first formally authorized in the Food Stamp Act of 1964, although its conceptual origins go back to a surplus-commodity disposal program that ran from 1939 to 1943. Those who qualify under program rules are guaranteed benefits, in this case a specified dollar amount loaded onto a debit card that can be used only to purchase food.[25] If the number of households qualifying for SNAP benefits increases, so does program spending unless Congress caps its budget, which it has not done in decades.[26] While the USDA at the direction of Congress places some restrictions on SNAP use—no alcohol, no tobacco, no soap or paper goods, no hot prepared or "take-out" foods except under special circumstances (such as the elderly who cannot cook)—it otherwise gives enrollees freedom to use their SNAP dollars to buy whatever foods they wish at over 250,000 participating food retailers, from Walmart to the local convenience store. Benefit levels are based on a "Thrifty Food Plan" of two dozen food types (such as eggs, cheese, and dried beans), with the expectation that meals are prepared at home and calibrated based on net household income after deductions for basic living expenses and some assets (such as a car). The average benefit in mid-2021 was around $120 per person per month—about $1.40 per meal. Underlying assumptions in the Thrifty Food Plan about how low-income households prepare and eat food were revised in October

2021 for the first time since 2006, resulting in a roughly 21 percent increase in basic benefits—and program costs.[27]

Who does SNAP serve? Prior to the onset of the pandemic in March 2020, roughly 81 percent of SNAP households were classified as living in poverty, which in 2021 meant that a household of four had a total annual income below $26,500 (the threshold jumped to $30,000 in 2022 due to the inflationary effects of pandemic supply-chain disruptions and spikes in oil prices following the Russian invasion of Ukraine).[28] While over 60 percent of these households had some type of earned income, it was not enough to buy sufficient food through an entire month. Around 50 percent of SNAP households relied on Social Security retirement or supplemental disability benefits, while 7 percent received some form of federal or state cash "welfare," such as under the federal government's comparatively miniscule Transitional Assistance for Needy Families (TANF) program, spending on which is capped by law at $16 billion a year. Over 80 percent of SNAP households included children, the elderly, or someone with a disability. SNAP use was not unknown among the active military, particularly in households with children headed by low-paid junior-rank service members.[29] While most immigrant adults who are not yet naturalized citizens are ineligible, any children born in the United States—and thus "birthright" citizens—can obtain benefits for the household. Popular views about poverty notwithstanding, SNAP enrollees were as likely to live in rural areas as in cities, and two-thirds of SNAP households got benefits for three years or fewer.[30] The "typical" SNAP household, if there is one, was a working mother with children.[31]

SNAP is designed to be "counter-cyclical," with enrollment and benefits fluctuating with broader swings in employment and income. So, for example, SNAP worked as intended as COVID-19 shut down the economy and propelled millions of suddenly under- and unemployed people into sudden income *and* food insecurity. While the most immediate response came from the nation's network of food banks and food pantries, SNAP benefits soon kicked in for anyone eligible who applied—although many who were eligible did not apply, a story in itself. Congress added billions of dollars to expand SNAP benefit levels and extended "Pandemic EBT" benefits to many not otherwise eligible, notably families with children cut off from subsidized school meals.[32] As a result, rates of food insecurity remained stable through 2020–22.[33] In this regard, and despite being targeted to buying food, SNAP is as much an *income* supplement as a food supplement; in budget terms, it is now the federal government's second-largest antipoverty program for the nonelderly, just behind the Earned Income Tax Credit.[34]

Like many US social-welfare programs, SNAP is implemented through the states.[35] While the federal government funds all benefits and sets eligibility rules, states pay half of the program's administrative costs and in return are granted flexibility over procedures on applying for and renewing benefits (such as whether to require in-person interviews) and the stringency of work rules for able-bodied adults. Some states make it easier to obtain rightful benefits, and others make it harder, leading the fifty states to vary in the percent of technically eligible residents who actually enroll.[36] In fiscal year 2019, the most recent for which full data are available, the states of Delaware, Illinois, Oregon, and Washington enrolled nearly everyone who was eligible, while Wyoming enrolled only a little over half, so where you live matters.[37] States seeking to maximize enrollment tend to view federal SNAP dollars in stimulus terms, with estimates that each $1.00 in SNAP spending generates $1.50 to $1.70 in overall economic activity.[38] Finally, while SNAP directly helps millions in need of adequate nutrition, the tens of billions of SNAP dollars spent annually is a nontrivial, if indirect, taxpayer subsidy to food producers, processors, and retailers—even farmers.[39] That's a point to keep in mind as we proceed.

Not surprisingly, SNAP is controversial. To its critics, most of them more ideologically conservative, it is a form of "welfare" that creates perverse incentives against work and undermines individual moral character. They tend to push to impose stricter rules on who can obtain benefits, how much they can obtain, and for how long. To its defenders, most of them more ideologically liberal, SNAP augments the food-purchasing power of millions who simply do not earn enough to provide fully for their families, either because of personal circumstance or the vagaries of the capitalist market economy. They tend to push to make benefits more generous and easier to obtain. Critiques from both ends of the ideological spectrum that SNAP is as much "corporate welfare" for big food companies tend to get lost in debate.[40] The program's scale, combined with popular views of many of its enrollees as "undeserving," makes it an easy target. These debates often are infused with culturally freighted views on race and ethnicity, gender, and immigration status and reflect deep-rooted ideological disagreements over balancing individual responsibility with some notion of the common good.[41]

But SNAP never was meant to be an essential antipoverty program. In fact, its origins reside in a Great Depression–era effort to use up agricultural surpluses that deflated commodity prices and threatened farmers' ability to make a living. As we discuss in chapter 2, efforts to reduce surpluses by destroying crops and animals while hungry people queued in breadlines inflamed public sensibilities. Government purchase of surplus food for donation to the needy—The Box—was criticized as inefficient and of limited nutritional value, demeaning to those who had to stand in line for charity and unfair to local retailers who lost business whenever free food was handed out. After much consideration of their options, federal government experts, working with retailers, came up with the idea of having eligible households purchase orange stamps, which could be redeemed for any food at any participating store. For each dollar of orange stamps purchased, participants would get a "bonus" of fifty cents in blue stamps, which could be redeemed only on foods declared in surplus by the secretary of agriculture. The first food stamp program was rolled out in Rochester, New York, on May 16, 1939.

But how did SNAP evolve from a comparatively modest Depression-era effort to use up surplus agricultural goods to the nation's foundational food-assistance program, not to mention an essential antipoverty program? And why does SNAP survive, despite efforts in recent decades to pare back all forms of "welfare"? This book answers those questions by tracing SNAP's long journey, one of repeated encounters at that intersection between want and plenty.

How Our Story Unfolds

The story told over the next four chapters unfolds in a largely chronological form. In chapter 2 we examine the origins of food stamps in the late 1930s as a way to use up agricultural surpluses, support farmers, preserve market capitalism, and feed the hungry—in that order of stated priority. We look at the pathologies of agricultural production, the problem of surplus, and why a coupon system dreamed up by a small group of government and food-industry experts came to be seen as a politically viable alternative to government handouts of surplus foods on one hand and more cash assistance to the poor on the other. While the food stamp plan rolled out in 1939 proved more popular than contemporary views on welfare might suppose, it was phased out in 1943 as wartime demand shrank surpluses and as full employment reduced (but did not eliminate) hunger and undernutrition. Without the pressures of price-deflating surpluses, few in the farm sector, the USDA, or in the congressional farm bloc felt compelled to keep stamps around. Hunger relief was not their business. Those who sought to retain stamps as a targeted form of food assistance were neither as organized nor as well positioned as agriculture's patrons in government.

Even so, as we see in chapter 3, advocates for food stamps kept the flame alive through the postwar years, seeing some type of voucher system as a good way to get food to the hungry and undernourished not being reached by the period's general prosperity. Their efforts eventually were aided by a familiar conundrum, the reemergence of price-deflating surpluses and their negative impacts on farmers. Despite resistance by the Eisenhower administration and the congressional committees on agriculture, neither of which regarded stamps as useful in reducing surpluses, an expanding cohort of legislators from the nation's cities kept pushing to revive the one USDA program they saw as having helped poor people obtain an adequate diet. After years of legislative struggle, much of it between rural and urban Democrats, Congress in 1959 gave the USDA authority to run food stamp pilot projects similar to the original. While Dwight Eisenhower declined to follow through, John F. Kennedy took the tool off the proverbial shelf to address pockets of dire need he had encountered in the 1960 presidential campaign. Kennedy's pilot projects eventually paved the way for what became the modern Food Stamp Program. But what was it about the *idea* of food stamps that endured over those years in the political wilderness and made them attractive as a way to provide an adequate diet for those in need?

Chapter 4 details the legislative politics at the heart of the Food Stamp Program, from the struggle to enact the Food Stamp Act of 1964 to key moments in program expansion through the late 1970s. Central to this story is how program promoters in Congress finally overcame opposition by the rural conservatives then in control of key House and Senate committees. The legislative bargaining required to pass the Food Stamp Act and then to reauthorize it every few years would form the basis for an increasingly formalized marriage of mutual convenience in which rural conservatives voted for spending on food stamps and other nutrition programs in return for votes by urban liberals for programs subsidizing commodity production. The "farm programs + food programs" linkage in Congress embodied in successive farm bills remains key to the program's survival sixty years later, albeit with its fair share of marital strains.

Chapter 5 offers glimpses into the politics of food stamps as *welfare* from the 1980s to the 2020s, reflecting the program's growth and increasing centrality as an income supplement. We focus in particular on the impacts of welfare "reform" under the Personal Responsibility and Work Opportunity Reconciliation Act of 1996. For liberals who could not stop the evisceration of federal cash assistance with PRWORA, defense of the Food Stamp Program *as an income supplement* thereafter became the Hill on Which They Would Die—and take the farm bloc's coveted commodity programs with them if it came to that. If the shrinking number of legislators who represent farming areas have been unwilling to take that bet, others are less disinclined, and recent years have been marked by a hardening of political alignments around food stamps that mirror the general ideological and partisan polarization from Ronald Reagan through Donald Trump. Along the way SNAP's future hinges ever more on party politics even as it gains important allies in unexpected places, notably the nation's major food processors and retailers. Despite repeated conservative Republican efforts to restrict program scope and cut spending, SNAP survives—and was the backbone of the nation's food-assistance response when the pandemic hit.

In chapter 6 we pivot to analysis, asking four questions. First, how do we explain SNAP's political resilience over six decades? After all, SNAP isn't an untouchable "third-rail" of US social-welfare policy like Social Security and Medicare, portending political death to anyone who dares touch it.[42] The able-bodied poor, unlike senior citizens, typically aren't a protected class "deserving" of public support. So what is it about this program that enables it to withstand the largely antiwelfare atmosphere of recent decades? That SNAP is about food has a lot to do with it. But, as we will find, the answer also lies in how the program was constructed in the first place and by how it acquired political allies along the way.

Second, while SNAP is politically resilient, is it a *good* nutrition program? We look at studies on how program enrollees spend their SNAP dollars and whether they are all that different than any other low-income US consumer. We also ponder calls to make SNAP more prescriptive. Should enrollees be forbidden from using SNAP dollars on "bad" foods like sugar-sweetened sodas? Should the federal government go so far as to prescribe which foods enrollees get, such as through some version of The Box? The battle lines here often are less partisan than philosophical. Here we may find liberals *and* conservatives who think that SNAP should impose rules against bad foods, opposed by other liberals *and* conservatives who think such paternalism is bad policy. The food industry, for which SNAP spending is an indirect taxpayer subsidy, not surprisingly is on the "no food is bad food" side.

Third, is SNAP a good *income* supplement? When we were not looking, SNAP became an essential antipoverty policy tool. But does it make a difference? Here we compare SNAP to other forms of income assistance and ponder whether it creates incentives against work. We find that SNAP supplements the incomes of low-income households in ways that withstand charged notions of welfare, while SNAP spending generates jobs across the food system, from the meat-processing plant to the local bodega. In this regard critics like to point out that Walmart, the nation's largest food retailer, relies on minimum-wage workers *and* is the largest single redeemer of SNAP dollars.[43] So it's complicated.

Finally, we revisit the intersection of want and plenty and ask, *Can you do better?* Here we look at alternatives, from The Box at one end to direct cash assistance at the other. We conclude with the thought that SNAP, whatever its flaws, may be the only way that lawmakers can agree on how to provide food *and* income assistance to those who need both, especially when they don't particularly like poor people or trust them to do what is right. In this regard SNAP is classically American: suboptimal on efficiency, if you listen only to economists, but more politically feasible than the alternatives. Feasibility, last we checked, is a virtue.

Now on to our story. It starts with piglets.

2 "To Encourage Domestic Consumption"

Not many people realized how radical it was, this idea of having the government buy from those who had too much, in order to give to those who had too little.

—HENRY A. WALLACE, Secretary of Agriculture, 1941[1]

The Paradox

It started with piglets.

More to the point, it started with sensational newspaper accounts of slaughtered piglets and sows being "plowed under" at the behest of the US government on recommendations of the National Corn-Hog Committee of Twenty-Five, dominated by Midwest producers. (Hogs eat feed corn, hence the joint committee.) The slaughter and disposal campaign aimed to cut pork output by nearly 70 percent, or roughly one billion pounds over the 1933–34 gestation cycle, to bring supply closer to demand, which in turn would prop up wholesale pork prices and farm incomes.[2] Consumption of pork and most other agricultural commodities had not kept pace with production through the early 1930s as Depression-battered US households cut back on "luxury" food purchases. At the same time export markets that once absorbed much of US farm output shrank by an estimated two-thirds under the impacts of the global depression and congressionally instigated trade wars with Canada and countries in Europe. All the while, US farmers kept producing. Most had little choice, hoping that *this year* revenues might cover expenses. For the individual farmer, cutting production made no economic sense. But for each farmer who kept going, without increased demand the aggregate outcome of their individually rational decisions was only more surplus and continued pain down on the farm.[3]

One way to reduce a surplus is to destroy it. By some estimates nearly 80 percent of all pigs slaughtered in 1933–34 were destroyed or otherwise made inedible, and the campaign momentarily had its desired effect in boosting pork prices.[4] But such drastic—and visible—actions upset millions of Americans suffering from unemployment and hunger and were seen as immoral by millions more. How can you destroy *food?* Public criticism of the slaughter grew so intense that President Franklin Roosevelt directed Secretary of Agriculture Henry Wallace to find other ways to reduce the pork surplus—including using some of it to feed hungry people. To be fair, many in his administration, not to mention the always-influential Eleanor Roosevelt, had opposed the slaughter on moral grounds, and even Wallace admitted it was "a shocking commentary on our civilization."[5] Moreover, plans had been in place to distribute some surplus pork through the American Red Cross and local relief agencies, but the public outcry prompted an increase in the amount to be donated and not destroyed.[6]

The pig-slaughter controversy underscored the paradox facing the still-new Roosevelt administration, the same that had bedeviled Herbert Hoover's before it. On one hand, there was *too much* food.

By the 1920s advances in agricultural science and technology had made US farms productive "factories in the fields," but with perverse aggregate effects in the form of recurring surpluses that put downward pressure on commodity prices and erode revenues, forcing some farmers into bankruptcy and off the land. Such conditions first emerged in the 1920s with the end of the World War I–era boom in agriculture, as continued high production now outpaced domestic demand with the flattening of US population growth after the end of open immigration—and worsened after the stock-market collapse of October 1929 ushered in the Great Depression.[7] Wholesale wheat prices alone dropped by 50 percent between 1929 and 1932, a steep downward spiral that imperiled farmers who had to take out credit each spring to plant their crops.[8] While the government might not be able to or even should save all farms—and farmers—it wanted to ensure adequate incomes for the remaining most efficient producers and guarantee an adequate supply of affordable food for the nation.

On the other hand, there was *not enough* food, or at least not where it was needed. The other challenge for Roosevelt's "brain-trusters" was how to feed the "one-third of a nation ill-nourished," in the president's words, without undermining a market system that produced abundant food and employed many thousands, from farmers to retail workers. Such was the "paradox of want amidst plenty."[9] Not everyone saw the paradox this way. Critics on the left in particular viewed efforts to prop up farmers by destroying crops as a failure of capitalism. "We do not know how to manage it," Socialist Party leader Norman Thomas observed about the surplus, "and, therefore, by subsidized destruction, we return to familiar scarcity in order to give our farmers prosperity." We have, he memorably lamented, "bread-lines knee deep in wheat, and our principal effort is to reduce the supply of wheat."[10]

So how *should* Roosevelt manage apparently untamable surpluses? Without increased exports and higher domestic consumption, continuing the Hoover administration's laissez-faire approach to production only guaranteed more surpluses, more downward price pressures, and more misery in the fields, with consequent effects on rural America as displaced farm families migrated to proverbial (and often literal) greener pastures. Such were the tales of the "Okies" vividly evoked by Woody Guthrie in "This Land Is Your Land" and by John Steinbeck in *Grapes of Wrath*. At the other end of the policy spectrum was a more active government role in managing food production, processing, distribution, and sale than even the most ardent New Dealers could envision or that the generally conservative agricultural sector would abide. While Congress authorized a range of supply-management schemes under the Agricultural Adjustment Acts of 1933 and 1935, some which paid farmers *not* to produce some crops on some of their land, they were tricky to implement and disliked by major farm groups like the National Farmers Union, at that time dominated by Midwest corn and Plains-states wheat producers who opposed government "intrusion" in their growing decisions. (By contrast, the American Farm Bureau Federation, then dominated by southern cotton growers, supported government-enforced acreage restrictions that kept crop prices high.)[11] Policies designed to raise commodity prices also might come at the expense of urban consumers, a politically sensitive matter with so many under- and unemployed. Secretary of Agriculture Wallace summed up the challenge—and suggested a solution: "With farmers burdened by price depressing surpluses and with many persons in need of the very foods of which the farmers had a surplus, it seemed to thoughtful people, both within and without the Department of Agriculture, that we should

FIGURE 3. Federal surplus commodities—cabbage and potatoes—distributed to hundreds of Cleveland's eighty-seven thousand people on direct relief, May 1939. Source: Stock Image ID: 10705600a, Associated Press /Shutterstock.

expand our efforts to get these health-giving surplus foods to our under-nourished families."[12]

How to Bridge the Gap between Plenty and Want?

So the federal government would use surplus crops to feed those who needed food. But *how?* The simplest, most direct way, at least in the view of the newly created Federal Surplus Relief Corporation (later Federal Surplus *Commodities* Corporation), was to use its broad authority "to encourage domestic consumption" under Section 32 of the Agricultural Adjustment Act of 1935 to purchase commodities at a price sufficient to give farmers a reasonable profit and ship the food to states for distribution to eligible households.[13] Section 32 funds came out of annual customs tariff receipts, not general tax revenues, and soon became regarded as "farmers money."[14] While the FSCC bought some goods directly from producers, most times it worked through the Commodity Credit Corporation, created at that time to stabilize agricultural markets by purchasing and storing surplus commodities for future sale or use.[15]

Whatever its precise form, government purchase and distribution of surplus foodstuffs posed a range of challenges, the first being how to determine which commodities were "in surplus." Was it only under conditions of "physical" surplus, when unsold goods literally piled up in storage? That type of surplus had prompted the pig slaughter. Or was it when a commodity was in "economic" surplus? Such a condition existed, as USDA economist Samuel Herman defined at the time: "if, notwithstanding actual consumption of the commodity, the price that the producer received for the commodity was so low that, in the opinion of the Secretary [of Agriculture], the supply of the commodity exceeded the demand."[16] This definition would shape federal surplus-management policy over ensuing decades, although physical surpluses still recurred with price-depressing regularity.

A related dilemma was *which* surplus commodities to purchase, in what quantities, and at what price, without distorting commodity markets.[17] Poorly thought-out surplus purchase policies might induce farmers to boost production or switch crops, in expectation that the government invariably will buy up excess output to prop up prices and bolster farm incomes. Farmers were (are) not stupid and were (are) happy to "grow for the government" if it was (is) less risky and more profitable than navigating commodity markets. Not surprisingly, economists like Herman worried that direct purchase created too many perverse incentives for producers, a reality that later generations of policy makers seemed to rediscover time and again.

Having decided which commodities to acquire, at what price, and in what quantities, the next set of challenges came in getting that food to those in need. For one thing it was difficult and expensive to set up a parallel system to purchase, process, store, and ship bulk foods around the country. Even using established private-sector processing and supply chains incurred substantial costs. For another the local relief agencies to which commodities were sent often lacked the physical capacity, people, and funds to store, repackage, transport, and track the distribution of bulk quantities of food, especially perishables like milk. This particular problem soon would emerge with school lunch and milk programs designed to use up specific surplus foods.[18]

For their part, those needing food had to go once or twice a month to a government commissary or other distribution site, which might not be convenient or easy to reach, while not knowing how much of what foods they would get. For example, in May 1938 eligible Chicago families received "four pounds of prunes, two pounds of dried beans, four pounds of butter, twelve pounds of cabbage, eight stalks of celery, *thirty* pounds of oranges, and two pounds of rice," while in Cleveland that same month families got a box containing apples, butter, oranges, potatoes, and rice.[19] Getting any fresh food, while appreciated, created its own challenges. Recipients might not have adequate home storage, might not know how to prepare unfamiliar foods, or simply might not like what they got, so surplus food allotments were prone to waste (a dilemma not unfamiliar to anyone gazing on the kohlrabi in their Community Supported Agriculture shares).[20]

Then there were the effects on consumer markets, with retailers complaining about loss of business on foods declared in surplus and distributed nearby.[21] After all, why should anyone purchase at retail what they got for free? This was not a hypothetical: flour millers, bakers, and food retailers had been hurt by the sole Hoover-era food-relief effort: the donation of millions of tons of surplus wheat through the Red Cross.[22] Not surprisingly, proposals to expand surplus-commodity distribution were opposed by the National American Wholesale Grocers Association, the National Retail Merchants Association, and local chambers of commerce, as well as by labor unions fearing a loss of jobs throughout the established food chain.[23]

Finally, professional social workers saw surplus-commodity distribution as unpredictable, unwieldy, and demeaning to the needy who had to stand in line for their box. Such open reliance on "charity" rubbed against the deeply rooted individualism in US culture, especially when those in line were able-bodied men of working age who did not fit dominant narratives about the "deserving" poor.[24] As one social worker put it, commodity distribution "combines the worst features of the commissary, the grocery basket, and the breadline. . . . No welfare worker close into the administration of this backdoor federal relief really likes it."[25] Many preferred to provide cash so that their clients could buy food in local stores, like any other customer.[26]

In this regard one option floated by Secretary Wallace was a "two-price" system, under which qualified low-income consumers would pay a government-subsidized price on designated surplus-food products at special government-run markets.[27] However, the idea was technically complicated and politically toxic to retailers, even after Wallace suggested that it be run through their stores, largely because grocers did not want to bear the onus of validating which of their customers were eligible to buy specially marked discounted foods. Some industry leaders, such as the president of the National Retail Dry Goods Association, also worried that a two-price system would lead to "perhaps permanent segregation of society into two sharply defined strata."[28] Faced with retailer hostility, the idea was dropped. The last thing Wallace wanted was a fight with business over the constitutionality of surplus-disposal programs based on vague language in Section 32: "to encourage domestic consumption."[29]

Nor is there evidence that FSCC officials considered straight cash assistance to enable the poor to purchase more and, likely, more nutritious food. For one thing it was not clear that the corporation had legal authority under Section 32 to distribute cash. Moreover, even with limited federal cash assistance under the short-lived Federal Emergency Relief Administration and federal grants to states through the Aid to Dependent Children program authorized in the Social Security Act of 1935, "relief" still was a state and local matter, and local officials were wary of federal initiatives that might undercut their authority over the local poor. Such attitudes were especially entrenched in the Deep South, whose labor-intensive agricultural economy depended on low-wage workers and where powerful cotton planters kept (mostly Black) sharecroppers and tenant farmers in perpetual dependence, assisted over the winter months by the barest level of food hand-outs.[30] Similarly exploitive conditions were to be found in the fruit and vegetable fields of Texas and the coal towns of Appalachia.[31] Their members of Congress, backed by one-party dominance (at that time Democratic) and the fiercely defended norm of seniority on key committees, would not hesitate to block federal programs that threatened local power structures.[32] New Deal policies also viewed relief, particularly for able-bodied men, through the lens of work, as exemplified by the various Works Progress Administration jobs programs. Most such schemes were met with hostility by businesses, concerned that government would compete with them for labor, thereby raising worker wages, or would produce goods for use (such as processing surplus food for distribution to the poor) that might hurt local processors and retailers.[33]

To recap: destroying food in a time of dire need was wasteful and immoral, government management of commodity production created a range of perverse incentives, buying and distributing surplus food was seen as inefficient and shamed those who had to stand in line, and providing cash to the poor ran against prevailing views about self-sufficiency, individual responsibility, and work, not to mention local control. Any commodity-surplus diversion effort also met with complaints about competing with and undercutting the private sector and its workers. All the while US farmers kept producing, and a sharp recession in 1938 threatened to undo any gains made the previous five years. Supply-management programs authorized under the Agricultural Adjustment Acts had proven insufficient—and disliked by farmers who did not want to be told what or how much to produce—while worsening conditions in Europe and Asia further eroded already-shrunken export markets.[34] Mounting surpluses and slumping farm incomes bedeviled federal policy makers. At the same time too many Americans still lacked adequate food, with new concerns now raised about malnutrition among young men as prospects of military conscription became likelier.[35]

The "paradox of want amidst plenty" would not solve itself.

The Food Stamp Plan

We got a picture of a gorge, with farm surpluses on one cliff and
undernourished city folks with outstretched hands on the other. We set out to
find a practical way to build a bridge across that chasm.

—MILO PERKINS, President of the Federal Surplus Commodities
Corporation, 1939[36]

Out of this paradox came the first "food stamp" program. Precisely
who thought up the scheme remains a bit hazy. By some accounts
Secretary of Agriculture Wallace began to "think out loud" in late
1938—following hostile retailer reception to his two-price idea—
"about some sort of system whereby surplus farm products could
be gotten to people who cannot afford to pay the market prices for
them."[37] The idea for a coupon-based plan apparently grew out of
talks in early 1939 between FSCC officials and representatives of
the National American Wholesale Grocers Association, in whose
view existing surplus-disposal efforts posed unfair competition.
Wallace credited the former business executive and first FSCC
president, Milo Perkins, for coming up with the food stamp
concept—supposedly after a conversation among them and their
wives while on a Sunday drive. Perkins in turn credited Edward
Bartelt, commissioner of accounts in the Treasury Department, for
the plan's technical details.[38] Still others cited USDA agricultural
economist Fred Waugh, who would deny paternity all through his
fifty-year career with the department, and Carlyle Thorp of the
California Walnut Growers' Association, who suggested a stamp-
like scrip plan at about the same time. *Whoever* is to be credited, in
classic New Deal terms the plan that emerged reflected close col-
laboration between government officials and affected parties.[39] As
Perkins later recounted, Secretary Wallace "asked some of those

FIGURE 4. Poster promoting the use of food stamps. Source: Special Collections, National Agricultural Library, US Department of Agriculture, accessed February 18, 2023, www.nal.usda.gov/exhibits/speccoll/items/show/246.

who had a direct stake in this thing to get together and work out a sensible plan to move surplus foods through normal trade channels. . . . Ways and means were discussed with farm leaders, with people from many branches of the food trades . . . and with people responsible for public health and public welfare activities. Many government people outside the Department of Agriculture became interested. Men in the General Accounting Office worked overtime to help us get our forms approved."[40]

So keen was Wallace to gain business support that he presented the plan to the National Food and Grocery Conference Committee of food manufacturers, wholesalers, and retailers. "If this plan is fully successful," Wallace told committee members, "the time is not far distant when all of the people of the U.S. will be adequately nourished. . . . Gentlemen, it may well be that you are pioneers in one of the most significant public health movements of our time."[41] The committee voted its approval on March 14, 1939.[42] It must be observed that nobody apparently consulted with those the new program was intended to help.[43]

The Food Stamp Plan (its formal title) was rolled out in May 1939 in Rochester, New York—a "fairly typical city with a competently administered local relief program"—and was extended to five other cities in ensuing months, with stated goals to add three dozen more in 1940. The plan worked roughly as follows: participating local social-welfare agencies would determine eligibility based on enrollment in existing relief programs, such as aid to the elderly, the disabled, or families with children, or in various Works Progress Administration jobs schemes. Priority went to families headed by one or more adults, household units that FSCC experts felt were best equipped to use the foods, but a bias that critics argued punished single individuals. Those deemed eligible would

FIGURES 5 AND 6. The first food stamps, 1939–43. Sources: Bureau of Engraving and Printing, Wikimedia Commons, accessed February 18, 2023, https://commons.wikimedia.org/wiki/File:Orange-US-Food-Stamp-1939.jpg and https://commons.wikimedia.org/wiki/File:Blue-US-Food-Stamp-1939.jpg.

purchase from the administering local agency a specified dollar amount in postage stamp–sized orange stamps, which could be used on a dollar-for-dollar basis to purchase any domestic food product at participating retailers; stamps could not be used on imported foods like coffee, tea, or Italian olive oil. While participating households were expected to spend a minimum of $1.00 per week per person—a baseline USDA economists considered necessary to maintain an adequate diet—the minimum was reduced to fifty cents in much of the rural South due to that region's lower overall incomes, cheaper cost of living, meager relief programs and, no doubt, to curry favor with its powerful members of Congress.[44] Household purchases of orange stamps were capped at $1.50 per person per week to prevent trafficking in "excess" stamps.

For each dollar in orange stamps purchased, the buyer got a "bonus" of fifty cents in blue stamps, to be used *only* on foods declared in surplus by the secretary of agriculture. So, for example, if prunes were declared in surplus (which, some readers might be surprised to find, they sometimes were), a plan participant could redeem the specified denomination in free blue stamps for a box of prunes that the retailer had obtained through normal wholesale channels. Unlike Wallace's ill-fated "two-price" scheme, there would be no distinction in the quality, appearance, or price to the consumer of the box of prunes in question. The only difference was the form of currency used to purchase it. The list of surplus foods available for redemption with blue stamps would be posted by retailers and was subject to change month to month. Participating retailers would be compensated for the combined full value of the orange and blue stamps by authorized local banks or the relief agencies themselves, in turn reimbursed out of Section 32 funds earmarked for surplus disposal. The program would be administered by the Surplus Marketing Corporation (later Surplus Marketing Administration), successor to the FSCC.[45] Of note, participating localities were required to drop surplus-commodity distribution to make food stamps more acceptable to retailers, so the needy had no choice in the matter, although targeted forms of surplus distribution emerged about the same time as new school lunch and "penny milk" programs promoted by producers.[46]

The stated logic of the Food Stamp Plan was to *supplement* the food-purchasing power of low-income households and, by increasing overall food consumption, reduce commodity surpluses and boost revenues for everyone in the food system, from farmers to retailers. Milo Perkins laid out that logic in "Eating the Surplus," a June 1939 address to retailers: "No wonder farmers are having trouble finding a broad enough market for what they produce, no wonder malnutrition is a headache for the Public Health Service, and no wonder it has been a tough job for many of you to make a decent living when a third of your customers have done more window-shopping than cash buying."[47] Program designers above all wanted to maintain a household's "normal" level of food expenditures so that the bonus stamps spurred additional consumption and did not simply substitute one food dollar for another. Hence the purchase requirement, which as USDA economists noted, was intended "to maintain the out-of-pocket food expenditures of participants, so that the surplus products bought with the free blue stamps will represent a net addition to their food consumption."[48] In this regard, participating localities were required to retain existing cash relief programs to ensure that food stamps supplemented, not replaced, other forms of support. As Herman observed, the bonus blue stamps essentially discounted the cost of food, making it "a domestic two-price system made palatable to retailing groups."[49]

In fact, the plan quickly proved more "palatable" than most other forms of surplus disposal. To economists and retailers it got additional food into the stomachs of those who needed it without "running the risks of disturbing normal family economy, wasting unwanted but valuable foodstuffs and circumventing the normal channels of trade."[50] The president of the Independent Grocers Alliance of America called the plan "worthy of the wholehearted support" of all food retailers. As he reminded members of the Chamber of Commerce of the United States, "The regularly established channels of distribution will be used in this new procedure to dispose of farm surpluses and to reach those in need. I believe that what we call private business now has the opportunity to demonstrate its capacity."[51] For farmers food stamps would help to "eat up the surplus" by boosting domestic consumption. Participating

FIGURE 7. Sign in store welcoming food stamps. Source: Photo 53227(1770), Franklin D. Roosevelt Presidential Library and Museum, accessed February 18, 2023, www.fdrlibrary.marist.edu/archives/collections /franklin/?p=digitallibrary/digitalcontent&id=3266.

local relief agencies preferred stamps to bulk foods, even if ending commodity distribution might come at the expense of people too cash-poor to purchase orange stamps, a condition endemic among sharecroppers and other agricultural workers already excluded from most New Deal social-welfare programs. While frontline social workers still preferred cash assistance, which could be used for nonfood needs like soap, or even on rent, most saw redeeming stamps in retail stores as more dignified than standing in line for a box of surplus commodities and likelier to enable participants to obtain a healthier range of foods. In this regard, historian Rachel Moran argues, the plan's treatment of the needy as "proto-consumers" with additional purchasing power fit with New Deal notions of consumption-driven Keynesian economics.[52]

Until No Longer Needed

It was elementary dogma in the Food Stamp Plan that food was nutrition, that the added blue-stamp foods advanced low-income consumers toward a minimum adequate diet, and that a better-fed population was a better population.

—SAMUEL HERMAN, Economist, 1943[53]

The Food Stamp Plan ran from May 1939 to March 1943. At its height in mid-1941, it operated in 1,700 counties throughout forty-seven of the forty-eight states (covering roughly half of the country), the District of Columbia, and Puerto Rico. Only West Virginia did not participate, mostly because its state legislature refused to oblige the Surplus Marketing Corporation's mandate to waive state sales taxes on food "purchased" using the bonus blue stamps, which would have imposed additional (and regressive) costs on stamp users. Instead, West Virginia continued to rely on surplus-commodity distribution, which the state's powerful coal operators likely preferred since many paid miners in scrip that could be used only in company-owned stores, not in US currency that could be used to buy stamps.[54] Over its run the plan at one time or another supplemented the food-purchasing capacity of nearly twenty million people, with a peak enrollment of four million, shopping at some two hundred thousand retail outlets of varying types and sizes. Spending on the plan over its four years came to $260 million, nearly $5 billion in 2022 dollars.[55] However, to put that into perspective, the USDA spent nearly $118 million on commodity purchase and distribution in fiscal 1940 alone.[56] Even so, limits on Section 32 funds left out many localities seeking to participate.

The plan worked largely as its designers intended. Neither the purchase requirement nor the open link between stamps and surplus disposal met with much debate. While the Surplus Marketing Corporation gave some local relief agencies permission to provide free blue stamps to people too cash-poor to purchase orange stamps or not otherwise enrolled in relief programs, it tended to discourage such efforts.[57] As one observer noted, the corporation "is interested primarily and entirely in the problem of the moving of surplus foods through the increase of consumption of certain farm products. The Corporation is not concerned with helping Chicago or any other city solve its inadequate relief problem."[58] This being said, the need for food was so dire that around 40 percent of participants over the four years got blue stamps at no cost. Many were the rural poor, belying popular views of poverty as a city problem.[59]

Opinions about food stamps as a means to divert surplus foods to feed those in need were almost universally favorable. One 1939 survey by pollster George Gallup showed approval by 70 percent who had an opinion, and other surveys reflected support by social workers, labor unions, and retailers—even the US Chamber of Commerce, in marked contrast to its hostility to most New Deal programs.[60] The Democratic Party embraced food stamps in its 1940 election platform as a means to help "needy consumers," while Republicans confined their support to the role of stamps in reducing farm surpluses.[61] Individual farmers voiced approval, when asked, even as the official positions of their national associations varied. The American Farm Bureau Federation, dominated by southern cotton growers, still favored commodity distribution as a "farmers program" and grudgingly went along with the plan so long as it emphasized surplus reduction, not hunger relief.[62] Greater enthusiasm was expressed by specialized producer groups, ranging from peanuts to prunes, each wanting their crops included in the plan when market conditions led to surplus—and even when they did not.[63] Even cotton growers soon got the USDA to try out a cotton stamp to absorb *their* surpluses, with less success.[64] As federal government economist Joseph Coppock later summarized about the Food Stamp Plan:

> It was one of the most popular programs of the late New Deal period. The use of stamps as "special purpose money" appealed to the money cranks and other persons interested in monetary solutions to our economic problems. To others, primarily concerned with the relief of the hungry, the Plan appeared to be more of a special poor-relief program than a farm-aid program, although both aspects were involved. To farm groups, it appeared a highly conscionable political device for raising farm income or justifying other governmental efforts to that end. Retailers and wholesalers welcomed the program's dependence on the ordinary channels of trade.[65]

There were criticisms. While social workers dutifully administered the plan where instituted, most still favored cash assistance and worried that purchase requirements forced participants to forego critical nonfood needs or put stamps out of reach of the cashless poor. More than a few wondered if stamps indirectly subsidized low wages.[66] They also were reluctant to buy into the USDA's zeal to reduce surpluses and prop up commodity prices if that meant higher food costs for price-sensitive low-income consumers—a classic tension in any nation's agrifood policy making—and were little inclined to enforce program rules if local retailers were lenient on what customers could do with their stamps.[67] That bonus blue stamps could be used only on foods declared in surplus also meant that participants had to use orange stamps—or cash—on especially desirable foods, notably beef and chicken, neither of which showed up on the surplus list during the plan's four-year run.[68] Nor could stamps of either color be used for nonfood items like toilet paper or soap. Such restrictions led Herman to observe, "The lack of freedom to treat the stamp as money conflicted with the freedom to trade with any retailer, the privilege of a normal consumer with money."[69]

What did food stamp *users* think? Not surprisingly, studies sponsored by the USDA found that most enrollees preferred using stamps in retail markets to standing in line at relief centers for a box of surplus foods, enjoyed the greater range of choices available compared to monthly surplus allotments, and were able to eat healthier overall diets. Even so, comparatively low participation rates in some areas suggested problems with the purchase requirement, which for many diverted scarce cash away from other needs, and on prohibitions against using orange or blue stamps on nonfood items.[70] Such complaints were greatest in cities with higher overall costs of living. "How, in the name of humanity, can we large families cope with these situations?" asked one disappointed New York City homemaker in a letter to Eleanor Roosevelt.[71] But there was not a choice in the matter; localities that opted for stamps had to end commodity distribution, leaving some households actually worse off.

The Food Stamp Plan was terminated on March 1, 1943, despite its overall popularity, a victim of changed circumstance. The need to feed armies in the field and send food aid to allies dried up most surpluses, leaving Americans at home to confront food shortages, rationing, and off-the-book (or "black") markets. While nutritionists and advocates for the poor protested that the plan still met a need, given nearly 30 percent price increases for some basic foods, and that it could serve as a model for more equitable food rationing, its budget was diverted to other priorities. Few in Congress objected when the USDA rerouted half of the plan's $50 million in fiscal 1943 funding to purchase and distribute select surplus commodities (notably, milk) to schools and state welfare agencies.[72] As Herman observed in a 1943 postmortem, the plan's conception—and its primary sales pitch—as a means to reduce surplus made it expendable in the view of USDA officials once most surpluses disappeared, and its "continued presence in the Department of Agriculture did not permit freeing it from the economics, the pressures, the 'bloc-mind,' of farm production."[73] Coppock concurred, noting that "it was not to the advantage of the Food Stamp Plan to remain within the administrative province of and responsibility of the Department of Agriculture."[74]

Moreover, the plan had to go through congressional committees on agriculture and appropriations that saw food production as the priority, and "a nutrition program for low-income city dwellers" lacked the political clout of well-organized commodity producers and their business allies—even if it also served many small-town and rural communities. In fact, integration of the initially independent FSCC into the USDA over the protests of urban liberals "implied that surplus distribution was no longer an emergency activity but had become closely associated with the long-term purposes of the Department of Agriculture."[75] As if to underscore this point, in late 1942 the Surplus Marketing Administration was folded into a new Food Distribution Administration. With few surplus foods to divert, the Food Stamp Plan had outlived its purpose, although, Herman concluded, "it was an experience that might be revived and strengthened" should conditions ever warrant.[76]

Taking Stock

So the Food Stamp Plan was well regarded, but did it *work*? The answer depended on who asked what question. For the USDA, officially, the plan successfully diverted millions of pounds of price-depressing surplus commodities, propped up farm incomes, and supplemented the food-purchasing power of low-income Americans, all through "normal" market channels, until surpluses no longer posed a problem. In this regard, as Coppock concluded in his 1947 assessment, the plan "was a striking combination of theoretical ingenuity and practical sense."[77] Nutritionists saw benefits insofar that participants tended to use their bonus blue stamps on comparatively expensive proteins like eggs and pork, when available, and on fresh fruits and vegetables, underscoring the price sensitivity of low-income consumers.[78] Studies at the time showed that the stamps helped to improve the diets of participants compared to nonparticipants of similar incomes.[79]

The verdict was more mixed on the fiscal front. For the congenitally skeptical members of the House and Senate appropriations committees, the plan was a dubious success because it incurred higher direct costs for the USDA when compared to commodity purchase and donation, even if it lowered costs for local agencies that no longer had to maintain food storage and distribution systems.[80] The agricultural bloc in Congress also tended to favor direct purchase and distribution as a "farmers program" whose effects on reducing surpluses could be measured in the tons of food handed out. It was trickier to assess the efficacy of "special purpose money" in reducing surpluses and boosting farm incomes through the regular marketplace; Coppock, for one, calculated that more cash assistance to the poor would have had about the same effects.[81]

With the end of surplus, support in Congress for continued appropriations for stamps out of Section 32 funds quickly dissipated.

Even so, economists of the period saw the plan's success in supplementing consumer-purchasing power as outweighing its budgetary costs.[82] They were wed less to its orange stamp–blue stamp construction—a "structural defect" in Coppock's view—than to its overall effects in boosting food consumption among low-income families. The plan not only made poor people better off but also raised "the general level of economic activity in the community," with increased average sales per customer generating higher revenues for food retailers, if not farmers. Food stamps also had positive political benefits, he mused, insofar that this form of income assistance made participants "more willing to accept their economic lot."[83] A later generation of feminist scholars would see such "earmarked" monies as paternalistic efforts to make low-income women into better consumers and homemakers.[84] However, Coppock warned, an "economic system which stands only with the support of food stamps and other such props is not a permanently satisfactory system."[85]

Some critics pointed to episodes of "chiseling" by food retailers. Whatever the enthusiasm of their national associations, individual grocers were caught in the middle, expected to enforce strict rules about orange and blue stamps while dealing with cash-strapped customers who wanted to use bonus blue stamps for *any* food, not just those declared in surplus, or on nonfood items like soap. The dilemma was most acute for small independent grocers struggling to compete with new chain markets.[86] Most violations apparently were handled by yet another New Deal arrangement, a "food industry committee" composed of local wholesalers and retailers.[87] For its part, the USDA admitted futility in expecting perfect compliance among some two hundred thousand retailers of varying types and did not want to hurt needy people just because some grocers played loose with the rules, so it tended to avoid penalizing rule breakers.[88] A departmental audit system designed to prevent cheating by retailers later was judged as "expensive, elaborate, and rather ineffective."[89] More telling, aside from the odd newspaper story of people trading stamps for cigarettes, there was little apparent official concern about "chiseling" by food stamp users themselves. To supervise every transaction, Milo Perkins advised, "would have required a corps of Government auditors checking the sales of every corner grocery store in America."[90]

Then there were issues of equity. Budget constraints limited the plan's reach, and federal officials were confronted with difficult choices in deciding which localities could participate. A truly national program would have served nearly twenty million (about 15 percent of the population) annually, five times more than it ever reached at its peak, and at a corresponding cost. Moreover, the plan's decentralized structure left administrative decisions to local officials—and local politics. Such discretion started with deciding eligibility, and there always seemed to be more who were technically eligible than who were approved by local officials.[91] While the plan's use of household income as its sole standard for eligibility was seen as fairer to potential participants (notably racial minorities) than other New Deal programs, its efficacy and fairness in the end depended on the efficacy and fairness of local relief administration generally, leaving its reach and impacts up to the vagaries of the federal system.[92] By some estimates only 75 percent of those technically eligible participated in the plan, compared to over 90 percent for the less strictly monitored commodity-distribution program.[93] While the purchase requirement was a disincentive for some eligible participants, and a perennial point of contention among social-welfare advocates, "lack of understanding" about program rules likely contributed. A few initiatives designed to better educate the eligible, ease purchase requirements for the poorest, and mail stamps to rural participants never went very far due to budget constraints and resistance by local officials.[94]

Overall, though, the Food Stamp Plan was deemed a success. While not cash, it was cash-like enough to enable users to "purchase" food in any participating retail market, with some degree of choice in which foods they could obtain with either orange or blue stamps. While the currency differed, and plan rules imposed some limits on choice, stamp users could act just like any other consumer. Retailers liked the plan because it used the "normal channels of trade," and most local relief agencies preferred it to handling surplus commodities.[95] And it supplemented the food-purchasing power of the poor in the most socially acceptable way of all, as participants in the market economy.

Even so, the plan was terminated because it no longer addressed the "paradox of want amidst plenty" posed by surplus. US farmers now were encouraged to ramp up production to meet wartime demands, and with tight crop inventories the USDA discontinued most surplus-diversion programs. In this regard, it bears reminding: the primary aim of Depression-era food-assistance policy was to support farmers and, critics argued, prop up market capitalism itself. How the government fed hungry people was defined by its desire to divert surpluses without disrupting the "normal channels" of food production, processing, sales, and purchasing. As such, the design of any food-assistance program would reflect agricultural priorities first and foremost. The Food Stamp Plan was no different.

Scholars of US political development often ponder how the New Deal social-welfare system would have looked had it not been for the conservative and agrarian biases in Congress.[96] This much is certain: without the surplus, food stamps never would have existed. But, having been tried and found useful, the *idea* of food stamps would remain, worth reviving should conditions change. Such changes would come about soon enough. But, as we will see, bringing back stamps was not to be easy, or quick, largely because of the politics of postwar agricultural policy.

3   *The Paradox Anew*

Good times are likely to be followed by bad times, however, and a mechanism like the Stamp Plan can serve the general welfare if it is contracted to a mere skeleton in times of great prosperity, but kept alive so that it can be expanded in times of depression to help cushion the shock.

—MILO PERKINS, President of the Federal Surplus Commodities Corporation, 1939[1]

Tending the Flame

Even as the USDA ended the Food Stamp Plan in May 1943, its spirit was kept alive in Congress—at first only by a few legislators and then in greater numbers, with rising frustration over the nation's domestic food-relief efforts as surpluses reemerged. Inside the USDA many of the experts who had administered the plan continued to study ways to improve it even if their higher-ups no longer cared.[2] While these advocates in government were not numerous enough to counter the "agricultural mindset" pervading US food-assistance policy, that would change with renewed attention to the "paradox of want amidst plenty."[3]

Efforts to authorize a new food stamp program soon after the plan's termination reflected concerns in government about undernourishment among men of draft age, with estimates that 40 percent of inductees were rejected for health reasons. In fact, a National Nutrition Council for Defense convened by Roosevelt in 1941 recommended extending food stamps as a "vital cog in the national defense program."[4] The problem of poor diet was most acute among Blacks in the rural South, an issue even for the racially segregated armed forces. Others saw the spikes in wartime food prices as an argument for continuing some sort of relief program for the elderly, disabled, and others unable to provide for themselves.

Perhaps the prime impetus behind efforts in Congress to legislate a food stamp program was recognition that the USDA left to itself had little interest in one. With no commodity price-deflating surpluses to divert, the rationale for stamps no longer held, as far as the department was concerned, and wartime priorities to maximize production now held center stage. But any effort in Congress to establish a stamp program by law would have to go through the House and Senate committees on agriculture—or so was the presumption of the majority who still viewed food assistance as a byproduct of agricultural policy. For their part, the patrons of agriculture were disinclined to revive a program most only tolerated under prewar conditions of crop surpluses and weak farm incomes. Those days were over, for now.

The first-known bill authorizing a food stamp program was introduced in June 1943 by Rep. Christian Herter, Republican from Massachusetts, but the House Committee on Banking and Currency, to which the bill was directed (because stamps were seen as a form of money), took no action.[5] In January 1944 Senators George Aiken, a Republican from Vermont, and Robert LaFollette Jr., a Progressive Republican from Wisconsin, submitted a bill to create a National Food Allotment Plan that would enable any household to use up to 40 percent of its income to buy vouchers for a prescribed basket of nourishing foods at a subsidized price. Poor families would get vouchers at no cost. Aiken's stated purpose was to guarantee that all Americans had a nutritious diet at a time of shortages and high food prices, ensuring a healthy civilian population able to support the war effort. He pointedly advised that his "allotment" plan should not be confused with the "old stamp plan, which was used partly as a relief measure and partly as a means of utilizing surplus farm commodities."[6] Of note, Aiken's plan apparently had technical assistance from USDA economist Fred Waugh, who took a leave of absence without pay to help the senator "get it right."[7]

An ad hoc subcommittee of the Senate Committee on Agriculture held hearings on the Aiken-LaFollette bill, during which USDA economists detailed the nutritional challenges facing millions of Americans in wartime. While acknowledging this problem, senators struggled over the allotment plan's potential costs and over concerns that subsidizing food purchases at a time of already high prices would stoke inflation. They also were caught between opposing views about forms of relief. On one side were labor-union leaders and social-welfare advocates who in earlier times had supported food stamps but now prioritized price controls, consumer subsidies, higher worker wages, and more generous cash assistance to the poor. On the other were agricultural producers who saw Aiken's vouchers as a narrowly targeted means to address proximate conditions of hunger and undernourishment. To Ezra Taft Benson, speaking for the National Council of Farmer Cooperatives, the allotment plan "is a specific treatment and therefore has merit when applied wisely and properly to a specific problem."[8] Benson's parsing reflected the agricultural establishment's view that some form of food voucher was the lesser of evils compared to price controls and consumer subsidies. Food retailers supported the allotment plan but did not testify, lest their unpopularity at a time of rationing and high food prices harm the bill's chances. The White House, engaged with the war, did not weigh in, and the committee took no action.[9] LaFollette later that year tried to add a food-allotment plan through an amendment to a bill reauthorizing the Commodity Credit Corporation but was rebuffed by his colleagues.[10]

Aiken and LaFollette proposed similar allotment plans in each subsequent Congress of the 1940s, with no greater success. Despite recognition of pockets of need, such as among the elderly and disabled, the war's end saw the nation giving top priority to integrating millions of returning veterans into the economy. It also saw an end to rationing, and increased domestic food consumption plus efforts to feed millions in war-ravaged regions overseas soaked up agricultural production through the 1940s.[11] Even Aiken was realistic, concluding, "I have not felt that the time was propitious for asking Congress to act upon this proposed legislation."[12]

Too Many Amber Waves of Grain—Again

Whenever we talked about surpluses, we talked about food stamps.

—FORMER USDA OFFICIAL[13]

But surpluses soon were back, for many of the same reasons as before the war. New farming technologies, from more powerful machines to improved seed hybrids and synthetic chemical

FIGURE 8. Surplus grain storage, 1950. Source: Photo by Frank Scherschel. Stock Image ID: 11959089a, Life/Shutterstock.

pesticides, enabled an ever-shrinking number of farmers to produce ever more food on the same land with less labor.[14] Corn yields alone went from twenty-eight bushels per acre in 1940 to thirty-seven in 1950 and to fifty-one by 1958 (one bushel equals about fifty-six pounds).[15] Farmers also were left free to produce as much as they wanted under generous—and supposedly temporary—fixed "parity" price supports put in place during the war and fiercely defended by farm groups and their congressional patrons for years after.[16]

Largely unchecked production soon swamped domestic consumption, while exports softened with the recovery of foreign agricultural sectors and the trade-dampening effects of the Cold War with Soviet bloc nations. The agricultural establishment once again faced its old foe, especially for crops (like corn, potatoes, and dairy) consumed largely on home soil. In response, the USDA under Harry Truman and, especially, Dwight Eisenhower turned to the surplus reduction strategies already in its policy toolbox. The Commodity Credit Corporation bought up ever more surplus wheat and corn, annual federal purchases of which ballooned from 1 million bushels in 1949 to *880* million in 1954 (yes, that is correct), with some 1.8 billion bushels now in storage. The situation became so dire that the CCC was compelled to store purchased grain in recommissioned World War II merchant ships.[17] The department also resumed surplus distribution to state and local relief agencies, increased commodity donations to the National School Lunch Program (created in 1946), and in 1955 devised a Special Milk Program to prop up dairy prices by getting children to drink more of it.[18] The department in one instance also authorized the destruction of 25 million bushels of potatoes—with little apparent public reaction.[19] However, there was no serious thought in the upper USDA echelons to bringing back food stamps as a means to bolster consumption, save for a momentary consideration in 1950 by Truman's secretary of agriculture, Charles Brannan, and only out of his frustration with congressional and farm-group hostility to his production-management reform plans.[20]

The disinclination of USDA leadership to revive food stamps even with the reemergence of massive surpluses can be explained by changing contexts and, increasingly, by ideological differences over agricultural policy. For one, the nation was experiencing general prosperity, with the national unemployment rate throughout the 1950s hovering around 4 percent, in stark contrast to 19 percent in the late 1930s.[21] Any pockets of dire need were largely out of public view, with no Depression-era images of breadlines to prick the public conscience.

Moreover, food assistance continued to be framed through an agricultural-policy lens. In this regard most Republicans opposed resumption of New Deal production-management schemes designed to prevent surpluses to begin with. Eisenhower's secretary of agriculture, Ezra Taft Benson, instead pushed unrestrained production, and, when demand lagged, the USDA would purchase surplus commodities for domestic donation or foreign sales, the latter criticized as little more than market-distorting dumping. As Jonathan Coppess observed in his analysis of the evolution of US agricultural policy, Benson embodied an "abundance" view that "emphasized support for production through flexibility and less federal intervention, coupled with assistance to the consumer to help bolster purchasing and consumption."[22] If Benson in his former role as executive director of the National Council of Farmer Cooperatives once endorsed Aiken's food-allotment plan, he did so because producers preferred vouchers that supplemented consumption to the price controls and consumer subsidies others promoted at that time. With such wartime concerns long receded, many (but not all) commodity producers backed Secretary of Agriculture Benson's "farm-centric" production and surplus-disposal strategies.[23]

By contrast, most farm-sector Democrats still favored some form of production management that minimized surpluses up front, but the differences between them and Republicans were as often along crop lines as ideological ones.[24] The dominant fault line, Coppess points out, was midwestern corn versus southern cotton. Midwestern Republicans tended to represent larger and better-capitalized corn (and later soy) operations, whose scale and efficiency gains from technology made them suited to navigating fluctuations in commodity markets. Corn growers also worried that high commodity prices hurt their primary customers, the pork and beef producers who used corn as feed. As such, they tended to favor Benson's more market-oriented flexible price supports.[25] Southern Democrats, conversely, supported continuation of acreage restrictions and fixed price supports that kept cotton prices high. (Plains-states wheat producers fluctuated between the two poles, depending on market conditions for their crop.) Members from both parties in other regions represented highly perishable fruits, vegetables, and dairy, most characterized by smaller, less well-capitalized producers who suffered fast and hard from price-deflating surpluses and who were likelier to favor programs that reduced farmers' risks or compensated them for losses from disasters (natural or market-based). That Republicans Aiken and LaFollette represented quintessential dairy states, Vermont and Wisconsin, likely mattered more than their party affiliation.

Moreover, any legislation on food assistance still had to go through the committees on agriculture. While the southern Democrats and midwestern Republicans, who dominated the panels throughout this period, clashed—often viciously—over commodity-production policies, they agreed that food relief was outside the USDA's mandate and budget. As Rep. Harold Cooley of North Carolina, chair of the House Committee on Agriculture during most of the decade, put it, "We do not want to put the Secretary of Agriculture in the relief business."[26] Cooley came to support food stamps as a means to get surplus foods to the needy—and to obtain the votes of urban Democrats for southern crop supports—but he never stopped worrying about "relief" being charged to agriculture's budget.[27]

The unwillingness of the "agricultural bloc" to rethink food assistance even as surpluses grew did not deter efforts to bring back stamps in some form. In fact, they intensified, driven by recognition that, while most Americans were far removed from the Depression's misery, there still was need, if one looked. In 1955, by one USDA estimate, around 12 percent of American families, or about 7.5 million people, were suffering from poor to very deficient diets, largely as a result of poverty.[28] Other studies suggested especially high levels of deprivation among the elderly, disabled, families with children, racial minorities, and Native Americans. In response a growing number of legislators expressed support for targeted food coupons, such as to supplement the purchasing power of the elderly on Social Security. Senator Aiken (who would represent Vermont until 1975) submitted his "allotment" bill in each Congress throughout the 1950s—with Senator Hubert Humphrey, Democrat from Minnesota, as lead cosponsor—now promoting it as a means by which underconsuming Americans could eat more of the surplus.[29]

In the House, efforts to establish some form of food stamps increasingly were driven by urban Democrats like Rep. Leonor Sullivan of St. Louis, who, upon entering Congress in 1953, submitted the first of a series of bills authorizing a stamp program and soon became known for her relentless focus on food assistance.[30] As Sullivan later explained, "I became deeply concerned by the accounts of undernourishment among needy schoolchildren and others in St. Louis at about the same time the main concern on agricultural matters here in Washington seemed to be the unmanageable surpluses of food. The more I thought about this contradiction the more indignant I became."[31]

When not trying to move a food stamp program through the legislative process, Sullivan also regularly reminded Secretary of Agriculture Benson that he already had authority to run one under Section 32, as Henry Wallace had in 1939.[32] But Benson was not

Wallace. Indeed, to the frustration of advocates for directing more of the surplus to domestic relief, the USDA under Benson consistently underspent available Section 32 funds, opting instead to use the Commodity Credit Corporation to purchase and store surplus commodities for later foreign sales.[33] By 1955 the costs to do so had climbed to $382 million a year (around $4 billion in 2022 dollars), giving Benson's critics ample opportunity to promote food stamps as a surplus-disposal strategy.[34]

Food stamps even emerged as a minor issue in the 1956 presidential campaign, with Democratic candidate Estes Kefauver, a senator from Tennessee, arguing for their revival as a means to attack "mountainous" surpluses and feed those not being reached by Benson's "Needy Families" commodity-distribution program.[35] While Kefauver failed to get his party's nomination, Democrats led by Representative Sullivan included language supporting food stamps in their 1956 party platform. The Republican platform, by contrast, emphasized expanding commodity distribution, school lunch, and school milk programs as needed to deal with specific surpluses.[36] Eisenhower's easy reelection would mean no near-term change in the status quo.

Leveraging the Urban Vote

Through the mechanism of an efficiently operated food-stamp program a larger part of our current food surpluses now being channeled into Government warehouses and finally disposed of overseas can be put to use building better bodies and healthier citizens of our own country.

—REP. VICTOR ANFUSO, Democrat from New York, 1958[37]

The persistence of large and increasingly expensive surpluses through the late 1950s intensified efforts in Congress to revive food stamps, as seen in the number of bills proposed (an average of twelve in the House per each two-year legislative cycle) and efforts to use whatever points of leverage presented themselves. Faced with continued resistance by the committees on agriculture, proponents tried to get the Senate Finance Committee to include a food stamp program in the Social Security amendments of 1956, to be administered by the Department of Health, Education, and Welfare. While the effort had the support of religious and social-welfare organizations, labor unions, and the National Farmers Union (which by now tended to represent small-scale producers), it was opposed by the Eisenhower administration, the business community, and the American Farm Bureau Federation, now firmly in the grip of antistatist Midwest corn growers. The Finance Committee ultimately voted nine to five against the amendment, with conservative farm-state Democrats joining Republicans in opposition. Similar proposals to shift food assistance out of the USDA grew through the decade, largely in response to Benson's views that surplus disposal should prioritize sales, not relief—the latter being a "welfare" program outside the department's primary mission.[38]

Another point of potential leverage came during negotiations between the House and Senate over the Agricultural Act of 1956, the latest renewal of the "farm bill" that authorized commodity programs.[39] The persistent Sullivan took advantage of acute intercrop and interchamber divisions on commodity programs as an opportunity to bypass an intransigent House Committee on Agriculture and persuade sympathetic conference committee negotiators to add language authorizing the USDA to run a food stamp program. The compromise bill passed both chambers with the help of votes by urban Democrats, who supported food stamps, only to be vetoed by Eisenhower over a number of disagreements, one of them over Sullivan's amendment. The House, split along crop-specific policy differences as well as party lines, sustained Eisenhower's veto. Congress then passed a revision, which Eisenhower signed, directing the USDA to analyze the *feasibility* of a food stamp program. The department did as mandated, with apparent reluctance. While the staff experts who wrote the January 1957 report acknowledged the potential of food stamps to enhance nutrition and even suggested ways to improve on the original plan (notably, by simplifying the two-stamp structure), USDA leaders nonetheless advised against a new stamp program on grounds of potentially high costs and modest impacts on surplus reduction.[40] Sullivan was unimpressed by their logic, given the millions being spent to purchase and store surplus commodities: "I am sorry the Department of Agriculture has resisted so strongly, so continuously, so cruelly, the idea of channeling some for the mountain of surplus commodities to these really poor Americans. True, there is in existence a surplus food-distribution program, but to characterize that program in a word, I would say it is wretched."[41]

Per Sullivan's gibe, heightened interest in food stamps in part reflected greater public attention to the costs of purchasing and storing ever-rising piles of surplus commodities, which by fiscal year 1960 came to $4.4 billion (equivalent to $42 billion in 2022), roughly two-thirds of the department's total annual budget and one of the federal government's largest nondefense budget outlays.[42] It also reflected growing awareness of the limited range of foods provided in monthly USDA surplus-commodity allotments, which tended to be heavy on grains and dairy, and complaints raised by local relief agencies and retailers about the free-food program that would have been familiar to the designers of the original Food Stamp Plan.[43]

Sullivan's strategy of attaching a food stamp program to any commodity support measure in the legislative pipeline recurred in 1957 through a floor amendment to a bill reauthorizing the Agricultural Trade Development and Assistance Act of 1954, better known as Public Law 480, which funded US donation of surplus commodities as foreign food aid.[44] While Sullivan's amendment got a 196 to 187 plurality, it fell short of the two-thirds majority required to override a House Committee on Rules ban on floor amendments.[45] But in that failure was clear evidence of the growing importance of urban House Democrats in agricultural and food-policy decision making. Among them was Rep. Victor Anfuso of New York City (Brooklyn, actually), the then-rare big-city House member to get a seat on the Committee on Agriculture; even Representative Sullivan never did. Anfuso also chaired the Subcommittee on Consumers Study, its only panel not organized around specific commodities or production programs.[46] With Chair Cooley's approval, Anfuso convened his subcommittee in April 1958 to consider "the possibilities of a soundly conceived, efficiently administered food-stamp program in the United States."[47] The hearings served as a forum in which social-welfare, food-industry, and agricultural-economics experts examined the technical details for a food stamp program that most felt would come sooner rather than later. Of note, there is little evidence that subcommittee members considered cash as an alternative; they, like most members of Congress, continued to view food assistance through an agricultural lens.

Several votes in the House in 1958 showed the increasing clout of urban Democrats on agricultural issues, often in conflict with their rural colleagues over balancing support for commodity production with programs aimed at consumers. The first came in consideration of the Agricultural Act of 1958. In June the House Committee on Agriculture for the first time worked up an "omnibus" (or "catch all") farm bill that included a food stamp program devised by Anfuso's subcommittee. Committee chair Cooley in particular foresaw the need to gain the support of urban Democrats in any floor vote on commodity programs, especially those supporting southern crops. However, committee Republicans, at the behest of the Eisenhower administration, used parliamentary maneuvers to block action until rural Democrats took out the food stamp program to save their commodity programs. The stripped-down bill then went down to defeat on the House floor, with urban Democrats joining most Republicans in opposing commodity supports sought by southern Democrats.[48]

A month later came another attempt at passage, during which the House Committee on Agriculture again included a food stamp program only to see it taken out by the Committee on Rules, itself dominated by conservatives opposed to expanded food relief. The full bill went to the House floor, where the required vote to permit consideration was defeated 171 to 214, with forty-four members not voting. As Sullivan later observed,

> A majority of the members of the Committee on Agriculture voted for . . . a food stamp proposal several weeks ago. They voted to make it part of the omnibus agricultural bill. I think it only fair to point out that when the food stamp amendment was subsequently dropped out of the omnibus bill, many Democratic members from urban districts voted against the rule to take up the agricultural bill. . . . It is obvious that the absence of a food stamp plan was one of the major causes for the failure of the catch-all farm bill to pass the House last month.[49]

The Committee on Agriculture, again with Cooley's support, soon after reported a stand-alone bill authorizing a multiyear, $1 billion food stamp program. It was the first time either committee on agriculture had done so, and the bill was seen as an effort by Cooley and other rural Democrats to appease their urban colleagues prior to another go at the Farm Bill. However, the Committee on Rules refused to allow the bill to go to the House floor.[50] Cooley sought a suspension of the rules to permit a floor vote and got a 196 to 187 plurality, but not the needed two-thirds. While the vote was largely along party lines, with 82 percent of Democrats in support and 85 percent of Republicans opposed, it also lay bare divisions between rural southern Democrats, many who did not vote at all, and northern urban Democrats, who voted in near-unanimous support.[51] A pattern was emerging: with Republicans united largely behind Eisenhower and against most forms of production management, farm-sector Democrats needed the votes of their urban colleagues, who in turn wanted rural Democratic votes for food stamps. If the latter were not yet forthcoming in sufficient numbers, the gap was narrowing.

Breakthrough—Of Sorts

In 1959 Representative Sullivan inserted language into yet another renewal of PL 480, directing the USDA to run food stamp "demonstration" projects. This tactic had been unsuccessful two years earlier, but the legislative landscape had changed with the 1958 midterm elections, which saw Democrats increase their control of the House by forty-eight seats and the Senate by thirteen, their largest majorities since 1940. Democrats made their greatest gains in eastern and midwestern cities, in the process shifting the congressional party's balance of power away from its long-dominant rural southern wing.[52] The impacts were evident during House floor consideration of Sullivan's amendment. While rural Democrats still regarded food stamps as "welfare," they also supported PL 480 foreign food aid as a "farmers program" and recognized that their urban colleagues now had the votes to block reauthorization if Sullivan's amendment was left out.[53] Sullivan made clear the strategy:

> Standing by itself, my bill might be vetoed. The Republican members of the Committee on Agriculture solidly opposed it—every one. Mr. Benson says he does not want it. He already has the authority to institute a food stamp plan such as called for in this amendment, but he won't initiate it on his own authority. He has told Congress . . . that if the Congress wants him to run a food stamp program, it must enact legislation for such a program. Placing such legislation on this bill is the best way to comply with that demand, and establish a more readily intelligent system of distributing surplus food to our needy.[54]

Democratic leaders were eager to avoid an intraparty fight heading into the 1960 elections. House Speaker Sam Rayburn of Texas apparently asked Representative Sullivan what she wanted, "and I told him."[55] After no small amount of maneuvering, the sides agreed on a compromise: largely along party lines, and with many southern Democrats not voting, the House in late August 1959 passed an amendment authorizing—but not requiring—the USDA to run food stamp "demonstration" projects and up to $250 million per year over two years to fund them. The Senate approved the amendment soon after, also largely along party lines.[56]

Eisenhower reluctantly signed because PL 480 food aid was key to his Cold War–era foreign-policy goals but stated that he would not follow through on food stamps. Secretary Benson dismissed the need: "The food stamp plan is a depression program. There is no need for it now. There is no depression. The economy is running near full capacity."[57]

Benson had little worry about any political costs for his continued intransigence. Rural legislators in both parties were content to let farm policy lie going into a presidential election year, especially given sharp divisions between Democratic cotton and Republican corn. Efforts by Sullivan and other urban Democrats to get Congress to order USDA to produce a plan for food stamp pilot projects went nowhere in the committees on agriculture that did not need their votes at the moment. It still was an imbalanced fight, at least while Eisenhower was in office. "With no activist federal relief administration to speak for the poor and poor people themselves unorganized and politically unconscious," as Janet Poppendieck observed about that moment, "no pressure was exerted on the department to take their interests seriously."[58]

At the close of the 1950s, then, most forms of food assistance pioneered in the Depression era—commodity purchase and distribution, school lunch and school milk programs—along with international food aid under PL 480 were revived and expanded as surpluses continued to pile up. But not food stamps, despite the efforts of their proponents, for whom the *idea* of stamps still possessed virtues that made them useful two decades earlier. In addition to helping to "eat the surplus" and bolster farm incomes, even if those direct effects were modest, food stamps promised to supplement the purchasing power of low-income Americans, who could shop at regular retail shops and enjoy some freedom on what foods to buy. If the proponents of stamps still lacked sufficient political leverage to overcome opposition by the USDA, key agricultural producers, and their patrons in Congress, a presidential election was about to tip the scales more in their favor.

(Re)Discovering Hunger

We can use our huge food surpluses for their only sensible purpose—to feed hungry people. We can demand that the Secretary of Agriculture use the food stamp plan that Congress has provided—and if he won't, we can get an Administration that will. I am convinced that, at very little cost, we can make far better use of our surpluses and provide far more help to the people that need them.

—SENATOR JOHN F. KENNEDY, Democrat from
Massachusetts, 1960[59]

If you read the *New York Times* in 1959, you usually encountered the term "hunger" in reference to People Not Here. They were Out There, in famine-stricken parts of India, Congo, Haiti, or some other "Third World" country to which the United States was shipping surplus grain via the newly renamed PL 480 Food for Peace program.

But hunger in America? Judging from the roughly 150 articles in 1959 with that term, you would not think there was much of it. In fact, the only *Times* article touching on domestic hunger was in January on Depression-level misery in the coal regions of eastern Kentucky and southwest Virginia, where thousands of miners were losing their jobs to mechanization, labor disputes, and the accelerating switch from coal in home heating. Impoverished families in Harlan, Kentucky, were subsisting on packages of USDA surplus rice, flour, cornmeal, cheese, and powdered milk, while at school

FIGURE 9. Family hauling home surplus food, Harlan, Kentucky. Source: Photo by Paul Schutzer. Stock Image ID: 12508187a, Life/Shutterstock.

their children were fed donated cabbage, sweet potatoes, corn-bread, powdered milk, and macaroni and cheese; the milk and cheese came from surplus federal stocks.[60]

A year later hunger at home *was* a problem, largely because can-didate John Kennedy said so after seeing it for himself during campaign stops in hard-hit West Virginia coal towns.[61] Senator Kennedy's "discovery" of hunger there no doubt was spurred by his tense primary-election competition with Senator Hubert Humphrey of Minnesota, who by 1960 had a national profile on hunger as an architect of PL 480 foreign food aid and lead cospon-sor of Senator Aiken's food-allotment bills.[62] If the senator from Massachusetts showed little interest in agricultural and food issues early in his political career, by 1960 he criticized Eisenhower's surplus-disposal policies and supported food stamps in Senate votes.[63] How much the Senator's newfound focus on hunger reflected political calculations versus personal convictions did not matter; Kennedy the president put hunger relief at the center of his early domestic and foreign-policy priorities.

Like Kennedy, more Americans by 1960 were more aware of hunger at home, although a fully developed sense of hunger's depths and impacts took several more years to coalesce.[64] In social-science terms, we call the "discovery" of hunger in the 1960s the heightened "salience" of a condition that may have existed for a while but was hidden from mass awareness or concern because it affected relatively small and marginalized segments of the population, because other priorities dominated the agenda of attention, or both.[65]

But why now? It helped that the still-new mass medium of television enabled candidate Kennedy to highlight conditions of poverty and hunger among West Virginia mining families and would play an even more profound role as the 1960s unfolded. Putting a "face" on hunger would matter to how Americans responded, just as newspaper photos of desperate men in breadlines alongside images of slaughtered pigs illuminated the "paradox of want amidst plenty" in the 1930s. Moreover, as we will consider more fully in the next chapter, it also helped that voices not attuned to the "agricultural mindset" were emerging as advocates for the hungry, in contrast to Senator Aiken's resigned observation years earlier, and were heard in the new administration.

But why was Kennedy's response to hunger at home the revival of a food stamp program discontinued nearly twenty years earlier? After all, to echo Ezra Taft Benson, there was no depression. While the economy in 1960 technically was in recession with a national unemployment rate at around 6.5 percent, the highest in a decade, and even with pockets of rural and urban despair, most Americans were not in dire straits. Still, those pockets of deprivation served as searing contradictions to the widely promoted view that US capitalism—and US democracy—worked for everyone, particularly when it was being compared to Soviet communism.[66] As such, images of hunger in America likely would prick the public conscience, just as they had during the Great Depression.

It also mattered that some of the conditions in agriculture that led to the creation of food stamps in 1939 were back, and in public view. Primary among them was the vexing problems of overproduction and underconsumption, particularly for wheat and feed grains like corn and soybeans, which by 1960 were costing taxpayers roughly $500 million a year (about $4.7 billion today) just to store. Or, as Kennedy's new secretary of agriculture, former Minnesota governor Orville Freeman, put it, "The problem of agricultural surplus comes down to too much wheat and too much feed grain—much too much of both." Freeman's solution, on the surface not that different from Benson's before him, was to get as much of that surplus into the "bellies of as many as possible of the world's hungry people" through the Food for Peace program.[67]

At the same time—and in contrast to images of rural innovation and prosperity that Iowa governor Herschel Loveless promoted to Soviet general secretary Nikita Khrushchev during his 1959 tour of the United States—conditions down on the farm were not great. Despite generally good commodity prices through the decade, higher costs of production had actually eroded net farm income, leading Democrats in 1960 to assail Republicans for production-maximizing policies that impoverished smaller producers and fueled a new rural "depression." Indeed, the number of farms in the United States had plummeted from around 5.5 million in 1950 to 4.0 million in 1960, accelerating an agrarian consolidation that started in the 1930s and continues to this day.[68] Solutions proposed by Democrats in their 1960 party platform included "farmer controlled" production management at one end and expanded surplus disposal at the other, including the food stamp program just authorized by Congress.[69] For their part, Republicans stuck with the policies promoted under Eisenhower, adding a "strategic food reserve" to be tapped in case of a nuclear attack or other national emergency.[70]

So, by 1960, the nation again confronted commodity surpluses and economic pain for many farmers and was about to rediscover hunger at home, even if not at the scale seen in the 1930s: the "paradox of want amidst plenty," back in view. But, to restate the question: *Why food stamps?* Was it because other forms of relief, from surplus-commodity distribution to cash assistance, were tried and found wanting? The various legislative hearings on food relief held during the late 1950s had compared the efficacy of different approaches (except for cash, it seems), so most in Congress likely had reached some conclusion about food stamps when they approved Representative Sullivan's pilot projects. Or maybe stamps were now the default setting for urban Democrats, who had come to despise surplus-commodity distribution but also knew that expanded cash relief was a nonstarter for their more conservative colleagues. "When Kennedy was elected," Representative Sullivan later recalled, "I had a letter written so it was on his desk in 1961 the day he was inaugurated, reminding him that he was for the idea of food stamps while in the Senate."[71] Or maybe it was because policy makers tend to stick to known ideas, even if flawed, rather than try to come up with new ones. Rare are the true innovations in policy design, and the original Food Stamp Plan may have been one of them.[72] It would be easier to revive and adjust a program done once before, even decades earlier, than to start from scratch.

Moreover, there were those inside government, including USDA economists like Fred Waugh, who had tended the food stamp flame over the intervening years, driven by a familiar set of concerns.[73] On the one hand, the nation was buried under literal mountains of surplus commodities. On the other, it had citizens who needed food, although how many were "truly" hungry as versus "merely" undernourished was a matter of some dispute.[74] What remained to be decided was how best to get more food to those who needed it, whether to link food relief to surplus disposal, and how to do all of this without stumbling over the politics of "welfare" or clashing with powerful agricultural and business interests—the paradox anew.

Taking the Tool off the Shelf

The Secretary of Agriculture shall take immediate steps to expand and improve the program of food distribution throughout the United States, utilizing funds and existing statutory authority available to him . . . so as to make available for distribution, through appropriate State and local agencies, to all needy families a greater variety and quantity of food out of our agricultural abundance.

—PRESIDENT JOHN F. KENNEDY, Executive Order 10914, January 21, 1961

So important was West Virginia to Kennedy's ascent to the White House that no one was surprised that his first official action as president was to direct the Department of Agriculture to do more about moving surplus foods to the needy. Through Executive Order 10914, signed the day after Kennedy's inauguration, the USDA boosted distribution of surplus commodities to Americans at home through the school lunch and school milk programs and doubled the size of food packages provided through local relief agencies.[75] His second executive order detailed the responsibilities of the director of the reformulated Food for Peace program, to be led by a former House member from South Dakota by the name of George McGovern.

Kennedy also acted quickly on food stamps. His campaign stops through Appalachia had left him unimpressed with the variety and quality of surplus foods provided under Eisenhower's Needy Families commodity program. In 1958 a not-atypical allotment provided in one month to a family of four in West Virginia contained ten pounds of flour, ten pounds of cornmeal, two pounds of rice, nine pounds of powdered milk, four pounds of butter, and ten pounds of cheese—the preponderance of dairy in particular was evidence of surplus-disposal policy trying to offset the effects of surplus-inducing commodity policy.[76] In 1960, the last year of commodity distribution under Eisenhower, the monthly package contained only pork lard (a rendered fat used in cooking), rice, flour, butter, and cheese. While Secretary Freeman quickly expanded the allotment to include peanut butter, canned meat, and dried eggs, few in or outside of the USDA thought it adequate for a nutritious diet.[77] Moreover, commodity distribution did not reach everyone; eleven states (including Representative Sullivan's Missouri) did not participate at all, and in another seven the program reached only 10 percent of those on public assistance.[78] Food stamps offered a solution, as Kennedy suggested in a special address to Congress two weeks after his inauguration: "We are committed to expanding the variety and quantity of surplus foods distributed to persons who, in a nation of unparalleled agricultural bounty, lack adequate diets. . . . I have instructed the Secretary of

Agriculture, consistent with the bill enacted last year authorizing establishment of pilot Food Stamp Programs, to proceed as rapidly as possible. . . . It is my hope that this pilot program, while providing additional nutrition for those now in need, will pave the way for substantial improvement in our present method of distributing food."[79]

On advice of experts in the USDA's Agricultural Marketing Service, Kennedy soon opted not to rely on legal authorization through Sullivan's 1959 amendment, which would expire at year's end, but on the broad authority under Section 32 on which Henry Wallace had created the original Food Stamp Plan. At Kennedy's behest, and with Freeman's prodding, the AMS by May rolled out eight food stamp pilot projects in six "areas of maximum chronic unemployment"—among them McDowell County, West Virginia— the results of which "will furnish operating experience necessary for our determination of the most effective kind of food allotment program."[80]

Of note, the new program would be led by AMS agricultural economist Isabelle Kelley, who joined the department just out of graduate school in 1940 and, over the ensuing two decades, was instrumental in launching its nutrition initiatives, including the Special Milk Program. Kelley was one of the four AMS experts tasked by Freeman to develop the pilot program and later was appointed the first director of the Food Stamp Division, the first woman in USDA history to direct an action program.[81]

As political scientist Jeffrey Berry amply details, Kennedy's food stamp pilot program was put together by a small team of AMS experts, some of them veterans of the Food Stamp Plan, working almost entirely unguided. The rules they devised reflected lessons learned from its Depression-era predecessor but also anticipated points of potential trouble with the ideologically conservative committees on agriculture and appropriations whose support, and funds, they would need.[82] Notably, the new program retained a purchase requirement; AMS officials were adamant that participating households should put up the amount of money they normally spent on food to get "bonus" stamps that would spur additional consumption. On the other hand, echoing Joseph Coppock's critique from fourteen years earlier, they did away with the mix of orange and blue stamps, arguing that the old two-color stamp system created unnecessary complexity, that restricted-use blue stamps never made an appreciable dent on surpluses, and that stamp users and retailers hated the restrictions anyway.[83] The social workers, food retailers, and bankers consulted by an AMS task force concurred, although, it must be noted, nobody apparently checked with the program's intended users.[84]

Under the new system there were only different denominations of currency-sized coupons that participants bought at a discount based on household income and "normal" food expenditures (for an average 40 percent discount) as calculated by AMS economists based on assumptions about what constituted an adequate food budget given "thrifty" shopping, home cooking, and eating habits.[85] Stamps could be used for any "domestically-produced" food. If that distinction left out coffee, tea, cocoa, and bananas (Puerto Rico apparently did not count as a domestic producer) and imported goods like Italian-made *parmigiano,* it no longer limited users to foods "in surplus." Any link to surplus disposal was now more symbolic, AMS director Howard Davis admitted, with the new program representing "a basic shift in emphasis from the attempt, under the old Stamp Plan, to move specific 'surpluses,' to one of generally increasing the consumption of perishables."[86]

FIGURE 10. A food stamp from the 1960s. Source: Photo by the author.

On May 29, 1961, Kennedy sent Secretary Freeman to Welch, West Virginia, to deliver ninety-five dollars in food stamps purchased by Alderson and Chloe Muncy, he an unemployed coal miner, to feed them and their thirteen children.[87] Mrs. Muncy famously first used the stamps to buy a large can of pork and beans at a local market. Freeman told the assembled crowd that food stamps were a "pioneering effort" that reflected President Kennedy's "very deep concern that there should be anywhere in this great land of ours less than full use of our abundance." The administration's goal, said Freeman, was a "full nutritional diet" for all Americans.[88]

USDA analyses of purchasing patterns in the first wave of pilot projects over 1961–62 indicated predominate use of stamps on meats and perishable foods not in surplus, as expected.[89] Studies of effects on nutrition indicated positive results on household capacity to meet minimum daily allowances through higher consumption of proteins, fruits, and vegetables, although assumptions about a "thrifty" food diet were shown to need adjusting as it became clear that AMS economists had little practical experience with the shopping habits of the poor.[90] Use of one type of stamp cut down on administrative complexity, consumer confusion, and conflicts with retailers. Despite anecdotes of participants trying to trade stamps to buy forbidden items such as cigarettes, the scandal-wary AMS concluded that "there is no evidence that such violations are so numerous that they would impair effectiveness of the program." Nor were there many reported instances of "cheating" among some four thousand participating retailers, largely because of the elimination of blue stamps, and retailers reported higher overall sales to stamp users. As expected, impacts on surplus commodities, where possible to calculate, were modest, although one AMS analysis suggested that expanded consumption of perishable foods led to higher returns for those producers.[91] Finally, poverty researcher Maurice MacDonald notes, "as a program for which income was the sole condition of eligibility, the stamps were reaching needy people who did not fall into categories eligible for other forms of public assistance," a nontrivial effect.[92]

The analyses also signaled potential problems. Most concerning was a drop in food program–participation rates, sometimes by two-thirds, when counties switched from commodity distribution to stamps, either because the poor did not see stamps as worth the cost compared to free food or because they were too cash-strapped to afford even the two dollars per person, per month, minimum. For many the graduated income and stamp-discount scale devised by AMS overly complicated decisions on whether to buy stamps or go without. Moreover, the new program had tighter administration compared to commodity distribution, under which both the USDA and local relief agencies cared more about moving surplus stocks than enforcing eligibility rules. Such a cavalier attitude was not possible under the closely watched stamp pilot program.

Despite such concerns, the AMS remained opposed to free stamps, and neither Freeman nor Kennedy saw a problem in its stance. Requiring participants to purchase stamps meant that the poor would spend more than their "normal" amount on food, increasing their consumption. The AMS position also reflected the general view, in Berry's encapsulation, that this was a self-help program, "and everyone would pay something for the stamps."[93] A decline in food-relief-uptake rates when a county moved to stamps perhaps indicated that many who had benefited from free food were not as needy as supposed or were making rational decisions that stamps weren't worth the cost.[94] Whatever the case, in the view of the AMS, uptake rates could be improved by adjusting purchase requirements, not by eliminating them outright.

Opinions about the food stamp pilots echoed the reception to the original plan. Most participants liked having greater choice and reported being able to provide more nourishing food to their families. Local relief agencies favored stamps over commodity distribution, and retailers simply wanted fewer restrictions on stamp use. While many local officials still evinced concern about the purchase requirement, they preferred stamps to cash assistance because stamps were targeted at improving nutrition. An AMS survey of moderate and higher-income families in Detroit and West Virginia found support for stamps over commodity distribution and, of note, cash assistance, attitudes reflecting prevailing views that the poor might not spend cash wisely.[95]

The pilot program's apparent success led Kennedy to expand it to twenty-five additional sites by late 1962, reaching 328,000 people.[96] Save for Detroit, the first wave of projects had focused on more rural coal, iron, and copper-mining regions hit by sector-specific disruptions (and, critics noted, were important Democratic strongholds). The second wave included Cleveland and St. Louis, large cities suffering from pockets of chronic unemployment and poverty, notably among Black migrants from the rural South displaced by the ongoing mechanization and consolidation in cotton. These cities also had high housing costs and were in states with meager cash-welfare systems. St. Louis was selected so that Representative Sullivan could observe program implementation firsthand.[97] Disturbingly weak uptake of stamps in these cities, and Sullivan's direct lobbying with Freeman, prompted the AMS to adjust purchase rules to account for housing and other expenses, such as childcare costs for working mothers. Program participation improved a bit as a result. Such "hardship" exemptions, Berry observed, eventually redefined household income "to mean *disposable income* after certain necessary expenses were paid."[98] But these adjustments came only after much trial and error.

In January 1963 Kennedy called on Congress to authorize a national food stamp program and appropriate funds to operate it. The president was convinced, in Secretary Freeman's words, that stamps represented a "better and more efficient means than commodity distribution for channeling more of the abundance of American agriculture to families in economic need."[99] The administration's bill to formally authorize the food stamp program was submitted in the House by Representative Sullivan on April 22, 1963. However, the task of shepherding the bill through Congress would be left to Kennedy's successor, Lyndon Johnson. Doing so would hinge on uniting otherwise incompatible partners, a marriage made not in heaven but in the committee rooms of Congress.

4   Farm Programs + Food Programs

During my tenure, we made the food stamp bill part of the farm bill. It was a carefully calculated thing which was done a long time ago to try and unite urban interests with agricultural interests, in common support of the bills, that had been fighting each other over. You got a food subsidy program, you got a farm subsidy program. Each in their own are unpopular with the other segment of society, but you put them together and you can get a lot of people who will vote for both of them that way.

—House Committee on Agriculture member, recalling the early 1970s[1]

"A Change Is Gonna Come"

By the early 1960s the politics of food stamps reflected a political landscape that had changed much over the previous decade.[2] The greatest shifts were demographic. While the coal towns of West Virginia helped Kennedy win the 1960 Democratic nomination, his narrow general-election victory over Richard Nixon depended on big city voters, punctuating the postwar shift in population, and political power, away from rural America.[3]

The effects of this shift were felt in agricultural policy making. Kennedy had criticized Eisenhower for spending vast public sums on commodity programs going to an ever-smaller number of farmers, sentiments shared by the expanding cohort of members of Congress from the nation's big cities, most of them Democrats, for whom farmers were just another "special" interest whatever their privileged status in American culture.[4] Where agricultural policy long had been the technically convoluted preserve of commodity producers and their patrons in the USDA and the congressional committees on agriculture, voices not attached to the "agricultural mindset" now began to demand a say.[5]

For their part, the shrinking cohort of farm-sector legislators—the core of the bipartisan "conservative coalition" that dominated Congress from the 1930s through the 1960s—worried about maintaining support for commodity programs on which producers had come to depend.[6] They were right to worry: by 1960 only 12 percent of House districts represented farming areas, down from 38 percent just a decade earlier.[7] Their concerns would intensify as the Supreme Court in *Baker v. Carr* (1962) dismantled much of the rural bias in how state legislatures allocated US House seats and as Congress, in passing the Voting Rights Act of 1965, enabled federal oversight of state election systems that long excluded racial minorities from the ballot box. Both reforms would erode rural America's artificially inflated hold over the House in particular—the Senate's constitutionally rooted rural bias remains—giving urban voters political power more commensurate with their numbers. Glimpses of the new politics were seen in the late 1950s as the committees on agriculture grudgingly gave ground on food stamps. It would crystalize with the fight over the Food Stamp Act of 1964, ushering in an arranged (even forced) marriage that endures to this day, albeit with its share of awkward moments.[8]

FIGURE 11. Lyndon Johnson signing the 1964 Food Stamp Act, Washington, DC, August 31, 1964. Source: US Department of Agriculture, accessed February 18, 2023, www.fns.usda.gov/snap/short-history-snap.

Scene 1: The Food Stamp Act as a Shotgun Marriage

An Act to strengthen the agricultural economy; to help to achieve a fuller and more effective use of food abundances; to provide for improved levels of nutrition among economically needy households through a cooperative Federal-State program of food assistance to be operated through normal channels of trade; and for other purposes.

—Preamble to the Food Stamp Act of 1964[9]

Kennedy's decision to ask Congress to authorize a national food stamp program had political risks, even with Democratic majorities in both chambers, but so did continuing to rely on Section 32 discretionary funds, given the hostility to stamps by the conservative southern Democrats who had controlled key House committees throughout most of the previous thirty years. Of particular concern was Rep. Jamie Whitten of Mississippi, longtime chair of the House Subcommittee on Agricultural Appropriations and known colloquially (if not fondly) as the "Permanent Secretary of Agriculture" for his near-feudal hold over USDA spending.[10] Whitten's antipathy to food stamps lay in not wanting to use "farmers money" for "relief" and reflected the culture of cotton in his Mississippi Delta district, where sharecroppers and tenant farmers subsisted on commodity handouts in between growing seasons. Whitten's subcommittee regularly approved less money for the pilot programs than Kennedy requested, and his grip over the food stamp program would be loosened if its status could be made permanent. Another was Howard Smith of Virginia, an avowed segregationist opposed to federal programs that might undermine "states' rights" and who, as chair of the Committee on Rules, used its role as House "traffic cop" to block floor votes on food stamps throughout the late 1950s. Smith's intransigence on civil rights finally provoked House leaders in 1961 to expand the Committee on Rules to include more liberals, but he still could throw up roadblocks with the support of the "conservative coalition" of Republicans and southern Democrats.[11] With most Republicans opposed to food stamps as "welfare," the real fight would be among Democrats.

By the time Rep. Leonor Sullivan submitted Kennedy's food stamp bill to the House in April 1963, pilot projects reached some 335,000 people in thirty-three areas, at an annualized budget outlay of approximately $20 million (see table 1 in the appendix). Kennedy now proposed a national program reaching around four million people within five years, when it was expected to cost around $360 million annually for benefits (around $3 billion today), funded out of general appropriations, not Section 32. Food stamps would supplant surplus-commodity distribution, which by 1963 reached some seven million people at an annual cost of $200 million but was criticized as nutritionally inadequate, poorly administered, unfair to retailers, and open to manipulation by local officials accustomed to lax USDA oversight.[12] While the administration's bill did not explicitly end commodity distribution, it was assumed, with Secretary of Agriculture Orville Freeman claiming that program costs would be offset "in substantial part by the discontinuation of Federal food donations to needy households in political subdivisions participating in the food stamp program." In his testimony to the House Committee on Agriculture in June, Freeman framed the new program as addressing inadequacies in commodity distribution and as having learned lessons from the original plan: "Recognizing these weaknesses, we revived the idea of a food stamp program which first had been tried shortly before the Second World War. In most respects, what we have done is to lift up the radiator cap and drive a whole new machine under it. The prewar food stamp program was a good idea, but it suffered badly from administrative problems both in design and in execution. Realizing that the memory of problems still hung over the food stamp concept, we began slowly with a few pilot projects."[13] Following a series of hearings, House Agriculture chair Harold Cooley appointed a special subcommittee to study the plan. Panel members made field trips to pilot project areas and reported out a revised bill in August, which went to the full committee for deliberation.[14]

The path to committee approval was narrow, despite Democratic control of the larger body. For one thing, most House Agriculture members saw stamps as relief for the urban poor, not as aiding agriculture. Even Cooley, who supported stamps, asked if "some way could be found to charge this up to welfare and not the farmer." Such concerns were situated in his fear the public had the wrong idea about who benefited most from federal farm policy: "With a $6 billion budget, the city people criticize us and complain that the farmers are a bunch of parasites, bloodsuckers, and many other unwarranted epithets. As a matter of fact, more of this goes to the cities than it does to the country people. The benefits are more for the city people."[15] This was not quite true. By late 1963 only seventeen of the forty-three areas in which pilot programs operated contained a population more than 50 percent urban, but the image of food stamps as "for the city people" was fixed in the minds of rural legislators and for many in the national press for whom urban (and Black) poverty was most visible. That only two members of House Agriculture—Democrat Cooley of North Carolina and Republican Robert Dole of Kansas—had food stamp pilots in their districts reinforced such impressions.[16] Committee Republicans even wondered if the Department of Health, Education, and Welfare should administer such a "welfare" program, an idea of some allure to committee Democrats so long as their committee retained control.

Another obstacle arose out the deepening divisions among congressional Democrats on civil rights. Southern Democrats worried that the proposed food stamp program gave the USDA too much authority over the states that, while free to set eligibility standards, "shall not discriminate against any household by reason of race, religious creed, national origin, or political beliefs"—making food stamps a potential federal lever against segregation.[17] Freeman's efforts to crack down on racial discrimination in commodity distribution reinforced their fears.[18] Committee Republicans, still furious at southern Democrats for insisting on preferential treatment for cotton during a failed effort to pass a farm bill in 1962, even pushed for explicit language barring racial discrimination by retailers, which skeptics regarded as little more than a ploy to further divide Democrats and kill the food stamp bill outright.[19]

The House Committee on Agriculture revisited the bill in October, but action stopped until 1964, with new president Lyndon Johnson taking over from his assassinated predecessor and stating support for food stamps as part of his "war on poverty." Orville Freeman stayed on as secretary of agriculture, in part to help to move the food stamp bill through Congress. Even so, that February House Agriculture voted nineteen to fourteen against it. The outcome came as a surprise insofar that three of the five southern Democrats who joined Republicans in the majority had pledged support but now voted no to express disapproval of Johnson's civil rights efforts.[20] Their "betrayal" angered urban Democrats, who earlier had acceded to party leaders and voted on the House floor for a controversial cotton-price support bill, over Republican opposition. Representative Sullivan promptly declared that she would force floor votes on any bill involving commodities unless the Committee on Agriculture reported out the food stamp bill, a threat with teeth if urban Democrats joined Republicans against commodity supports, especially any aiding southern crops.[21] They soon targeted a bill to fund research on the health hazards of smoking that Cooley, from a tobacco area, was eager to get in the wake of the January 1964 surgeon general's report on smoking and health. The tobacco bill went to the Committee on Rules, which late in February voted to block floor consideration; the panel's urban Democrats now joined Republicans against a program aiding a southern crop and in clear retaliation for the Committee on Agriculture's rebuff of food stamps.[22] The Committee on Rules reserved its right to reconsider, "implying that it could be saved given favorable Agricultural Committee action on the food stamp bill."[23]

The Senate, meanwhile, had attached a wheat-management program sponsored by Senator George McGovern, Democrat from South Dakota (and former director of Kennedy's Food for Peace program), to the cotton program sought by southern Democrats and sent the combined bill back to the House.[24] Faced with prospects that urban Democrats would join most Republicans in opposition, House leaders conceived of a strategy, in the words of political scientist Randall Ripley, "tying the wheat-cotton bill to some bill that would appeal to urban Democrats. In short, they wanted to arrange a trade."[25] President Johnson, trying to manage the growing schisms in his party, backed the deal: rural Democrats would vote the Food Stamp Act out of committee or watch the wheat-cotton bill go down to defeat on the House floor.[26] The threat was particularly worrisome in light of ongoing divisions over commodity supports that had nearly scuttled a farm bill two years earlier. Political scientist John Mark Hansen describes what happened next: "Under President Lyndon B. Johnson's not-so-gentle prodding, House Agriculture Committee chairman Harold D. Cooley pried an authorization for a permanent food stamp program out of his committee, which had long been inhospitable to any welfare programs that did not benefit farmers. On the floor, the urban liberals insisted that the food stamp vote precede the farm bill vote, lest unrepentant conservatives defect. The script went as planned."[27] Ripley, in his study of House passage, observed that there never was a formal deal to link the food stamp and commodity-support bills: "Instead, and this is typical of the operations of the House, it was a matter of a favorable psychological climate. . . . The more the individual members and the press talked about a specific trade of rural votes on food stamps for urban votes on wheat-cotton, the more firmly the exchange became implanted in the minds of the members."[28] One Democrat from the Committee on Agriculture recalled, "You never used the word 'deal.' But Mrs. Sullivan talked to Cooley, she talked to me, and it was pretty well understood that there would be this type of help."[29] Even so, per Hansen's assessment, it did not hurt that Johnson twisted a few arms; "I think most of you know what's going on here," Howard Smith complained on the House floor.[30]

The committee voted out Sullivan's bill 16 to 14, along with a Republican amendment requiring that states participate and provide matching funds in line with the federal-state arrangement on cash assistance under the Aid to Families with Dependent Children (AFDC) program. That amendment was seen by food stamp supporters as a "poison pill" that would ensure defeat by senators wary of any new mandate on the states, and it was voted down on the House floor. The ensuing vote on the Food Stamp Act was 229 to 189, with 216 Democrats and 13 Republicans in the majority against 163 Republicans and 26 Democrats, most of them southern (13 other Democrats voted "present" or did not vote).[31] While members of either party from rural areas were least likely to support food stamps, those whose districts hosted pilot projects voted more favorably.[32] The House soon after approved the wheat-cotton bill by a narrower 211 to 203, also largely along party lines, with some urban Democrats not voting.[33]

This "logroll" on two otherwise imperiled bills sent a clear message: among Democrats at least, no legislation supporting commodity programs would get enough votes beyond the committees on agriculture unless it did something for nutrition.[34] As Ripley summarized, "The food stamp program was the one food program that had even a partial urban orientation to it. Urban members skeptical about billions for farm programs could receive at least mild comfort from the prospect of millions for the urban needy."[35] Intraparty divisions added to the equation, with southern resistance on civil rights stiffening northern Democrats against any help for southern crops. While most urban Democrats held up their end of the bargain, defections on the wheat-cotton bill were enough to underscore a spreading antipathy to commodity supports, a threat that members of the congressional farm bloc now fully appreciated.[36]

Jamie Whitten voted with the majority each time; he still disliked food stamps but knew that his own power in the House sometimes required going along with party leaders. In this regard, Ripley argued, Whitten was a "reliable trader."[37] Whitten's views on food stamps would soften over time, in no small part due to the rising number of Blacks voting in his district with the end of Jim Crow laws, and by the mid-1970s was in synch with fellow Democrats. He would go on to influence agricultural policy until his retirement in 1995, at that time the longest-serving House member in history.[38] In recognition Congress renamed USDA's headquarters building after him. Howard Smith voted no twice, opposing the wheat-cotton bill for its costs, and two years later suffered a surprising primary defeat to a liberal challenger, who in turn lost in the general election to a Republican—a harbinger of the partisan realignment to come.[39] Harold Cooley barely escaped an upset defeat in 1964 but lost to his Republican challenger two years later. Of note, while Cooley's tobacco bill never left the Committee on Rules, funding for it was folded into an agricultural appropriations bill that passed soon after with little opposition.[40] A deal was a deal.

The bill moved to the Senate. The Committee on Agriculture and Forestry chair, Allen Ellender, a conservative Democrat from

Louisiana, was as hostile to food stamps as his House counterparts but knew that his liberal colleagues had sufficient leverage to overcome his opposition. Besides, the ever-persuasive Johnson wanted this program.[41] With less doubt that the Senate would pass a bill, Ellender's committee focused on reviewing the House draft and hearing from an array of organized groups with by-now established positions. The American Farm Bureau Federation opposed stamps; the National Farmers Union voiced support. Producer-group stances depended on the extent to which they benefited from surplus-commodity distribution; milk producers opposed stamps, potato and dry-bean producers supported them. Labor unions and social-welfare organizations backed stamps as part of the War on Poverty, although some opposed the purchase requirement as unfair to the very poor and expressed concern about the administrative discretion being given to the states. Local relief officials wanted mostly to get out of the business of distributing commodities. The US Chamber of Commerce opposed a new federal "welfare" program even as some local chapters saw stamps as boosting their economies. Food retailers just wanted few restrictions on what foods could be purchased with stamps.[42]

The committee soon reported out an amended version, which the Senate approved by voice vote on June 30.[43] Its bill deleted a House provision to ban stamp use on soft drinks and other "luxury" foods, which the USDA and retailers opposed as administratively unwieldly, and inserted clear language halting commodity distribution where stamps were adopted. The House accepted the Senate version by voice vote soon after, to avoid delay as the fall elections neared. In his August 31 signing statement, Johnson called the new program "a realistic and responsible step forward toward the fuller and wiser use of our agricultural abundance. . . .

As a permanent program, the Food Stamp Plan will be one of our most valuable weapons for the war on poverty. It will enable low-income families to increase their food expenditures, using their own dollars."[44]

The Food Stamp Act of 1964 (PL 88–525) did not create new policy, Jeffrey Berry notes, so much as "it legitimated and ratified the administrative guidelines already in effect."[45] In codifying Kennedy's food stamp program into law, Congress—or the USDA for that matter—could not terminate the program unless Congress repealed the act itself. On the other hand, Congress limited program authorization to three years, guaranteeing a review in short order. Congress also would decide annual program budgets through appropriations processes still dominated by Whitten and other patrons of agriculture, among whom perceptions that food stamps took "farmers money" never dissipated. Their reluctance to fully appropriate funds authorized by law would constrain program expansion in its initial years (see table 1 in the appendix).[46] Local politics did as well, insofar that states (and even counties, with state permission) could decide whether to participate, an option poverty researcher Maurice MacDonald argues was kept so that "congressmen from conservative areas could vote for passage, secure in the knowledge that their constituents could still decide not to offer the program."[47] States opting out of stamps could keep surplus-commodity distribution, which at its peak in 1971 reached some four million households, or could forego any federal food assistance whatsoever.[48] States also decided eligibility standards for people not covered by AFDC or other forms of public assistance, had flexibility in adapting income rules to local conditions, and would bear around 70 percent of all frontline administrative costs, a requirement proponents feared would dampen state interest in participating but which congressional budget overseers saw as fair, given full federal funding for the benefits. If the new Food Stamp Program was not everything its proponents sought, it now was authorized under law. As such, it would be harder to eliminate, in contrast to its predecessor's reliance on USDA discretion and the whims of congressional appropriators.

Scene 2: The "Hunger Lobby" Demands More

Why does the government pay the Mississippi plantation of a U.S. senator more than $13,000 a month not to grow food or fiber, and at the same time why does the government pay a starving child in Mississippi only $9 a month, and what are you doing about it?

—REV. RALPH ABERNATHY, President, Southern Christian Leadership Conference, 1968[49]

All government programs have unintended consequences.[50] Sometimes they result from faulty initial assumptions, sometimes from underfunding, and sometimes from ineffectual or discriminatory frontline administration. Sometimes the consequences aren't unintentional at all if program designers knew what *could* happen but proceeded anyway for political or bureaucratic reasons. The new Food Stamp Program suffered from all of these in its first years.

Chief among the program's unintended consequences was its apparent role in *worsening* hunger where it replaced commodity distribution. Such effects were most acute in the Deep South, where mechanization and consolidation in cotton, accelerated by congressionally mandated commodity-management programs, disrupted traditional (if exploitive) systems of sharecropping and tenant farming, driving now-surplus labor to northern cities—with resulting increases in urban poverty there and deeper deprivation among those left behind.[51] Southern states also had meager welfare systems, with relief often limited to surplus commodities.[52] As journalist Nick Kotz argued in *Let Them Eat Promises,* his searing indictment of hunger, poverty, and race in America, ending paltry but free commodity allotments exacerbated conditions for the worst off: "In theory, the food stamp plan sounded simple and workable, and should have been an enormous improvement over commodity distribution. . . . In practice, though, the food stamp plan amounted to virtual extortion from the poor; it was no accident that the stamp payment formula produced the outcries, 'We can't afford the stamps' and 'The stamps run out after two weeks.' Following their congressional leaders' twin desires of helping the farmers but not providing welfare for the poor, Agriculture Department bureaucrats had designed a food stamp program so conservative that reformers call the plan 'Scrooge stamps.'"[53]

More neutral observers came to similar conclusions. The economics of being very poor made purchasing a prescribed dollar amount of stamps at the start of each month a gamble for households with irregular incomes and limited capacity to meet other expenses. Getting free surplus commodities had at least allowed the poor to preserve what cash they had. But the poor were faced with a hard choice wherever food stamps replaced commodity distribution: spend meager cash up front on stamps and hope to make it through the month or forego food assistance altogether. For many the prospect of being required to spend 40 to 50 percent of their incomes on stamps, compared to 17 percent being spent on food per capita in the United States overall, made it no choice at all.[54] With free commodities no longer an option, many were left worse off than before.

The result was an average 40 percent decline in participation in federal food programs when states switched from commodity distribution to food stamps, hovering around 16 percent of those eligible in the early years of the Food Stamp Program (FSP).[55] The problem was exacerbated by other program rules. While the USDA set stamp-purchase and benefit-level formulas, states had discretion in setting eligibility standards for monthly allowable incomes and assets, usually tied to their often-punitive criteria for public assistance. Seven states did not participate, content to rely on commodity distribution. Such latitude led to considerable variation in participation rates across states and even counties within states.[56]

Criticism of the FSP, and of its designers' assumptions about the poor, grew, but within a fast-shifting political context. How to feed hungry people always had been left in the hands of government experts, with little input from those affected or even those claiming to speak on their behalf. Nor was there much national publicity on or rallying around the Food Stamp Act, negotiations over which had been an "insider" game of bargaining among Secretary Freeman and key members of Congress.[57] That game was about to change with the emergence of advocates for the hungry and poor, including (uniquely) the poor themselves.

Any number of books detail the politics of hunger and nutrition in the late 1960s.[58] All point to the pivotal role of members of Congress outside the farm bloc, led by Senators Robert Kennedy of New York and Joseph Clark of Pennsylvania, who in 1967 used a special Subcommittee on Poverty to investigate shortcomings in the FSP and ended up exposing dire conditions of poverty, malnutrition, and outright hunger in the Mississippi Delta—to the fury of Jamie Whitten and other southern conservatives. Sometimes overlooked was the role of the labor movement, of churches and synagogues, and of young civil rights activists, many from the South. Also critical was a newly organized Citizens Board of Inquiry into Hunger and Malnutrition in the United States, whose Field Foundation–funded study, *Hunger U.S.A.*, laid out in damning detail evidence of hunger and malnutrition throughout the country.[59] That study in turn got national exposure by CBS, arguably the most influential of the nation's three broadcast television networks. In its visually compelling May 1968 special, *Hunger in America, CBS Reports* also charged that Freeman was reluctant to take stronger action for fear of antagonizing the USDA's congressional overseers, whose support Johnson needed for the escalating war in Vietnam.[60] Also critical was the Poor People's Campaign, led by the Reverend Ralph Abernathy after the April 1968 assassination of the Reverend Martin Luther King, which weeks after King's murder engaged in widely (if not always sympathetically) publicized demonstrations at USDA headquarters in Washington to protest its "collusion" with local political and economic elites.[61]

Pushed by new advocates and magnified by televised images of starving children, the problem of hunger jumped into the national spotlight. But Congress did little. For one thing Vietnam now overshadowed most domestic problems—save, possibly, fears of "civil disorder" with racial unrest in the nation's cities. Gone were the heady (for liberals) days of Johnson's Great Society, replaced now by concerns about the budget with rising spending on the war. Absent pressure from Johnson, who always may have been lukewarm about a food stamp program long identified with his predecessor, the conservatives in control of the committees on agriculture and appropriations were content with marginal changes—and furious at "outside agitators" making trouble.[62] Few of *their* constituents were rallying for more relief, and any who did were not being paid much mind, so

FIGURE 12. Resurrection City, Poor People's Campaign, Washington, DC, 1968. Source: Collection of the Smithsonian National Museum of African American History and Culture, Washington, DC, © Jill Freedman.

food stamp advocates had little leverage in the absence of votes on commodity programs. Only once, in late 1967, was Representative Sullivan able to hold a peanut program hostage in exchange for a two-year FSP reauthorization rather than the one year sought by a House Committee on Agriculture determined to keep the program on a short leash.[63] The committee treated food stamps "like dirt," she later complained, "an abomination that must be tolerated as the price for getting urban cooperation in the House on farm subsidy legislation."[64] At the behest of Johnson, who just wanted the issue off his desk, Congress authorized a National Nutrition Survey to gather data supporting, or refuting, the findings in *Hunger U.S.A.*

For its part the USDA was caught between its congressional overseers and growing outside criticism of its antihunger efforts.[65] Department officials pointed to FSP expansion, now to over eight hundred counties despite congressionally imposed budget constraints, and blamed state welfare systems for providing too little cash to allow the poor to buy stamps. Expectations about the program were unrealistic, they felt, and resented criticisms after years of trying to feed the needy when few others cared. "No one told us that this was a program to feed *all* the poor," complained one.[66] Pressure from liberal senators and increasingly visible "hunger lobby" activists, plus input by Freeman's own advisory committee on civil rights, spurred the secretary to find funds to boost benefit levels and to reduce purchase requirements for households earning less than $30 a month (the median monthly income in 1967 was $600).[67] However, Freeman deflected pressure to tap $300 million in unspent Section 32 funds, unwilling to incur the wrath of Whitten and other guardians of "farmers money."[68] Johnson, needing congressional support for his budget and tax priorities but with reduced Democratic majorities in both chambers after the 1966 midterms, rebuffed Freeman's request to add more funds to food programs.[69]

Even so, hunger-relief advocates saw some gains. Especially important was the Senate's vote to form a Select Committee on Nutrition and Human Needs, to be composed of members of the generally liberal and urban Committee on Labor and Public Welfare and of the generally conservative and rural Committee on Agriculture and Forestry.[70] The new panel would be chaired by George McGovern, a liberal Democrat from South Dakota who directed the Food for Peace program under John Kennedy.[71] Creation of the Select Committee was made possible in part by the support of key southern Democrats, notably Herman Talmadge of Georgia, who, like

McGovern, also sat on Agriculture and Forestry. So did newly elected Republican Robert Dole, a conservative from Kansas who had supported federal school-lunch programs when serving in the House. Dole and McGovern were partisan and ideological opposites—and bitter foes in 1972 when McGovern ran for president and Dole chaired the Republican Party—but their shared experiences as World War II combat veterans and memories of hard times during the Great Depression would unite them in fighting hunger at home and abroad.[72] While the committee had no authority to report out legislation—that function remained with standing committees like Agriculture—over the next decade it would shine a light on hunger and its roots in poverty, keep pressure on the USDA to improve program outcomes, and act as a counterweight to antirelief biases in the farm bloc and, increasingly, the Republican Party as a whole.[73] In the House, liberals settled for using the more accommodating Committee on Education and Labor to hold hearings on hunger. This was done over the strenuous objections of new House Agriculture chair W.R. "Bob" Poage of Texas—first elected to Congress along with Lyndon Johnson in 1936—whose antipathy about food stamps was matched by his determination to keep the program under his committee's jurisdiction. But if control over the Food Stamp Program still lay with the patrons of agriculture, they no longer operated unchallenged.

Scene 3: Hitching Food Stamps to the Farm Bill

The best way to get those food stamps is to threaten the farm program!

—SENATOR ALLEN ELLENDER, Democrat from Louisiana[74]

The intertwined problems of poverty and hunger did not feature in the 1968 presidential election after the assassination of Robert

Kennedy. Democratic nominee Hubert Humphrey, the former senator from Minnesota now serving as Johnson's vice president, instead focused narrowly on alleviating hunger, which Republican nominee Richard Nixon, vice president under Eisenhower, mentioned only once.[75] Few in the "hunger lobby" expected much once Nixon was elected.

They were to be surprised. For one, public attention to hunger (if not poverty) was reawakened in early 1969 with the release of the previously authorized National Nutrition Survey, which affirmed claims made in *Hunger U.S.A.* about conditions of hunger and malnutrition throughout the nation. George McGovern's subsequent strategic use of the Select Committee to publicize the survey's findings, highlighted by memorable testimony on hunger in South Carolina by its junior senator, Democrat Ernest "Fritz" Hollings, made national news and prompted more legislators to look closely at conditions among their own constituents. Many were sobered by what they found.[76] Others, not so much: fellow South Carolinian Strom Thurmond, a segregationist Democrat turned Republican, called the survey a "Democratic plot to get the Negro vote."[77]

Moreover, the politics of food stamps began to get more complicated in ways that ultimately aided program advocates. Liberal Democrats had held their tongues under Johnson, but with Nixon in the White House felt free to criticize the FSP's failings, and the modest boost in food stamp allocations they once wangled out of Orville Freeman no longer sufficed in the harsh light of the survey's findings.[78] At the same time farm-sector Democrats and producer groups fretted that Nixon would dismantle their long-defended system of commodity supports; concerned about losing leverage, they even had to urge incoming secretary of agriculture, Clifford

Hardin, to keep nutrition programs in the USDA when he mused about shifting food "relief" to the Department of Health, Education, and Welfare.[79] Hovering above all of this were the political ambitions of the new president. What Nixon really felt about hunger in America is anyone's guess, just as it was hard to know what he felt about many domestic problems.[80] What *was* certain was that Nixon would not be outflanked on any major policy issue being pushed by potential Democratic rivals for 1972.[81] On hunger—which Hardin called "the hottest item on the domestic front"—Nixon worried about McGovern and was not about to let the South Dakotan use the Select Committee to browbeat him into action.[82] He promptly authorized a White House working group to verify the survey's results and got Hardin to float the idea of paying for boosts in food programs with reductions in commodity supports, an idea sure to unnerve farm-bloc Democrats. But the money had to come from somewhere; Nixon, like Johnson, was under pressure to cut domestic spending to pay for the ongoing war.

McGovern and other senators—including liberal Republicans like Jacob Javits of New York—kept up the pressure in widely publicized field visits to pockets of rural and urban poverty and in Select Committee hearings highlighting the dire conditions they encountered. Not wanting McGovern to gain more traction, Nixon in April 1969 authorized an added $270 million in all federal food-program spending for fiscal 1970, to go to $1 billion for fiscal 1971, and directed that the money be added to the USDA budget.[83] A month later, in a "Special Message to Congress Recommending a Program to End Hunger in America," Nixon proposed, among other actions, amending the Food Stamp Act to set uniform national eligibility standards, reduce purchase-requirement prices, and provide more free stamps to the poor. The message also announced the establishment of a Food and Nutrition Service to enable the USDA to better coordinate its expanding portfolio of nutrition programs.[84]

While antihunger advocates expressed concerns about budget-driven income-cutoff limits for free stamps, the Senate in September 1969 adopted the administration's proposals through a set of amendments to the Food Stamp Act. But movement stopped at House Agriculture, where Bob Poage declared that he was holding the amendments hostage, in trade for concessions on commodity programs when the Farm Bill went up for reauthorization the following year.[85] Poage and other farm-bloc House Democrats were concerned that under stricter budget constraints more funds for food stamps would be at the expense of farm programs, so tying the two into a single legislative package would keep urban Democrats in the fold against Republican opposition to spending on either. That Democrats like Rep. Shirley Chisholm of New York—the first Black woman elected to Congress (and first to run for president)—now had seats on House Agriculture precisely to promote food stamps factored in his calculation.[86] Poage even proposed that the Food Stamp Act be brought formally into the Farm Bill, a suggestion neither Nixon nor the Senate took up.[87] For Poage and other House Committee on Agriculture members, the proverbial shoe was now on the other foot: an ever-shrinking cohort of House members from farming areas *needed* nutrition programs to keep their commodity supports, and the Food Stamp Program was their bargaining chip.[88]

Faced with this roadblock, and with McGovern keeping a drumbeat of criticism on the eve of Nixon's December 1969 White House Conference on Food, Nutrition, and Health, the president had Secretary Hardin issue a set of administrative rules to increase food stamp allotment levels to better meet basic nutritional needs, reduce purchase prices for most participants, and extend the program to areas not already participating.[89] Whitten and Poage were unhappy with the new rules when informed by Hardin about them, but they also were weary of being portrayed as villains and soon would need urban liberals' support on commodity programs. Neither opposed Hardin's request for funds to cover the extra costs, and otherwise budget-conscious congressional Republicans acceded to Nixon's wishes. In their essential capitulation, Ronald King argues, the "period of conservative opponents using spending allowances as a means of limiting food stamp expansion was coming to an end."[90] Nixon's rules changes would lead to the most significant expansion in Food Stamp Program coverage and spending since its inception, with enrollees' benefits on average *doubling* from 1970 to 1972.[91]

A critical political factor in all of this was the concurrent failure of Nixon's Family Assistance Plan, which would have replaced a patchwork federal-state welfare system with a minimum monthly cash income for all families.[92] The plan's graduated "negative" income tax structure would provide incentives to work without risking sharp cuts in support, in stark contrast to the rigid "benefits cliffs" in AFDC and state general-assistance programs. However, the White House underappreciated the already essential role of food stamps for many poor families, and its proposed "cash-out" of stamps for those getting a guaranteed income raised alarms. While antihunger and social-welfare advocates agreed that cash was superior to the "in-kind" support of food stamps, they saw Nixon's plan as insufficient, given an emerging consensus that the poor should not pay more than 30 percent of household income on food. Eliminating stamps might *reduce* total monthly support for those already on assistance, particularly in states with comparatively generous relief programs.[93] Moreover, because food stamps were not fully adjusted for the cost of living, they were a comparatively good deal for rural America, so even some rural legislators were wary of losing them.[94] Critics attacked Nixon's plan just as his White House Conference on Food, Nutrition, and Health convened in early December, prompting the administration to promise that families getting a guaranteed income could still purchase stamps. It did not matter: the Family Assistance Plan soon died in Congress. While most liberals supported the plan despite their misgivings about its benefit levels, it failed because moderates in both parties were split while conservatives uniformly opposed a guaranteed income for anyone who should be working.[95] Ironically, as Jeffrey Berry concludes, Nixon's prior boost in food stamp benefits played a part in fracturing congressional support for a guaranteed family income: "In fact, food stamps had come to resemble a guaranteed annual income. The December 1969 administrative reforms had made benefits equal throughout the country. Eligibility was based solely on income and assets. Both the nonworking and working poor could qualify, and a liberal benefit reduction rate of 30 percent preserved the incentive to work. The cost of the benefits provided to enrollees was borne totally by the federal government. Food stamps had turned into . . . a 'mini-negative income tax.'"[96] In this regard, even if many rural Democrats still were lukewarm about them, food stamps at least were tied to supplementing food consumption and, indirectly, production. With the demise of the Family Assistance Plan and with Nixon's intent to phase out commodity distribution, stamps now were more essential than ever as a nutrition *and* income supplement.

They also were an increasingly valuable bargaining chip for the beleaguered patrons of agriculture struggling to hold onto their commodity programs. In a reversal of the politics behind the initial passage of the Food Stamp Act, Poage released his hold on Nixon's proposed amendments in return for liberals' votes for commodity programs in the Agricultural Act of 1970, which Congress approved in late November. Passage of the amendments to the Food Stamp Act took longer due to differences between a more generous Senate bill and a more restrictive House version, but Congress approved a compromise on January 1, 1971, a day after program authorization technically expired. In addition to formalizing the changes made by the USDA, the amendments reflected necessary legislative bargains. On one hand, Congress expanded eligibility for free stamps and extended the program to Puerto Rico, Guam, and the US Virgin Islands. On the other, at Poage's insistence it instituted a work requirement for able-bodied adults, excluding mothers with small children—the first such "workfare" provision in program history.[97] The USDA, uninterested in being a welfare agency, did little to enforce it.[98]

A year later Secretary of Agriculture Earl Butz, who took over after Hardin resigned, declared his intent to make major changes in commodity programs when the Farm Bill came up for renewal in 1973.[99] Butz had served under Ezra Taft Benson in the 1950s and was just as ardent in his belief that markets alone should drive production decisions. The secretary's vow to kill off the last vestiges of New Deal production management was made politically palatable by overall good times in the fields; commodity prices and farm incomes were strong, and once-massive corn and wheat surpluses had evaporated with higher domestic meat consumption and increased foreign sales.[100] In fact, rising consumer food prices (which also generated more need for food stamps) was now of greater concern, making subsidies for well-off farmers less defensible.[101] With most Republicans opposing fixed price supports, Democrats representing crops that still depended on some form of production management (notably cotton and dairy) needed allies in nutrition programs that many long regarded as little more than urbanites' extortion of "farmers money."

Their solution was brilliant, if infuriating to nutrition advocates eager to detach food assistance from agriculture's grasp and to Butz, who disdained food stamps and wanted the USDA out of "relief" altogether.[102] But the patrons of agriculture were not about to throw away a strong playing card: in putting together the tactically named Agriculture and Consumer Protection Act of 1973, the committees on agriculture formally made the Food Stamp Act its own title in the Farm Bill. Accommodating food stamps created few political problems, John Mark Hansen observed, even for the more conservative House committee: "The leadership created a subcommittee, staffed it with members sympathetic to food stamps, let them work out their program, and then bundled their proposals together with all the rest. . . . Politically, food stamps were just another commodity."[103]

Just another commodity, one to be combined with (and offset divisions between) corn, cotton, dairy, and wheat programs into an omnibus legislative package encompassing enough to get needed votes in an increasingly urban and suburban Congress. Given its growing scale and importance, the Food Stamp Program was a particularly valuable commodity and ripe for bargaining. When negotiators were done, the amendments to the Food Stamp Act contained in the 1973 farm bill expanded program eligibility and mandated that all states make stamps available to all who qualified. (A year later Congress increased to 50 percent the federal share of state administrative costs, making statewide implementation easier.) While participants still had to purchase stamps, the Farm Bill's new nutrition title nevertheless extended the program to more people than ever; guaranteed that anyone who met program rules could get stamps; and, to satisfy producers, processors, and retailers, made more foods eligible for food stamp purchase.

Of note, the program was authorized through the Farm Bill's full four years, with no fixed ceiling on spending, in stark contrast to the short reauthorizations and strict spending limits of the previous decade.[104] *Just another commodity.*

Scene 4: Renewing Vows and Ending Purchase Requirements

We have forged a real, working urban-rural coalition. Urban members are beginning to care about the problems of rural members and the future of the family farmer, and rural members have graphically demonstrated that they care about what happens in the cities. The average city fellow, up to now, has automatically voted against every farm bill.

—REP. FRED RICHMOND, Democrat from New York, 1977[105]

The adjustments made in Nixon's first two years led to dramatic increases in program enrollments, from 2.9 million in 1969 to 11.1 million by the end of Nixon's first term in 1972 (see table 1 in the appendix). Even greater increases came in the mid-1970s with the deepest recession since World War II, which also caused inflation in food costs for all Americans. The resulting spike in program spending—from $1.9 billion in fiscal 1972 to $4.6 billion in fiscal 1975—and elimination of strict budget caps soon prompted fears that spending on food stamps was "out of control" and forced program advocates to tighten its rules even as they sought to eliminate purchase requirements altogether.

Cost concerns prompted the new Ford administration to try to restrict eligibility and reduce spending, but it typically lost in court when sued by a new set of antihunger advocacy groups, led by the Food Research and Action Center, for which lawsuits became a key tool in getting the government to adhere to the law.[106] One FRAC lawsuit prompted a reluctant USDA to enforce a requirement in the 1973 amendments that states employ full-time food stamp outreach coordinators, whose efforts (as Congress intended) led to higher enrollments among those eligible and more program spending.[107] On the legislative front Ford was stymied by enlarged Democratic majorities in the wake of the 1974 "post-Watergate" midterm elections. In one notable instance Congress in February 1975 overwhelmingly voided new USDA rules to increase the cost of stamps, in the process signaling more intensive legislative interest in program administration.[108]

More far-reaching effects of the 1974 elections were felt by the conservative rural Democrats who long controlled key House committees. The greatest shock was Bob Poage's ouster as chair of House Agriculture for his insufficient fealty to the party caucus, specifically on food stamps.[109] Poage was replaced by Thomas Foley of Washington, who was more typical of a new generation of committee Democrats; while his district's economy was based in agriculture, most of his constituents lived in and around Spokane, making Foley equally sensitive to consumer needs. The future House Speaker also was the first northerner to chair House Agriculture in over fifty years and did not share his predecessors' attitudes that poverty and hunger were rooted in individual moral failings or genetics. Foley soon expanded committee staff expertise in nutrition programs.[110] Jamie Whitten survived the purge, the threat of removal further moderating his position on food-programs spending even as their costs rose. In the Senate, Agriculture and Forestry chair Talmadge now had to manage an expanded Democratic committee majority that now included liberals Hubert Humphrey (back as a senator from Minnesota), Patrick Leahy of Vermont (succeeding the just-retired George Aiken), and, of course, George McGovern, who also still led the Select Committee on Nutrition and Human Needs.

Even with rapid FSP growth, McGovern and other Senate Democrats wanted to further extend its reach by finally eliminating purchase requirements that most felt were unfair to the poor, administratively burdensome, and open to abuse by food stamp vendors who sometimes pocketed the cash. Republican Robert Dole shared their views and, with McGovern, authored amendments to the Food Stamp Act to provide free stamps on a sliding income scale and to improve what both saw as lax USDA and state administration.[111] The latter focus came out of growing awareness that the spike in enrollments focused attention on program costs, not impacts. Despite USDA data that the majority of enrolled households fell at or below the federal poverty line, public support for stamps in addressing hunger was being eroded by media-fueled portrayals of fraud and abuse, particularly by able-bodied adults, middle-class college students, unionized strikers, and others who did not fit the "deserving" frame for relief, even in a recession.[112] Complaints from inflation-burdened consumers on seeing stamp users buy steaks and other "luxury" foods (which was their right) grew. Even if charges of fraud and abuse were found to be exaggerated or untrue, program defenders recognized the at least symbolic need for tighter eligibility rules, more effective frontline implementation, and stronger USDA oversight.[113] But neither the Dole-McGovern bill, nor one by conservative House Republicans to

FIGURE 13. Republican Robert Dole *(second from left)* and Democrat George McGovern *(second from right)*, hearing before the US Senate Select Committee on Nutrition and Human Needs, Washington, DC, 1980. Source: Robert and Elizabeth Dole Archive and Special Collections, accessed February 18, 2023, https://dolearchivecollections.ku.edu/?p=digitallibrary/digitalcontent&id=1827.

restrict eligibility and cut spending by 40 percent, went anywhere in Ford's two years in office. The White House sought political advantage by attacking program "fraud, waste, and abuse," even if most of it was due to administrative error, and by intentionally underestimating program costs in annual appropriations requests, calculating that any overspending narratives would work against its opponents when Congress was forced to provide more money as the weak economy spurred still-higher enrollments. Given the circumstances, food stamp advocates decided to wait it out until after the 1976 election.[114]

Their strategy paid off. While Jimmy Carter was not as liberal as other Democratic candidates, his appointments of Rep. Robert Bergland of Minnesota as secretary of agriculture and of nutrition advocates in key roles at Food and Nutrition Service signaled his sympathies on nutrition programs. The "hunger lobby" was now on the inside, shaping program rule making. For his part Bergland had supported eliminating purchase requirements when he served in the House and, as a farmer himself, was well positioned to build coalitions on farm and food programs.[115] In Congress, House Agriculture chair Foley supported an end to purchase requirements but Senate Agriculture chair Talmadge did not and in fact proposed to replace stamps with cash grants administered by the Department of Health, Education, and Welfare. Echoing concerns raised with Nixon's Family Assistance Plan, few thought such an idea feasible without comprehensive welfare reform. Carter soon signaled his support for eliminating purchase requirements as the Farm Bill came up for reauthorization later in 1977.[116]

That May the Senate passed a farm bill containing the McGovern-Dole food stamp plan 69 to 18, largely along party lines (13 senators did not vote).[117] A few midwestern Republicans argued that eliminating purchase requirements severed any connection between stamps and food production, but most senators by now favored the change—no doubt aided by concurrent favorable action on corn and wheat target prices. The House, as before, required explicit vote trading: chair Foley first moved amendments to the Food Stamp Act, approved by a 320 to 91 floor vote, and then a bill reauthorizing commodity programs, approved 294 to 114, each largely along party lines. Key to both votes was an urban-rural coalition assembled by Rep. Fred Richmond, Democrat from New York, who—not unlike fellow Brooklynite Victor Anfuso twenty years before—leveraged his role as chair of the House Agriculture Subcommittee on Nutrition to pull together long-antagonistic factions, now to overcome opposition by a growing cohort of nonrural conservative Republicans, some of them former Democrats who left the party over civil rights and social issues. Richmond convinced rural Democrats to support ending purchase requirements and oppose rigid work rules by getting urban Democrats to back commodity supports, including a sugar subsidy Carter opposed.[118] When asked about this coalition, Richmond remarked, "I organized it. It functioned on the farm bill, and now it is functioning on food stamps."[119] Following negotiations between House and Senate conferees, both chambers easily approved an omnibus farm bill that included the Food Stamp Program. While Carter expressed concerns about the costs of the bill's commodity supports, especially those on dairy and sugar, he signed to get the food stamp program reforms he wanted.[120]

The 1977 amendments to the Food Stamp Act, nested within the omnibus Food and Agriculture Act, reflected a classic balancing of interests. On one hand, Congress eliminated all purchase requirements. From then on stamps were provided without cost based on a sliding scale according to household income adjusted for some living expenses and deductible assets. On the other, Congress sought to bolster program legitimacy with new administrative mechanisms for certifying eligibility and preventing fraud, narrower eligibility for college students, and pilot programs to test the efficacy of work requirements for the able-bodied. Of particular importance, legislators tightened most forms of "categorical eligibility" by eliminating automatic enrollment in food stamps for households getting support from AFDC or Supplemental Security Income, effectively removing nearly one-half million from the program. That provision would be reversed in the Food Security Act of 1985, reinstated in passage of "welfare reform" in 1996, and reversed yet again six years later (see chapter 5), illustrative of vacillations between more and less restrictive program rules that reflected the legislative bargains of the moment.[121]

All programs in the Food and Agriculture Act were authorized for four years, through fiscal 1981, despite Carter's wish to authorize food stamps only for two. *Just another commodity.* However, to address cost concerns Congress imposed fixed caps on annual FSP spending, which Carter opposed as impractical.[122] They *were* impractical: enrollments rose by nearly four million over the next three years due to the end of purchase requirements and the impacts of a still-weak economy on jobs and income. More who were entitled to stamps now signed up, with highest growth rates among the elderly and rural poor previously dissuaded by purchase requirements. More effective administration would not offset escalating costs, from $5.5 billion to $9.2 billion in Carter's last year in office. Congress was unwilling to cut benefits, so it had to pass "emergency" supplemental appropriations each year to make up the difference, thrusting food stamps into a broader ideological debate on "uncontrollable" federal spending.[123] In fact, by 1980 spending on nutrition programs now surpassed that on agricultural programs as a percent of the annual USDA budget.[124]

A side note: at the end of 1977 the Senate eliminated the Select Committee on Nutrition and Human Needs as part of an overhaul of its committee system. Jurisdiction over hunger and nutrition went to a new Subcommittee on Nutrition within the renamed Committee on Agriculture, Nutrition, and Forestry, to be chaired by George McGovern, with Bob Dole as ranking minority member.[125] While both opposed the Select Committee's termination, the new subcommittee at least gave their agenda a more permanent institutional home, from which they now could craft and report out legislation.

A Marriage Made in . . .?

Ending purchase requirements marked a turning point in the two-decade long evolution of food stamps from a narrowly targeted antihunger effort to a truly national nutrition *and* income supplement.[126] It also affected the tactical marriage between advocates of food stamps and defenders of commodity programs.[127] While that arrangement continues—the Supplemental Nutrition Assistance Program is still run by the USDA and remains under the jurisdiction of the committees on agriculture—holding it together requires ever more effort, especially in today's House. The fewer than three dozen House members who represent farming districts have to work harder than ever to seek the support of urban and suburban legislators for commodity programs they might otherwise oppose for their generosity to the less than 2 percent of Americans who actually farm. Similar dynamics play out in the Senate, even with its structural bias in favor of rural states. In return, promoters of food stamps continue to get the grudging support of their more conservative rural colleagues. Sixty years after passage of the Food Stamp Act of 1964, the politics of the Farm Bill still embodies classic notions of legislative reciprocity.[128] Everyone gets something.

However, unlike swapping votes on infrastructure projects— "you vote for my bridge; I'll vote for your subway line"—the "farm program + food program" marriage is a tenuous bond between partners with otherwise incompatible interests and values, more reminiscent of Ingmar Bergman's *Scenes from a Marriage* than Rob Reiner's *When Harry Met Sally*. By the end of the 1970s the quiet trading in congressional committee rooms had been replaced by a more public, more partisan, and more ideological politics, as food stamps became identified less as a farm program—*just another commodity*—and more as welfare.[129] Soon the "politics of discomfiting allies," to borrow from Ira Katznelson, that long supported food stamps would run up against forces not so enamored with the marriage in the first place, starting with the next occupant of the White House.[130]

5 *Welfare Politics*

There must be a safety net, basically, for eating, for nutrition, a safety net against starvation in this country.

—SENATOR RICHARD LUGAR, Republican from Indiana, 1995[1]

Who Is Deserving? Of What?

The Food Stamp Act of 1977 made stamps available to anyone needing them, at no cost, with monthly allotments based on adjusted household net income. The "bonus" stamps no longer supplemented "normal" food expenditures but instead freed up cash for other uses. In so doing, the program's income support or "welfare" function now was front and center, with political consequences that endure to this day.

For conservatives in the burgeoning suburban and Sunbelt wings of the Republican Party, shrinking a social-welfare safety net stitched together since the New Deal would be a singular passion.[2] Given a degree of ideological consistency in their views about individual responsibility and small government, Ronald King argued, conservative critics of food stamps "could no longer be dismissed simply as intransigent Southerners and plantation farm interests," although the racialized framing of many conservative attacks on the welfare state suggested deeper biases.[3] In the four decades from Ronald Reagan through Donald Trump, conservative Republicans led repeated attempts to narrow access to food stamps or eliminate the program entirely. For its part a Democratic Party largely rid of its rural conservative wing would become more unified in defending food stamps, even if it required compromises that made the program more complex and administratively burdensome.[4] Under such polarized circumstances, and with the ongoing decline in the overall number of farm-sector legislators, the politics of food stamps would be far less easily managed by traditional coalition-building tactics.

Even so, as per the conceit of this book, food stamps—now the Supplemental Nutrition Assistance Program (SNAP)—not only have survived but are more consequential than ever to the nation's social-welfare safety net. The question, again, is *how?* What is it about this form of assistance that has proven so resilient despite general public antipathy to "welfare" (in the abstract, at least) and the sustained hostility of the most potent US political movement of the past fifty years? It cannot simply be due to the "food programs + farm programs" marriage that lingers on in Congress—can it?

This chapter details three episodes over the past forty years that embody the politics of food stamps *as welfare:* (1) Ronald Reagan's use of the federal budget process to force program cuts in 1981, (2) the effects of welfare "reform" with the passage of the Personal Responsibility and Work Opportunity Reconciliation Act (PRWORA) of 1996, and (3) repeated attempts by House Republicans to reduce program enrollments and benefits by pulling SNAP out of the Farm Bill in 2014 and 2018.[5] In each instance program detractors claimed that food stamps went to the wrong people, undermined incentives to work, or simply were unafford-able. In each instance they seemed to have the upper hand. In each instance they ultimately failed. *Why?*

Reagan and the "Truly Needy"

The Food Stamp program will be restored to its original purpose, to assist those without resources to purchase sufficient nutritional food. We will, however, save $1.8 billion in fiscal year 1982 by removing from eligibility those who are not in real need or who are abusing the program.

—PRESIDENT RONALD REAGAN, 1981[6]

In his 1980 victory over Jimmy Carter, Ronald Reagan pledged to cut taxes, build up the armed forces, and balance the federal budget. To achieve the last objective, even with his vows that tax cuts would generate jobs and greater tax revenue, more money for defense meant cuts in domestic programs. But, as Reagan soon found, middle-class entitlements like Social Security and Medicare were politically untouchable, even with his own supporters, so attention focused on programs comprising the social-welfare safety net for the poor. Here Reagan promised that savings could come through reducing what he claimed was widespread and costly fraud, waste, and abuse, without harming the "truly needy."[7]

Food stamps topped Reagan's list of targets as he took office in 1981. For one thing annual program spending had nearly *doubled* during Carter's term in office, from $5.5 billion in 1977 to $9.2 bil-lion in 1980, because of the elimination of purchase requirements and the ongoing effects of a weak economy on the need for food assistance (see table 1 in the appendix). One in ten Americans were getting food stamps by 1980, Ardith Maney noted, "a much broader universe than any other means-tested welfare program."[8] More important than this fact was how Reagan framed its meaning. His campaign attacks on "welfare queens" and "young bucks" scamming the system, even with (or because of) their racial overtones, reflected his insight that many in the beleaguered (and largely white) middle class were ill-inclined to coddle anyone "undeserving" of their support.[9]

Moreover, the "problem" of hunger had changed. The clutch of federal nutrition programs assembled over the preceding two decades—food stamps, targeted commodity distribution, subsidized and free school meals, the Special Supplemental Nutrition Program for Women, Infants, and Children—*had* alleviated most of the worst forms of hunger and malnutrition. "The public perceives that hunger is no longer a serious problem in America," Jeffrey Berry observed at the time. "Consequently, discussion of the food stamp program has focused on issues such as eligibility and fraud."[10] In this regard the visibility of the colored paper coupons themselves made for a fair bit of tsk-tsking at cash registers, and numerous "steak and shrimp" anecdotes bolstered public support for tighter program rules. Lamented one program advocate, "Every time you see someone in the checkout line using food stamps, and you're not, you've been lobbied against the program. It's out in the open in every supermarket every day."[11]

Reagan's crusade against social-welfare spending could not succeed without Congress; in this regard he benefited from the concurrent Republican takeover of the Senate for the first time since 1954. Democratic losses in 1980 were heaviest among farm belt liberals, with George McGovern's defeat a particularly poignant symbol of the end of an era. The resulting partisan reshuffle shifted leadership of the Senate Committee on Agriculture, Nutrition, and Forestry from the by-now moderately conservative Herman Talmadge (who

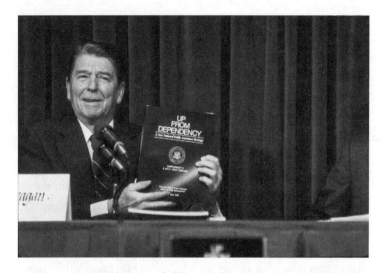

FIGURE 14. Ronald Reagan holding *Up from Dependency*, an executive-branch self-help catalog, while participating in a welfare-reform panel discussion, February 11, 1987. Source: Photo by Dirk Halstead. Editorial 50586009, Getty Images.

also went down to defeat in 1980) to the very conservative Jesse Helms of North Carolina, a former television commentator who vowed to get rid of "the parasites who have infested the food stamp program."[12] The task of chairing the Subcommittee on Nutrition went to Bob Dole, who had to balance his long support for food programs with loyalty to his party and president. Democrats kept control of the House but lost nearly three dozen seats, most in rural districts, leaving the House majority more urban, more liberal, and, for the first time, more supportive of food stamps than the now more conservative Senate.[13] Even so, Reagan's broad overall popularity would enable a coalition of House Republicans and conservative southern "Boll Weevil" Democrats to push through the president's initial budget and economic plans.[14]

From a playbook developed in the Nixon administration, decisions on food stamps in Reagan's first years were made in the White House and the Office of Management and Budget, not in the USDA, where Secretary of Agriculture John Block had little interest in the program and ousted the hunger advocates installed by Carter. Nor were they made in the committees on agriculture. Instead, the White House and its allies in Congress set hard budget ceilings and imposed across-the-board cuts in "discretionary" domestic spending through previously underused "reconciliation" authority through the Congressional Budget and Impoundment Act of 1974.[15] Reconciling spending on every program to hard overall budget limits fundamentally disrupted the bargaining inherent in distributing federal monies and "made urban-rural logrolling difficult," Kenneth Finegold observed, "as every interest sought to prevent its programs from being cut to meet the overall budget goals."[16] It worked: Congress went on to approve Reagan's fiscal 1982 budget despite individual members' opposition to specific cuts.

The Omnibus Budget Reconciliation Act of 1981 (OBRA) made over $50 billion in cuts in domestic nondefense spending for fiscal year 1982 (October 1, 1981, to September 30, 1982), a roughly 7 percent reduction from fiscal 1981 and one of the deepest cuts in year-to-year domestic program spending in US history. Nutrition programs saw deeper proportional cuts, with school and summer meals programs slashed by over 30 percent.[17] While the Food Stamp Program fared a bit better, it also saw a roughly 15 percent cut, around $1.8 billion, through narrower eligibility rules, reduced deductions, delays in adjusting benefits to increases in the cost of living, tighter administrative regulation, and prohibitions on using federal funds for program outreach. Combined, these changes dropped around one million from program rolls and reduced benefits for remaining enrollees.[18] Hard caps on program-budget authorization were set through fiscal 1985 and, in a pointed rebuke of the routine overrides under Carter, Reagan declared that he would oppose "emergency" supplemental appropriations; the program would have to live within its budget.[19] It could do so, Reagan pledged, by reducing fraud and waste.

Social-welfare advocates were stunned at the severity of combined cuts in Aid to Families with Dependent Children (AFDC), food stamps, subsidized school meals, housing vouchers, and Medicaid, which for many revealed the fragility of public support for programs serving the poor, especially under budget rules that favored politically powerful constituencies—including those defending commodity programs. Critics countered Reagan's claims that the cuts would not harm the "truly needy," pointing out that the households most affected were composed of children, single parents, senior citizens, and the disabled. Others were the "working poor"—those at or just above the poverty line—for whom the combined impacts of program cuts and rules changes made it harder to take part-time or low-paying jobs because the resulting loss of benefits would make them worse off.[20] But such arguments did not resonate with fellow citizens facing their own economic stresses and convinced that their tax money was being wasted on or abused by people not like themselves.

Of note, OBRA also replaced Puerto Rico's participation in federal nutrition programs with a food-assistance block grant, which came with an immediate 25 percent cut in total federal food support for the territory's residents, who are US citizens.[21] That cut took years to reverse, and overall funding for the block grant remained flat for decades, until increased under the Biden administration.[22] Nutrition advocates to this day point to Puerto Rico in opposing proposals to convert federal food programs into block grants to the states, more about which we discuss later in this chapter.

For defenders of food stamps, it could have been worse. In his role as chair of the Senate Agriculture Committee, Jesse Helms tried to move the Food Stamp Act out of the 1981 farm bill, reasoning that severing its ties to commodity programs would enable deeper cuts, even reinstatement of purchase requirements. But Bob Dole, as chair of the Subcommittee on Nutrition, worked with committee Democrats to block Helms and report out cuts that met the administration's budget goals but were less severe than demanded by the most conservative Senate Republicans. In the House new Agriculture Committee chair Eligio "Kika" de la Garza of Texas kept food stamps in the Farm Bill to balance cuts in commodity programs, only to see a coalition of Republicans and conservative Democrats use floor votes to make deeper cuts in food stamps. Those votes were met with retaliation by urban Democrats, who in other floor votes sided with Republicans to kill peanut and sugar programs.[23] The final conference bill, agreed to only after six weeks of stalemate over commodity programs and passed by only two votes on the House floor, authorized commodity programs for four years but food stamps for one. This tactic, political scientist John Ferejohn observed, combined with rigid overall spending limits, further split the "farm programs + food programs" coalition and "undermined the omnibus approach that characterized it."[24]

The cuts, spending caps, and stricter rules imposed between OBRA and the 1981 farm bill effectively froze Food Stamp Program spending at roughly $11 billion annually over the next four fiscal years. However, efforts to obtain even more savings were blunted as yet another recession drove up unemployment to nearly 11 percent in 1982, the first double-digit rate since 1940. The resulting spike in demand for food assistance, especially among newly laid-off manufacturing workers, forced Reagan to acquiesce to supplemental appropriations, despite his earlier pledge, but never beyond the budget caps. At the same time the "farm programs + food programs" coalition in Congress pulled itself back together, with rural legislators once again eager to lock in the votes of their urban colleagues as fiscal 1983 appropriations for commodity programs came up for consideration. It also was a midterm election year, and the political ramifications of the recession were apparent for members going before the voters. In considering the fiscal 1983 budget, the committees on agriculture reconnected food programs to commodity supports. Dole led the Senate in softening another round of proposed cuts and put Food Stamp Program reauthorization back on track with commodity programs through 1985: *just another commodity.* In the House rural and urban Democrats renewed their vows and rebuffed Republican demands for more cuts in food stamps and commodity programs, the latter now defended amid what would soon be the worst farm recession since the 1930s. The conference version, accepted by both chambers and, reluctantly, by Reagan, split the difference on spending and made no new changes in the Food Stamp Program. Equally important, Congress formally brought it back into the Farm Bill. Their experience in 1981 reinforced the aim of urban and rural legislators, whatever their other differences, to renew an arrangement that, Ferejohn noted, afforded a "substantial degree of insulation from electoral events outside their control."[25]

FIGURE 15. Cover of a food stamp booklet from the 1980s. Source: Photo by the author.

Government Cheese

At a time when American families are under increasing financial pressure, their government cannot sit by and watch millions of pounds of food turn to waste. I am authorizing today the immediate release of 30 million pounds from the CCC inventory. The cheese will be delivered to the States that request it and will be distributed free to the needy by nonprofit organizations.

—PRESIDENT RONALD REAGAN, 1981[26]

The recession of the early 1980s was especially brutal for working families caught in the tectonic shifts of deindustrialization, with "Rust Belt" communities from Allentown, Pennsylvania, to Flint, Michigan, facing acute food need as steel, auto, and tire companies shuttered plants that long anchored local economies and moved manufacturing jobs to lower-cost (and nonunion) states, a precursor of even greater economic dislocations to come.[27] But the program cuts and spending caps imposed in 1981, even with some supplemental appropriations, straightjacketed Food Stamp

Program enrollments and left substantial gaps in coverage. Efforts to attack alleged fraud and waste also saw the USDA penalizing states that erroneously enrolled claimants, leading frontline administrators to deny benefits as a default setting.[28] More households now needed food assistance for the first time but could not get it, and many getting assistance were not making it through the month.

At the same time the USDA was grappling with a historic, expensive, and increasingly embarrassing milk surplus, a consequence of generous dairy price supports enacted under the 1977 farm bill—the familiar "paradox of want amidst plenty," in liquid form.[29] The administration, pressed to respond to alarming media reports of hunger but not wanting to increase spending amid a ballooning budget deficit, saw in the dairy surplus an opportunity that would have sounded familiar to Henry Wallace or Ezra Taft Benson in their times: give it away. Three days before Christmas in 1981, Reagan announced the release of millions of pounds of cheese and butter sitting in Commodity Credit Corporation–leased cold storage for distribution to qualified local agencies. In 1982 alone the USDA shipped out 150 million pounds of cheese and 50 million pounds of butter to the states, which sent the products to local governments and charitable organizations able and willing to accept them.[30] In many instances households on some form of public assistance got entire five-pound blocks of American cheddar, thus situating "government cheese" in the lexicon of relief, if not haute cuisine.[31]

The White House saw the dairy giveaway as a one-off action to get rid of a specific surplus foodstuff, not a revival of The Box handed out each month under the old commodity-distribution program. But the dairy flood soon surfaced familiar tensions. Food stamps by now had supplanted most forms of commodity distribution, and the system for getting surplus foods to those in need had atrophied. Local governments and an array of new and largely volunteer-driven community organizations, from church soup kitchens to labor union–hall food pantries, now found themselves with truckloads of dairy products but little guidance or funding, leading to widespread complaints about haphazard planning and makeshift delivery systems, not to mention the costs to resize and distribute blocks of cheese and butter for household use. Food retailers and the dairy industry complained about lost sales, while the recipients, many of them newly unemployed factory workers, openly expressed their shame at being obliged to stand in the cold for cheese that sometimes was moldy from poorly managed storage.[32] Administration critics were quick to point out that the $2.2 billion to purchase and store surplus dairy in 1982 alone was not much more than what was just cut from the food stamp budget.[33]

Media accounts of rising hunger paired with complaints about the dairy giveaway prompted Congress and the administration in early 1983 to agree on a Temporary Emergency Food Assistance Program (TEFAP), introduced by Senator Dole, that added surplus rice, cornmeal, and honey to dairy and provided a one-time allocation of $100 million to cover processing and distribution costs incurred by states and local relief organizations. The White House had become sensitive to reports detailing the negative impacts of the 1981 budget cuts on the social-welfare safety net and saw a comparatively modest sum to distribute food the federal government already owned as an inexpensive remedy. But public and congressional concern about hunger remained, with special attention paid to the "new poor" in hard-hit industrial towns and, ironically, farming households facing bankruptcy as the 1980s farm credit crisis worsened. Reversing the cuts to food stamps was off the table so far as Reagan was concerned, but harsh criticism about his seeming callousness, including from some Republicans, forced matters. Late in 1983 Congress and the administration agreed to extend TEFAP for another year. But the need for food assistance never seemed to abate, and appropriations to enable the USDA to distribute surplus commodities and to purchase food for distribution when surpluses dried up (as when the cheese mountain got whittled down by a federal buyout of dairy herds) continued through the decade. In 1990 Congress finally took the "Temporary" out of TEFAP; forty years later *The* Emergency Food Assistance Program continues to fund USDA dissemination of surplus and purchased commodities to qualified charitable organizations.

Among them was a relatively new entity, the food bank, first created in Arizona in the late 1960s to "rescue" unsold food being tossed out by grocery stores for distribution to the needy. By 1979 it had grown in number to 13 regional operations linked together through a new national network, Second Harvest (now Feeding America). TEFAP soon would provide a comparatively modest (roughly $750 million annually before the 2020 pandemic) but critical stream of federal money that enables food banks to process surplus commodities and purchase additional food for distribution to local food pantries and social-service agencies.[34] With TEFAP and other government support, including tax breaks for companies donating "surplus" foods, the number of food banks exploded to 180 by the end of the 1980s. Thus did "government cheese" beget a permanent "emergency" food system.[35]

The Existential Crisis: Food Stamps and Welfare Reform

We must replace the welfare state with an opportunity society. The balanced budget is the right thing to do, but it doesn't, in my mind, have the moral urgency of coming to grips with what's happening to the poorest Americans.

—REP. NEWT GINGRICH, Republican from Georgia, 1995[36]

The battles over food stamps in Reagan's early years gave way to a truce, mostly because the bipartisan coalition that supported the across-the-board budget cuts in 1981 had fallen back into more predictable alignments. The urban-rural partnership supporting food stamps and commodity programs reasserted itself in putting together the next farm bill, the Food Security Act of 1985, amid an ongoing farm recession brought on in part by the previous decade of largely unchecked production and heavy farmer reliance on credit.[37] Defenders of commodity programs, especially in the House, again needed the votes of nutrition-program supporters, in part to overcome their own divisions. The Democratic House and Republican Senate loosened the hard caps imposed on Food Stamp Program spending, restored some benefits cut in 1981, and reestablished the automatic (or "categorical") eligibility for households getting AFDC or Supplemental Security Income that was eliminated in the 1977 amendments to the Food Stamp Act. In exchange conservatives obtained additional work requirements for able-bodied adults.[38] The administration, reluctant to continue what had become a losing battle, thereafter allowed for incremental increases in enrollments and benefits to better meet need.

With renewed Democratic control of the Senate after the 1986 midterms, the partisan divide between Congress and the White House reinforced stalemate, and food stamps largely fell off

Reagan's policy agenda through the remainder of his presidency. In fact, the period saw Congress make a series of adjustments designed to improve benefits and expand enrollments: the Stewart B. McKinney Homeless Assistance Act of 1987 improved benefits for and outreach to the homeless; the Hunger Prevention Act of 1988 raised baseline benefit levels, reversed OBRA's restrictions on the use of federal monies for outreach, and provided funds to states to educate eligible low-income households on program benefits; and the Mickey Leland Childhood Hunger Relief Act of 1993 allowed for higher deductions in shelter costs.[39] Much of the impetus behind these initiatives came out of the House Select Committee on Hunger, established in 1984 and chaired by Mickey Leland, Democrat from Texas, until his death in a plane crash in 1989. Under Leland and his successor, Tony Hall of Ohio, along with ranking Republican member Bill Emerson of Missouri, the committee played much the same role in publicizing the problems of hunger and malnutrition at home and abroad as had its Senate counterpart under George McGovern and Bob Dole in the 1970s. As befell its Senate counterpart, the House disbanded the Select Committee on Hunger in 1993, this time in response to Republican charges that the chamber was spending too much money on specialized panels.[40]

Of note, the 1990 farm bill authorized funds for state pilot projects on innovations in outreach but otherwise preserved the Food Stamp Program status quo. Ongoing conflicts between southern and northern crops, paired with a general antipathy among nonrural legislators about "welfare for farmers," put the farm bloc on the defensive, and the patrons of agriculture largely avoided picking fights with nutrition-program supporters, whose votes they needed to stave off conservative attempts at radical reforms in their own programs.[41]

With rules and spending caps loosened, relatively modest program growth resumed early in the presidency of George H. W. Bush but soon jumped, from $16 billion in fiscal 1990 to $24 billion in fiscal 1993, during the post–Gulf War recession that cost Bush reelection.[42] That spike in spending amid ongoing concerns over the federal deficit fed into renewed ideological and partisan tensions over entitlement programs during the presidency of Bill Clinton. Ironically, annual Food Stamp Program spending remained level, at around $24 billion per year, in Clinton's first years in office despite efforts by liberal Democrats to expand eligibility and benefits. Faced with Clinton's own concerns about the deficit and constrained by congressional budget rules that narrowed their options, advocates contented themselves with relatively minor adjustments.[43] Moreover, a 1993 expansion in the Earned Income Tax Credit was pulling a significant number of single mothers into the workforce and off other forms of assistance, including food stamps.[44] Even so, the program's growth over the previous decade fit conservative narratives about "uncontrolled" entitlements that drove Republican gains in the 1994 midterm elections and gave the party control of both chambers of Congress for the first time in four decades. The new House Speaker, Newt Gingrich of Georgia, led Republicans to victory with harsh attacks on congressional Democrats—and on Congress itself—and promises in a widely publicized Contract with America to rein in "out of control" spending. But, as before, programs serving the middle class—the major share of entitlement spending—were untouchable, so Republicans again took aim at programs serving the poor.[45]

To achieve its objectives the new Republican majority sought to deploy the same budget-reconciliation process on which Reagan relied in 1981. A top target was cash assistance under the six

FIGURE 16. President Bill Clinton speaking on welfare reform at Vanderbilt University Medical Center in Nashville, Tennessee, October 27, 1996. SOURCE: Photo by Paul Richards. Editorial 51587584, Getty Images.

decade-old Aid to Families with Dependent Children program, which by 1995 served only the very poorest, few of whom worked. It was also seen as susceptible to fraud and criticized as fostering "generational dependence" among those it supported.[46] Negative public impressions about AFDC also no doubt were influenced by the racial and gender composition of its clientele, particularly single Black women with children—about whose identity as caregivers *or* wage earners the dominant culture is especially conflicted.[47] Such criticisms were shared by centrist Democrats like Clinton, who in running for president had promised to "end welfare as we know it." But attention also turned to the Food Stamp Program, both because of its costs—now roughly equal to AFDC in annual federal spending—and attendant negative views on the deservedness of its enrollees, especially the able-bodied unemployed poor who automatically qualified based on enrollment in AFDC and who by now made up a little over 30 percent of all food stamp households.[48]

The House Republican Contract with America proposed to repeal the Food Stamp Act and fold it and other federal nutrition programs into block grants to the states, whose funding levels would be set at 95 percent of the aggregate amount of current program spending and allocated based on a state's proportion of eligible poor.[49] Proponents contrasted the purported flexibility of block grants with the detailed rules governing federal food programs—rules instituted largely to ensure adequate nutrition while minimizing fraud and waste—and argued that states freed of federal "micro-management" could serve the needy better and at a lower cost. Opponents weren't so sanguine, arguing that block grants simply allowed the federal government to wash its hands of responsibility in ensuring equitable treatment for all Americans, regardless of residence, and that the proposed funding formula would erode the value of the grant over time and undercut government's capacity to respond to increased need if economic conditions worsened.[50]

Congress eventually chose a different path.[51] Apart from the most ardent conservatives, Republicans who supported a block grant for cash assistance hesitated when it came to food. For one thing, proposals to block grant AFDC had come with assurances to retain food stamps as a federal safety net, and even many Republicans worried that without strong federal oversight states might "race to the bottom" to keep benefits and costs low, allegedly to avoid attracting new claimants from other states. "If you happen to be a citizen of one of those States," declared Senator Richard Lugar, Republican from Indiana and new chair of the Committee on Agriculture, Nutrition, and Forestry, "you are out of luck."[52] Lugar initially supported a food-program block grant but grew warier the more he looked at its ramifications, not the least for his own state. By contrast, the Food Stamp Program ensured a basic level of food security nationwide. It also mattered that food stamps were in-kind, cash-*like* but not cash, a distinction that hindered antipoverty advocates fighting to save AFDC but that also made it easier for many Republicans to support continuing vouchers tied to food consumption.[53]

Moreover, AFDC had few friends, an especially debilitating problem in a "winner-take-all" political environment under budget reconciliation. While by 1995 it already provided less support to poor people than any other antipoverty program—including the Earned Income Tax Credit, food stamps, Section 8 housing vouchers, and Medicaid—to critics it symbolized the failures of the welfare state.[54] By contrast, food stamps and other federal nutrition programs had friends beyond the usual hunger and nutrition advocacy groups. They included Republicans on the committees on agriculture—*just another commodity*—as well as agricultural producers and food retailers concerned about lost business if block grants replaced food stamps and school meals programs. Such support beyond the largely liberal "hunger lobby" enabled House Committee on Agriculture chair Pat Roberts of Kansas to get Speaker Gingrich to not push the block grant, a task made easier when a proposed block grant for child nutrition programs sparked a political firestorm and made Republicans look heartless, especially when critics pointed to subsidies going to wealthy farmers.[55]

With Republicans split and Democrats united in opposition, attempts to convert food stamps to a block grant were defeated in House Agriculture, on the House floor, and in the Senate.[56] Subsequent efforts by the Republican leadership to package the block grant and a range of program cuts in an omnibus fiscal 1996 budget bill and a separate welfare "reform" bill failed to survive Clinton vetoes, in no small part because of public perceptions that Republicans were waging war on the poor.

Having fended off the block grant, by early 1996 the committees on agriculture focused on a new farm bill that would include Food Stamp Program rules changes designed to incentivize work and reduce benefits fraud, give states greater discretion in administering the program, and impose new caps on program spending to achieve the budget cuts demanded by Republican leaders. At the same time they were considering the most significant changes in commodity programs since 1973, and House Agriculture chair Roberts in particular needed votes from urban Democrats to offset expected opposition by farm-sector Democrats. Several of the newer House Republicans had replaced southern Democrats who long defended regional crop interests, opening the way for radical changes in commodity policy as well. As before, the Food Stamp Program was an invaluable bargaining chip. Gingrich, under pressure from his caucus to deliver on promised entitlement cuts but aware of the tenacity of the urban-rural coalition supporting food stamps, initially sought to sever it from the Farm Bill, as Jesse Helms had tried in 1981. Roberts, fearing a fatal loss of support for his commodity reforms, convinced Gingrich to back a final conference version of the Federal Agricultural Improvement and Reform Act of 1996 (FAIR) that contained a two-year reauthorization of the Food Stamp Program, even as commodity programs were authorized for seven.[57] For his part Lugar got Senate Democrats to support additional restrictions in food stamp eligibility, more work requirements, and new caps on program spending. While unhappy about changes that made the program more restrictive and more administratively complicated, Senate Democrats accepted the deal as preferable to even deeper cuts being sought by conservative Republicans. Two-thirds of House Democrats refused to back the conference bill, but the votes of the rest helped Roberts offset defections by farm-bloc legislators upset about changes in commodity programs. Clinton, with an eye on farm-state voters as he sought reelection, made no mention of food stamps in signing FAIR into law.[58]

That legislative battle stood in stark contrast to what happened to cash assistance under AFDC. The Personal Responsibility and Work Opportunity Reconciliation Act of 1996 (PRWORA), signed into law by Clinton after over a year of intense partisan conflict and two presidential vetoes, replaced the federal-state arrangement under AFDC with a Transitional Assistance for Needy Families (TANF) block grant to the states. In doing so TANF essentially ended federal cash assistance to the nonelderly able-bodied poor. Its block grant, as welfare advocates feared, was highly permissive, and states subsequently spent it on a wide variety of activities that purportedly enabled work and fostered a way out of poverty, even if they provided no actual cash.[59] Moreover, as many feared, the block grant remains unadjusted from the roughly $16 billion per year first authorized in 1996; with inflation, its "purchasing power" in 2022 was effectively 38 percent lower than twenty-five years earlier.[60]

Passage of PRWORA also reshaped the Food Stamp Program. Free of the "farm programs + food programs" linkage in the Farm

Bill, Republicans leveraged welfare "reform" to make the most consequential changes in Food Stamp Program rules in two decades by eliminating eligibility for most legal immigrants and anyone ever convicted of a drug felony and severely limiting it for able-bodied adults without dependents who were not working at least twenty hours a week or enrolled in state work programs. Other new rules lowered benefits for remaining enrollees. States also gained greater flexibility in how they administered the program, leading some to impose even tighter rules on applying for and retaining benefits. Most important, the law ended categorical eligibility for food stamps that had been reinstated only a decade earlier, so anyone supported by TANF in any way would have to apply separately for food stamps, an administrative burden guaranteed to deter many otherwise eligible households.[61] Together these changes were expected to reduce Food Stamp Program spending by $23 billion over PRWORA's seven-year authorization. Nutrition and social-welfare activists fought these changes but had little leverage in defending a welfare program whose beneficiaries had low social and political standing. While Clinton expressed concerns about the bill's effects on food stamps, he signed PRWORA into law to get his broader welfare reforms.[62] It was, as his liberal critics bitterly acknowledged, a presidential election year.[63] Of note, in passing PRWORA, Congress also boosted funding for The Emergency Food Assistance Program; those losing food stamps at least could go to food pantries, assuming any were nearby.[64]

Even with its negative immediate impacts, PRWORA had an unintended benefit for longer-term Food Stamp Program viability. To limit fraud and abuse—such as when enrollees sold stamps for cash or retailers allowed stamp use on ineligible products—the law mandated that all states adopt Electronic Benefits Transfer systems, first authorized in 1990, by October 1, 2002. EBT debit cards soon replaced paper, making it harder to cheat and easier for the USDA to track purchases. For their part, users no longer had to pull out colored coupons whose visibility in checkout lines so frequently prompted shame and stirred antipathy to the program.[65] The *unintended* benefit was in the public face of program enrollees: armed with their debit cards, those spending food stamp dollars now looked just like every other consumer.

The Marriage Wreckers: Dividing Farm and Food Programs

In the end, it isn't real complicated. You can't get to 218 if you dismantle SNAP or farm programs.

—Agriculture lobbyist, 2017[66]

Liberals' bitter experience with PRWORA underscored the hard reality that defending cash assistance was a lost cause. But food stamps, if cash-like, were not cash and enjoyed greater public support so long as the program was kept free of scandal and focused on feeding fellow Americans. To these ends program advocates and the Clinton administration spent the next four years paying close attention to reducing benefits fraud and on making it easier for states to administer the program. They also focused on easing restrictions on the working poor and on families with children—largely sympathetic groups that saw disproportionate drops in food stamp enrollment immediately after PRWORA's enactment (see table 1 in the appendix)—and embraced a "make work pay" frame for able-bodied adults that enabled strategic alliances with moderates in both parties.[67] Liberals were not always happy with the direction of what they saw as a minimal entitlement for a decent society but largely accepted the changes as the cost for keeping the program going.

They also vowed to keep the program in the Farm Bill, where it would enjoy the kind of political cover that cash welfare never had. Their message thereafter was unambiguous—no food stamps, no Farm Bill.[68] For their part the committees on agriculture made no effort to decouple food stamps and commodity programs during the next two reauthorizations.[69] Passage of the Farm Security and Rural Investment Act of 2002 benefited from relatively low overall concern about federal spending—George W. Bush entered office in 2001 enjoying the first budget surplus since the 1960s—and, in pointed contrast to fellow Republicans like Gingrich, from Bush's support for reversing some of PRWORA's restrictions on food stamps as part of his "compassionate conservative" agenda.[70] With his encouragement the Republican House and the Senate narrowly controlled by Democrats agreed to deals that reinstituted some eligibility for legal immigrants, increased benefit levels for the working poor, and further simplified program rules to enable states to better serve enrollees. Despite clashes between regional commodity interests (with southern *Republican* cotton besting midwestern Republican corn) and complaints from conservatives about "excessive" spending on food and farm programs—the latter exploding after yet another cycle of deflated commodity prices following the 1998 Asian financial crisis—both chambers passed the omnibus farm bill by large margins. Bush's comments on signing it merit consideration:

> This bill is also a compassionate bill. This law means that legal immigrants can now receive help and food stamps after being here

five years. It means that you can have an elderly farm worker, someone here legally in America who's worked hard to make a living and who falls on hard times—that person can receive help from a compassionate Government. It means that you can have a head of a family who's been working hard, been here for 5 years, been a part of our economy, been legally working, and that person falls on hard times—our Government should help them with food stamps, and this bill allows that to happen.[71]

The context was much different in 2008. The expansions in eligibility and benefit levels made in Bush's first term largely undid the cuts made through PRWORA, boosted enrollments, and nearly doubled program spending from eight years earlier at the moment when large budget deficits reemerged with revenue losses from Bush's tax cuts and the expense of post-9/11 wars in Iraq and Afghanistan. The rising costs of commodity supports after 2002 also drew criticism. Moreover, both chambers of Congress now were controlled by Democrats, almost guaranteeing conflicts with conservative Republicans focused on cutting spending. However, most in Congress were in no mood for a major fight, and an unpopular president in his last year in office was ill-positioned to influence a bill important to legislators in both parties as the fall elections neared under conditions of a rapidly metastasizing recession. In passing the Food, Conservation, and Energy Act of 2008—over a Bush veto—Congress made only modest adjustments to commodity programs and slightly broadened eligibility for food stamps under a renamed Supplemental Nutrition Assistance Program (SNAP).[72]

That decade of successive expansions in program eligibility and benefits paved the way for the next big fight. SNAP enrollments and costs again had jumped dramatically with the macroeconomic effects of the Great Recession of 2007–9, the deepest and broadest since the 1930s, and with a temporary expansion in benefits under President Barack Obama's American Recovery and Reinvestment Act of 2009.[73] At roughly $70 billion, SNAP by 2010 made up nearly 80 percent of annual USDA spending, with predictable political ramifications. For conservatives attention once again was on the budget. As before, their narrative became "uncontrollable" social-program spending and on the deservedness of those being helped. Conservative media fixation with a "surfer dude" and other able-bodied enrollees again fueled an antiwelfare narrative.[74] As before, an election scrambled the political landscape, with 2010 seeing Democrats suffer a proverbial midterm beating following the contentious passage of Obama's Affordable Care Act, shifting control of the House to Republicans and giving "Tea Party" conservatives their best chance at sweeping changes in the welfare state since passage of PRWORA.[75] Several of these ideological heirs to Newt Gingrich had defeated Republican incumbents in party primaries, making the largest Republican majority since 1946 also the most ideologically conservative.[76]

This new phalanx of House conservatives promised to make good on their Contract with America–inspired "Pledge to America" to cut discretionary federal spending back to pre-2008 levels, at minimum.[77] As was the case in 1981, and in 1995, "discretionary" was understood to mean everything *but* national defense, Social Security, and Medicare. Achieving their goals would require an immediate 30 percent cut in all other domestic programs and more in years to come.[78] As before, their strategy would hinge on using the reconciliation process to set hard budget targets and to hold everyone else to them. However, this time House Republicans

FIGURE 17. Antitax protesters staging "Tea Party" rally, Federal Plaza, Chicago, April 15, 2009. Source: Photo by Brian Kersey. Stock Image ID: 12296005a, United Press International/Shutterstock.

faced a Senate still controlled by Democrats, not to mention Obama in the White House. As a result, the new House majority would resort to budget politics "hostage-taking," forcing successive votes on the debt ceiling (which sets federal government borrowing authority) and even shutting down the federal government itself to try to get concessions.[79]

All along, the toughest battles were among Republicans themselves. While some reflected ongoing tensions between regional commodities, others were more ideological. Most of the newer House Republicans hailed from homogenous suburban and exurban districts, the result of decades of demographic shifts and no small amount of strategic district line redrawing after each census. Most thought that their Committee on Agriculture colleagues did not go far enough in cutting SNAP and some resurfaced the idea of a nutrition block grant to the states.[80] For conservatives like Rep. Timothy Huelskamp of Kansas, "The real concern is that what is now a farm bill is really not that. *It's a food stamp bill.*"[81] Huelskamp's stance reflected the changed demographics of his sprawling western Kansas district: in contrast to when Bob Dole and Pat Roberts represented the "Big First," Huelskamp's voters were social conservatives in the suburbs of Wichita and Topeka, not the still shrinking number of farmers and residents of the district's small towns. For Huelskamp and fellow movement conservatives, the traditional distributive politics of the Farm Bill no longer adhered; many also opposed commodity supports. Such divisions were more muted in the Senate, where comparatively broader constituencies led more Republicans to support the longtime linkage. SNAP "helps get the farm bill passed," remarked Thad Cochrane of Mississippi, who, unlike his predecessors, supported the program. "I come from a state where we have higher-percentage participation," he observed. "It is part of my representation of the state that I make sure that those interests get represented. I have never had to apologize in Mississippi for supporting it."[82]

Such intraparty divisions played out in reauthorizing the Farm Bill over the next three years. While the Senate in mid-2012 easily passed a bill that made modest cuts in SNAP and commodity programs, the House was another matter. Republicans on the Committee on Agriculture approved provisions to tighten SNAP eligibility and cut spending by roughly $16 billion over ten years but sided with committee Democrats in rebuffing deeper cuts sought by party leaders.[83] Committee chair Frank Lucas of Oklahoma knew that going too hard at SNAP would alienate Democrats whose votes he would need on the House floor to overcome the determination of many conservatives to trim commodity programs as well. But his margin of error was slim, as two-thirds of House Democrats already resolved to oppose *any* cuts in SNAP, whose status as an entitlement ensured that it would continue even if the omnibus farm bill failed.[84] "I hope no one votes for it," said Rep. James McGovern of Massachusetts. "If we don't stand for the poor and vulnerable, what do we stand for?"[85] With the stalemate on the overall federal budget dragging on through the 2012 elections, Congress was forced to reauthorize most USDA programs by continuing resolution.

The 2012 elections did little to alter the equation. The Senate, despite regional divisions on commodity supports that threatened to derail floor consideration, again passed its farm bill in May 2013, again with modest cuts. But divisions among Republicans proved fatal once the House bill left the Committee on Agriculture in June. Following a party-line vote approving a controversial floor amendment enabling states to impose stricter SNAP work requirements on able-bodied adults—and letting states keep some of the money when benefits were terminated—the House promptly voted 234 to 195 against the omnibus bill itself, the first floor defeat on a farm bill since 1962 and, as Jonathan Coppess points out, "almost forty years to the day after the House had agreed to combine the two policies in the 1973 farm bill."[86] All but 24 Democrats voted no, the SNAP amendment the last straw in what they saw as a relentless campaign against the poor. More important, 58 conservative Republicans who approved the amendment subsequently voted against final passage because the bill did not cut spending enough.[87]

It was a stunning embarrassment for House Republican leaders unable to hold together their caucus and get the 218 votes needed (if all 435 members voted). "I just can't get over the fact that 58 Republicans voted for an amendment that would sink the bill," said minority leader Nancy Pelosi of California, reminding everyone that President Obama had promised to veto any bill containing these SNAP cuts.[88] Republicans thereafter abandoned any pretense of continuing the "farm programs + food programs" linkage and divided them into separate bills.[89] The move was applauded by conservatives as a way to isolate and cut back a food stamp program they deemed out of control and by a few commodity groups worried about the fate of their programs as fighting over SNAP stalled farm-bill reauthorization. But the tactic was seen as risky, given united Democratic opposition and weak support for commodity programs among most House members, and was opposed by most agricultural groups, even the American Farm Bureau Federation. Obama vowed to veto any farm bill not containing nutrition programs.[90]

But House Republicans soldiered on, hoping that their united front might somehow force the issue. A month later the chamber passed a "farm only" bill wholly along party lines, with all Democrats voting against. While Republican leaders praised passage of the first "pure" farm bill in forty years, farm-sector legislators were pessimistic about its chances in the Senate without nutrition programs. In September House leaders bypassed the Committee on Agriculture entirely and pushed through the Nutrition Reform and Work Opportunity Act of 2013 by a 217 to 210 party-line vote. The bill contained many of the program changes sought by conservatives and promised $39 billion in SNAP savings over ten years, ten times more than in the Senate farm bill.[91] The House bill also authorized SNAP for three years, compared to the five years for commodity programs. The Senate refused to adopt either House bill as a substitute for its own omnibus farm bill and simply waited. Finally, in late September the House, by another narrow party-line vote, put its two bills back together, despite complaints by conservatives about renewing the linkage. But, faced with complaints from normally supportive Republican constituencies, from farmers to food retailers, House leaders reluctantly concluded that no farm bill would get past the Senate—or Obama—without nutrition programs. The tactical separation had worked to get gain momentary approval from House conservatives but could go no further.

The final passage of the Agricultural Act stretched on into early January 2014, months after its authorization technically expired. Residing in the background during House-Senate negotiations was an end to a temporary increase in SNAP benefits provided by the 2009 stimulus package, the effect of which was an immediate $5 billion cut and another $6 billion projected. While expected, the roughly 6 percent decrease in benefits stiffened program advocates against additional cuts. Moreover, Senate Republican conferees did not see eye to eye with their House counterparts and signaled that they were comfortable with the modest cuts suggested by Senate Democrats, who in turn knew that *some* cuts were unavoidable, given Republican control of the House.[92] The final agreement offered something for everyone to dislike. On SNAP, conferees agreed to new rules that would cut spending by roughly $8.6 billion over ten years, more pilot projects to help enrollees get into the workforce, and more TEFAP funds to help food banks address "emergency" needs. The cuts infuriated some nutrition advocates. "They are gutting a program to provide food for hungry people to pay for corporate welfare," said Joel Berg, of the New York City Coalition against Hunger.[93] Others were more charitable, calling the outcome "relatively favorable" and certainly better than taking chances with another Congress.[94]

Whether the cuts were enough to appease a sufficient number of House Republicans remained uncertain. Following debate, the chamber voted 251 to 166 in favor of final passage, with most Republican and Democratic leaders supporting the deal.[95] Defections came from opposite ends of the ideological spectrum. The 103 Democrats voting no were largely urban liberals, while 89 Democrats, including most members of the Congressional Black Caucus, voted for the bill as a matter of practical politics.[96] The 63 Republican defectors were its most ideologically conservative, for whom the final bill did little to reform SNAP or save money.[97] Many also opposed continuing the "farm programs + food programs" linkage. To Rep. Marlin Stutzman of Indiana, a farmer himself, it was "just more business as usual and reverses the victory for common sense that taxpayers won last year. This logrolling prevents the long-term reforms that both farm programs and food stamps deserve."[98] The Senate approved the conference report by a bipartisan 68 to 32 vote; the 9 Democrats who voted no, largely from the Northeast, opposed further cuts in SNAP.[99]

Of note, in 2016 Representative Huelskamp suffered a primary-election defeat at the hands of Roger Marshall, who four years later went on to succeed Pat Roberts in the Senate, just as Roberts had moved from the First District to the Senate twenty years earlier and Bob Dole twenty years before that.[100] While Huelskamp's stances on social issues had endeared him to many conservatives, his obstinance on the Farm Bill ultimately proved his undoing in a district long identified with agriculture and keenly aware of the precarious political status of farm programs.

Once More into the Breach

Nearly the same story played out four years later, this time with a Republican Congress working with a Republican president, Donald

Trump. Annual SNAP spending, while falling from its historic high in 2013, continued at roughly $60 billion a year, putting the program squarely in the crosshairs of self-proclaimed "Freedom Caucus" Republicans, the ideological heirs to the Tea Party—and, in some ways, grandchildren of Gingrich—who now composed a substantial portion of all House Republicans. Given such favorable political alignments, one might have expected fundamental changes in SNAP during the next farm-bill reauthorization. Indeed, the Trump administration proposed a raft of program changes, from stricter work requirements and eligibility time limits to new restrictions on benefits for legal immigrants, designed to cut spending by $20 billion a year over ten years, and floated the idea of the Harvest Box as a way to get food to the needy at lower cost.[101]

But Trump never invested political capital into SNAP reform as farm-bill reauthorization wended its way through Congress. The Senate, as before, was largely content with the status quo, and its bill made only incremental adjustments in nutrition and commodity programs. The most conservative House Republicans again led the charge, and again encountered resistance from party colleagues, led by Committee on Agriculture chair Michael Conaway of Texas, who made clear that any changes had to promote program objectives, not just cut spending on assistance to poor people, even as Trump was bailing out farmers to compensate for the effects of his trade wars. Conaway tried to achieve some Republican goals by pushing to tighten eligibility for able-bodied adults but was caught between Democrats united against any new restrictions and conservatives wanting more. Despite a thirty-six-seat Republican advantage, the House soon found itself mired in stalemate. Again conservatives blocked floor passage because the committee's bill failed to make their desired cuts in food and farm programs and out of anger at the failure of House leaders to move a separate immigration reform bill (itself opposed by food-sector businesses reliant on immigrant labor).[102] Again House leaders split farm programs and food programs into separate bills, each passing along party lines.[103] Again the two bills were pulled back together, this time by a House-Senate conference committee. Again a midterm election scrambled the political equation, with 2018 handing control over the House back to the Democrats and hastening Republican determination to pass a bill before a new Congress convened. Again the final passage was stalled by a stalemate between the House and Senate over the federal budget, leading to yet another government shutdown—the first under conditions of one-party control.[104] The final passage of the Agricultural Improvement Act of 2018 proved anticlimactic and offered few substantive or budgetary changes in SNAP.[105]

Having failed in Congress, the administration spent its final two years trying to achieve its goals through administrative rule making, only to find its efforts sidetracked by the economic shocks of the COVID-19 pandemic or blocked in the courts until time ran out on the Trump presidency.[106] In fact, SNAP enrollment and spending jumped in 2020 with the pandemic and, in part, under successive stimulus packages negotiated between the White House and congressional leaders, over the objections of House conservatives. With the inauguration of Joseph Biden in January 2021, SNAP survived the Trump presidency largely unchanged.

That seemingly pedestrian fact punctuates the larger story of the past forty years and brings us back to the question that animates this book: *How* has SNAP survived four decades of "welfare politics," becoming arguably more essential than ever for the nation's social-welfare safety net? What is it about this program that enables its resilience amid often treacherous political undercurrents? To answer that question, in our final chapter we turn from our accounting of history to analysis.

6   *Let Us Now Praise the Food Stamp Plan*

In my view, the growth of the food stamp program . . . constitutes the most important change in public welfare policy in the United States since the passage of the Social Security Act in 1935.

—RICHARD NATHAN, former deputy undersecretary for welfare reform, 1975[1]

This chapter ends our journey. If in previous chapters we traced the path taken by the Supplemental Nutrition Assistance Program from its Depression-era origins to the present day, we now step back to evaluate, posing four broad questions: First, *how* has SNAP survived all of these decades, despite everything? What factors account for its longevity and its continued centrality to the nation's food and income-assistance safety net? Second, is SNAP a good nutrition program—that is, do benefits fulfill the program's primary objective and enable enrollees to obtain an adequate and nutritionally balanced diet? Third, is SNAP a good income supplement, helping enrolled households get out of poverty? Does it do the job? Fourth, and finally, compared to what? It is one thing to critique a program, another altogether to offer viable alternatives, so we conclude by asking: *Do you have a better idea?*

The Practical Politics of Food Assistance

Let's return to the question that motivated this book: *How has SNAP survived?* Based on our review of the program's decades-long history, here are a few thoughts, in order of their importance. First, and too often underremarked on, it's about *food*. In the end it's that simple. All the efforts over the past forty years to cut back on federal nutrition programs, SNAP in particular, were blunted or reversed after new surges in food insecurity, even outright hunger, due largely to economic conditions that each time resurfaced the "paradox of want amidst plenty," if not contradictions in market capitalism itself. Americans may not like "welfare" in some abstract sense, but they also do not want to see fellow Americans go hungry in a land where food is abundant and comparatively inexpensive.[2] In this regard, as political scientist Matthew Gritter argues, SNAP is seen widely, even among many conservatives, as the safety-net program of last resort.[3] Program advocates understand this and play the "hunger card" at every turn, leaving the more zealous program critics in the unenviable position of looking heartless, especially when those in need are children, the disabled, the elderly, or anyone else who fits mainstream notions of the "deserving." Even able-bodied adults down on their luck merit help getting food so long as they abide by culturally enforced rules promoting work and personal development. That SNAP work requirements may not make much of a difference or that states often seek to waive them (as we discuss later) is immaterial; they seal a deal with taxpayers that help is granted to those who help themselves, if they are able.

Second, while the SNAP dollars loaded onto EBT cards are cash-like, they still are not cash, a nuance grasped by those who designed the original Food Stamp Plan and reinforced by the demise of federal cash assistance with the enactment of the Personal Responsibility and Work Opportunity Reconciliation Act (PRWORA) in 1996. In that difference, even if the practical distinction is paper thin, paired with SNAP's formal connection to food, lies its survival. Many, perhaps most, conservatives can live with this form of targeted food relief and focus on narrowing program eligibility to the "truly needy."[4] Liberals may prefer outright cash assistance, but most will settle for making SNAP more generous and easier to access. That SNAP is not straight cash matters to its politics, just as it matters to similar forms of assistance, starting with the Earned Income Tax Credit and extending to Section 8 housing vouchers, discounted public transit passes, heating subsidies, and Medicaid.[5] One reason may be that conflicting sides can negotiate the rules for "in-kind" assistance more easily than for cash, which, once provided, can be used for any expense (although debit-card technologies could change that equation). While layering more "administrative burdens" on the program hinders the ability of some otherwise eligible households to obtain benefits, the opportunity to shape the rules makes it possible for critics to support the program at all.[6] Save for the failed Gingrich-led attempt in 1995 to convert SNAP into a block grant, it speaks volumes that the *dominant* politics of SNAP over the past forty years has been over its rules, not its existence.

Third, institutional factors favor SNAP in ways that never helped cash welfare. The most important resides in Congress, where, even with the constitutionally rooted rural bias of the Senate, farm-sector legislators in both chambers are in a distinct minority and need the support of their nonrural colleagues to maintain commodity supports going to a tiny cohort of often well-off producers. The most obvious way to do so is to maintain the "farm programs + food programs" linkage through the Farm Bill, keeping SNAP in the USDA and under the jurisdiction of the committees on agriculture. If Food Stamp Program supporters once were vexed at how the "agricultural mind-set" shaped US food-assistance policy, they now more or less accept the arrangement, as welfare expert David Super once explained: "With jurisdiction over food stamps lodged in the extremely conservative agriculture committees, liberal adventurism was obviously off the agenda. On the other hand, because the economic justifications of the agricultural subsidy programs dear to their constituencies' hearts rested on shaky ground, the committees were constrained from any conservative adventurism of their own: If they cut too deeply into the food-stamp benefit structure, they could expect swift and effective retaliation from legislators with liberal or fiscally conservative urban and suburban constituencies."[7]

The ideological polarization of recent years forces defenders of food *and* farm programs to play the Farm Bill card ever more tightly against their shared nemesis, the ideological conservatives who proclaim their desire to cut all forms of "discretionary" spending.[8] Despite it all, the deal endures, benefiting all sides. "To a greater degree than in other advanced democracies," political scientist John Ferejohn observes, "administrative programs in this country are required to maintain substantial legislative popularity to survive and expand. . . . Unless a popular basis can be built, the politics of the program will remain contentious and divided by ideological issues. This truth has faced the proponents of agricultural and welfare programs since the New Deal."[9] But the deal is *not* symmetrical. While SNAP and other federal food programs benefit tens of millions of low-income households, they are maintained in trades for commodity programs that offer greater direct proportional economic benefits to producers and, critics argue, raise food prices, also benefiting producers at the expense of consumers.[10]

That asymmetry extends beyond farmers and explains the fourth factor in SNAP's political resilience. Put simply, SNAP has many friends beyond the well-organized and influential "hunger lobby" of food banks, secular and faith-based food-relief organizations, nutritionists, and antihunger advocacy groups.[11] They include major food companies like Kraft and Pepsico, retailers from Walmart to dollar stores, financial institutions that process billions of dollars in EBT transactions, state and local governments that see SNAP dollars as "free" federal money, for-profit and non-profit providers of job training and placement services mandated by program work requirements, and public health and medical establishments worried about the health implications of inadequate nutrition, to name but a few.[12] For the food industry in particular, tens of billions of SNAP dollars bolster annual revenues in an often thin-margin business, and it is not about to let ideological conservatives cut too deeply into its subsidy.[13] Hence the industry's antipathy to accepting Sonny Perdue's Harvest Box, which would have diverted program funds from retailers, or to prescribing what foods SNAP enrollees are able to purchase with their benefits. Even the generally conservative American Farm Bureau Federation has taken a nuanced view on SNAP. "Food stamps have become a large part of the demand of the food that we raise as farmers," said the president of the Indiana Farm Bureau in 2014. "When you have one in five Americans on food assistance, that's 20 percent of the demand for food in this country."[14] For their part nutrition advocates are happy to align with corporate America on a common

FIGURE 18. Volunteers at the Bread of Life facilities unloading donated food from a truck for sorting in Malden, Massachusetts, April 28, 2020. Source: Photo by C. J. Gunther. Stock Image ID: 10633535j, EPA-EFE/Shutterstock.

objective, even if doing so mutes any criticism of other food-industry practices. What some label the "Walmart/Hunger Coalition" gives federal food programs the kind of political cover that cash welfare has never enjoyed, if at some cost to a more open accounting of who benefits.[15]

In sum SNAP endures because it still is about food—even if nobody today claims that it helps to "eat the surplus"—because it is harder to demonize as "welfare"; because it enjoys structural advantages that enable coalition building even amid broader political polarization; and because it has friends beyond the "hunger lobby" with their own stakes in the program's continuation. Barring a seismic shift in our politics—say, conservative Republicans win the presidency and amass congressional majorities large enough to overcome their internal divisions—the Supplemental Nutrition Assistance Program will remain at the center of the nation's nutrition and income-assistance safety net. And even if such a political reordering should occur, history suggests that SNAP probably will endure, in one form or another. SNAP now is the policy status quo, and its nearly sixty years in existence—more, if you go back to its Depression-era roots—grants it a legitimacy that makes it is easier to adjust to than to eliminate outright.[16]

Nutritionally Adequate

An Act to . . . provide for improved levels of nutrition among economically needy households.

—Preamble to the Food Stamp Act of 1964[17]

Okay, but if we are spending tens of billions in taxpayer dollars each year on food assistance for tens of millions of Americans, *does SNAP work?* Does the program fulfill its primary purpose and enable enrolled households to provide themselves with a nutritionally adequate diet?

This question is not as easy to answer as one might hope.[18] For one thing SNAP's rules do not prescribe which foods program enrollees can or cannot buy. Sure, you cannot use your EBT card on booze and ciggies and in most instances not on hot prepared or takeout foods because you are supposed to prepare meals at home, but otherwise you are free to use your benefits to buy any food you like at any eligible retailer, be it Sam's Club or the local 7-Eleven. SNAP is not like the Supplemental Nutrition Program for Women, Infants, and Children, better known as WIC, which *is* highly prescriptive (some say paternalistic) in limiting voucher use to foods selected by USDA nutritionists according to the federal government's current *Dietary Guidelines for Americans*. Such restrictions are intended to ensure that pregnant women, newborn infants, and children up to age five can obtain nutritionally balanced diets at critical stages of development.[19] So, for example, WIC vouchers can be used for specified quantities of unsweetened orange juice, plain yogurt, whole wheat bread, brown rice, domestic cheddar cheese, canned tuna, and dried lentils but not sugar-sweetened orange juice, processed cheese spreads, or yogurt with fruit or granola mixed in. Of note, WIC cannot be used on imported cheese, no doubt due to efforts by the National Dairy Council, the National Milk Producers Federation, and members of Congress from Wisconsin and other dairy states to protect domestic producers.

With SNAP, by contrast, food is food as far as the USDA is concerned, and SNAP dollars can be used on Pringles and a Diet Coke—or on imported parmesan—if enrollees so desire. That freedom of choice is absolutely fine with the food industry writ large, which historically disliked restrictions on food stamp/SNAP use. But it drives other interested parties crazy, and proposals to bar SNAP use on "bad" foods pop up each time Congress revisits the program. Such efforts go back as far as the initial passage of the Food Stamp Act, when the House barred stamp use on sodas and other "luxury" foods only to seek that provision stripped out by the Senate in response to USDA and food-retailer concerns about administrative complexity.[20] More recently proposed restrictions come from nutritionists worried about the prevalence of obesity and diet-linked diseases in low-income households and from conservatives who object to taxpayer dollars being spent on "bad" foods and who want to restrict what poor people can do with their benefits—hence the foods that were to be prescribed in the Trump administration's Harvest Box.[21]

Before we get into whether making SNAP more WIC-like would have desired nutritional and health effects, we should ask: What foods do SNAP households actually buy? The good news is that we have some idea. The universal use of EBT cards allows the USDA's Food and Nutrition Service to amass reams of household-level data on SNAP use, enabling a proverbial army of nutritionists and economists to study enrollee purchasing patterns (in the aggregate, to preserve privacy). The bad news is that even with such data it is difficult to establish the nutritional effects of SNAP on its own. As befitting its name, for most enrollees SNAP *supplements* other forms of food acquisition, from personal cash to other federal nutrition programs.[22] Many SNAP households are enrolled in WIC, have access to free or subsidized school meals, and fill the end-of-month "SNAP Gap" with trips to local food pantries. SNAP households also tend to spend more on food beyond their benefits, indicating that the program bolsters food consumption as intended, even without the old purchase requirement. Such effects are greatest for larger households with older children.[23] Finally, SNAP enrollees tend to be in worse health *before* they join the program.[24] Not surprisingly, those seeking benefits often are acutely food insecure, with all the nutritional deficiencies and diet-linked illnesses that come with being poor and not having consistent access to adequate food of any sort, much less fresh produce and high-quality proteins (which for most Americans mean meat, poultry, and seafood).[25] Overall, then, establishing SNAP's independent impacts on nutrition and health gets tricky.

Admitting such limitations on what we can prove, do SNAP households have demonstrably different diets than comparable non-SNAP households? Based on studies by the USDA and independent scholars, the evidence is, no: SNAP users are not that much different than other consumers of similar socioeconomic background or of average Americans in general.[26] They are no more, and no less, likely than comparable non-SNAP households to buy sugary sodas and highly processed convenience foods, largely for the same reasons, including the higher costs per calorie of high-quality proteins or fresh fruits and vegetables and, regardless of assumptions that still underpin the newly revised Thrifty Food Plan, limited time to cook meals from scratch.[27] *All* lower-income Americans, not only those in SNAP households, eat far too many ultraprocessed foods containing excessive sodium, refined carbohydrates, unhealthy saturated fats, and added sugar, largely because of their comparative affordability and convenience.[28] Program enrollees also tend to buy their food at the same places most Americans shop, notably superstores like Walmart and Costco and large-chain grocery stores like Kroger and Food Lion, assuming such retail outlets are nearby. If not, they're too often stuck with local convenience or dollar stores with only enough healthy options to qualify as SNAP retailers.[29]

If SNAP enrollees aren't so different in their purchase and consumption habits, would imposing WIC-like restrictions on them promote better overall nutritional outcomes?[30] Proposals to make SNAP more prescriptive are based on suppositions that enrolled households would consume less of these "bad" foods if barred from using program benefits on them. But most economists doubt that. Their examination of SNAP's "inframarginal effects" suggest that, faced with such restrictions, most program enrollees will substitute other dollars for those purchases. So, for example, should Congress ban SNAP use on sugar-sweetened soda, most program enrollees simply will use their "free" dollars to buy it. After all, soda is cheap, thanks largely to inexpensive high-fructose corn syrup used in most brands, so even poorer households can scare up $2.50 for a two-liter bottle of Pepsi at the local CVS or Family Dollar if they really want one.[31] The same logic applies for that 5.7-ounce box of Cheetos Cheesy Jalapeño Mac 'n Cheese mix you can pick up for $1.50 at Target, always good for a quick lunch even with its high sodium content. Despite assertions by some advocates, there is no conclusive evidence that such bans will prompt fundamental changes in enrollee purchase and consumption habits.

Such restrictions also would create considerable administrative complexity, starting with forcing the USDA (or Congress) to decide which of literally hundreds of thousands of food products found in retail markets are "good" or "bad" and according to what criteria. There is a reason the USDA—whose primary job, last we checked, is to promote food production and consumption in all forms—always looked askance at such restrictions. A department that props up the dairy industry by figuring out ways to get more Wisconsin mozzarella on top of *and* inside your Domino's pizza is not inclined to consign any food product to nutritional purgatory.[32] The other reason is outright political: just imagine the reaction of the National Potato Council, Potatoes USA, and the Alliance for Potato Research and Education, not to mention members of Congress from potato-growing states like Idaho, Washington State, and Maine, if USDA staff nutritionists declared Pringles or any other highly processed potato-chip product a bad food off-limits to SNAP households.[33] Observe the knockdown fights over which foods and food ingredients are allowed in federally subsidized school meal programs or in WIC, and you get the picture.[34] Even a seemingly easy target like sugary sodas stirs no small reaction from the soft-drink and snack-food industries, not to mention sugar producers of various types and their always responsive members of Congress, one reason why the USDA refuses to grant requests by states and municipalities to bar SNAP use for those beverages.[35] Such targeted bans also would confuse retailers and shoppers and cause uncomfortable scenes at checkout reminiscent of days when food stamps could not be used on coffee, tea, cocoa, or other imported foods. Overall, as economist Diane Schanzenbach summarized in testimony before the House Committee on Agriculture in 2017, "a ban will likely increase the administrative costs of the program to both the USDA and retailers, and increase the stigma faced by recipients when they use the benefits, but not have the benefit of inducing any behavioral change."[36]

If bans on bad foods pose all sorts of problems and might not produce desired results, what about "healthy incentives" programs that give SNAP enrollees "bonus" dollars to be used on comparatively more expensive fresh fruits and vegetables at farmers markets and other participating vendors? Starting from a "bonus bucks" program in Detroit in 2009 and a USDA-funded Healthy Incentives pilot program in western Massachusetts in 2011–12, the number and scope of such "double up" initiatives have expanded considerably. They now have financial support from some city and state governments and, since the 2014 farm bill, from the USDA's Gus Schumacher Nutrition Incentives Program.[37] These "healthy incentives" programs *do* seem to help, with SNAP enrollees using their bonus benefits to increase their consumption of fresh fruits and vegetables and in some places locally produced meat and seafood.[38] Such incentives seem to sidestep the landmines apparent with efforts to make SNAP more prescriptive. Moreover, while there is evidence that simply raising SNAP benefit levels would have much the same effect on household food-consumption patterns, the targeted nature of "healthy incentives" programs gives them widespread political support, from nutritionists and community activists to local farmers, farmstand operators, and other retailers.[39] In short, as most policy scholars will verify, incentives usually are more effective policy tools when compared to bans—even for poor people.[40]

Education also helps. The USDA runs a companion program, SNAP-Ed, that offers a range of services and grants to states and localities designed to help enrollees use their program dollars more effectively and with greater nutritional benefit, through in-person and online nutrition and cooking classes, seasonal food and menu guides, culturally relevant recipes, and other "capacity building" programs. Such initiatives seem to have some desired impacts, especially when they are targeted at children just starting to shape their lifetime eating habits.[41]

What, then, can be said about SNAP as a nutrition program? At its most basic SNAP reduces—although it does not eliminate—household food insecurity, an impact that *in itself* has critical immediate and long-term nutritional and health benefits, including positive impacts of improved diet in reducing household healthcare costs.[42] While any purported benefits of SNAP on its own are complicated by multiple factors, such as whether a household has ready access to a decent grocery store or a kitchen in which to cook meals, one can say that, at minimum, without SNAP the United States would see far greater food insecurity, even hunger, with all the attendant nutritional and health impacts, including psychological ones, that come with not having consistent access to food.

An Accidental Antipoverty Program

SNAP is an unusual income supplement. Unlike TANF and Social Security, SNAP benefits are made available solely as a function of net household income. As Kenneth Finegold observed, "an American can receive a subsidy for food just because he or she is poor. To qualify, poor people do not need to be old, disabled, veterans, or parents, as they do in other welfare programs."[43] SNAP also is unusual because it is not cash as such. Then again, as we have noted, neither is so much of the contemporary US social-welfare safety net.[44]

With the thought that SNAP's primary purpose is to supplement food consumption, does it also help to alleviate poverty? Answering this question also is complicated. For one thing SNAP benefits are calibrated on monthly, not annual, household net income after accounting for a range of deductions, and enrollees can enter the program in one part of a year, leave in another, and even reenter some months after that. After all, SNAP is designed to address proximate conditions—hunger and food insecurity—not causal factors like low wages, inadequate education, or lack of access to good jobs. "As a compromise between urban and agricultural interests," Marjorie DeVault and James Pitts argue, "the food stamp program was designed to define the problem in terms of food rather than income inequality. Thus, food stamps ended as a substitute for an adequate guaranteed income, leaving the structural sources of poverty unexamined."[45]

This being said, a few observations are possible. First, the program's benefit structure is largely progressive: benefits are highest for the poorest households and decrease incrementally as monthly household income improves toward the 130 percent of the federal "poverty line" adjusted net-income cutoff. (A household of four would be declared in poverty in 2023 if its total annual income fell below $30,000; higher thresholds apply in Alaska and Hawai'i.)[46] Prior to the 2020 pandemic, more than half of SNAP benefits went to households in deepest poverty, with the remainder spread out among households hovering at or just above the poverty line. At least one-third of all SNAP households comprise the "working poor," with at least one nondisabled adult who works, typically in comparatively low-wage retail and service-sector jobs or in jobs with erratic incomes (either of which describes many jobs in the food system, an irony in itself). Most of these households include children.[47] In this regard, as economist James Ziliak notes, growth in SNAP enrollment and spending in the decade after the Great Recession of 2007–9 reflected macroeconomic conditions of stagnant wages and risings costs, with program growth rates "most rapid among full-time, full-year workers, as well as part-time, full-year workers." As such, the composition of SNAP households has trended toward those with annual incomes just above the poverty line, suggesting that, in Ziliak's words, "SNAP has evolved into a work supplement for educated, near-poor households."[48] The economic effects of the 2020 pandemic and spikes in food prices in 2021–22 made this more so. By comparison, only around 7 percent of SNAP households get benefits of any kind from TANF, belying stubbornly held public perceptions about food stamps and welfare.[49]

SNAP's benefits structure—and its status as an entitlement program—also makes it an effective income stabilizer during economic downturns, so long as those eligible can obtain benefits in a timely manner, or at all (more on that later). As already noted in chapter 1, while the nation's food banks met the most immediate need as the pandemic eviscerated household incomes and food security, SNAP worked as designed once benefits kicked in. The program's countercyclical effects are greatest for poor households with children and at least one working adult and are particularly effective in reducing poverty in Black households. Moreover, SNAP benefits are adjusted regularly for inflation, so their buying power keeps up at least somewhat with rising costs. By comparison TANF has minimal antirecessionary effects, largely because the program's $16 billion per year block grant has remained unchanged since 1996. This contrast, not to mention the Puerto Rico's ongoing struggles with food security since Reagan put its food programs into a block grant, bolsters arguments against tampering with SNAP.[50] As Judith Bartfeld and colleagues conclude in their sweeping assessment, "The benefits of SNAP, including its capacity to respond to macroeconomic forces; its critical role in reducing the incidence, depth, and severity of poverty among both working and nonworking households; and its ability to reduce food insecurity would be severely jeopardized by shifting to a block grant."[51]

More to the larger point, as Laura Teihan, Dean Jolliffe, and Timothy Smeeding argue in their meta-analysis, "SNAP is our nation's most effective antipoverty program for the nonelderly . . . one that is especially good at reducing extreme poverty—by over 50 percent—and also especially effective for poor families with children."[52] If the program has not significantly lowered the nation's poverty rate, it has reduced its *severity*. Program benefits may target food consumption, but they also free up cash to enable enrolled households to pay other bills and not forego other necessary expenses, such as health care.

Such benefits have consequences beyond greater food and income security. For example, a 2016 study by Hilary Hoynes, Diane Schanzenbach, and Douglas Almond of households enrolled in the Food Stamp Program from 1963 through 1975 found that children in those households were likelier to graduate from high school, likelier to have better overall health, and, for women in particular, likelier to become economically self-sufficient than children from low-income households not enrolled in the program.[53] A 2017 analysis by Crystal Yang suggests that making program benefits available to newly released prisoners reduces the rate of recidivism.[54] In the end, then, SNAP helps to cushion against falling back into poverty and its attendant pathologies.

This being said, the whole question of SNAP as an income supplement brings to mind Joseph Coppock's observation in his 1947 review of the first Food Stamp Plan: "An economic system which stands only with the support of food stamps and other such props is not a permanently satisfactory system."[55] SNAP, in his sense, is but a halfway decent prop.

A Side Bar on Work Requirements

Even as they do some good, do SNAP benefits "disincentivize" work? The possibility that benefits are so good that enrollees are better off *not* working is a perennial worry among conservatives who profess concern about the moral character of poor people otherwise able to work, and it comes up each time the program gets reviewed in Congress.[56] As we saw, divisions over the stringency and universality of work requirements for able-bodied adults without dependents (our so-called ABAWDs) nearly scuttled two successive farm bills.

Putting aside the ideological argument, which comes with its fair share of racial and gender undertones, what does the evidence show? First, SNAP has less drastic benefit reduction rates—or "cliffs"—compared to TANF and state general-assistance programs that do make some households worse off if they earn any income. Even so, a SNAP household member who is offered $10.00 per hour for additional work might gain only about $7.80 per hour in total household resources after considering the reduction in SNAP benefits for each dollar earned above the baseline. In theory such benefit reductions could lessen that person's incentive to work. In *practice* economists calculate that the effects of SNAP benefits on labor-market participation are modest at best and vary considerably depending on the characteristics of the household in question.[57] Any such effects often are offset by work incentives in programs like the Earned Income Tax Credit, which, Teihan, Jolliffe, and Smeeding observe, "encourages work effort for low-wage single parents to a much greater extent than it is discouraged by SNAP."[58]

Even so, SNAP rules since the passage of PRWORA continue to impose a three-month time limit on the ability of ABAWDs ages eighteen to forty-nine to enroll during every thirty-six-month period unless they meet mandated work requirements, which can include specified types of community service or participation in state-approved job-training programs. How these requirements are implemented and enforced varies from state to state. Some do not provide any support services and simply cut off benefits after three months even if enrollees are actively looking for work or seeking job training. States can obtain USDA permission to waive work requirements and time limits under certain conditions, notably living in areas with stubbornly high "structural unemployment" (such as the closure of coal mines in eastern Kentucky) or seasonal fluctuations (such as those affecting farmworkers in California's Imperial Valley). Even before the pandemic, nearly every state sought a waiver at one time or another, some routinely, and not only due to persistently high unemployment; states also seek waivers because enforcing rules on ABAWDs is administratively complicated or because they want more time to set up training programs.[59] Such programs are resource intensive and do not necessarily save money.[60] States also can simply exempt 15 percent of ABAWDs from work requirements and time limits each year. Of note, the Families First Coronavirus Response Act of March 2020 suspended time limits and most work requirements nationally through the duration of the declared health emergency, which the Biden administration extended through early 2023.[61]

Overall, the evidence suggests that SNAP's work requirements and time limits are ineffectual policy instruments.[62] They do little to "incentivize" work, and states often seek to avoid enforcing them. But keeping work requirements appears to be the cost of doing business on Capitol Hill, the programmatically suboptimal being the politically necessary.[63]

Back at the Intersection of Want and Plenty— or, Can You Do Better?

We should all be ashamed that tens of millions of our fellow citizens don't know where their next meal will come from. America is a land of abundance. We have more than enough to feed everyone. What we lack is the moral vision and political will to act.

—REP. JAMES MCGOVERN, Democrat from Massachusetts, 2022[64]

On September 28, 2022, President Joe Biden convened the White House Conference on Hunger, Nutrition, and Health, the first such top-level gathering on hunger and nutrition since Richard Nixon hosted the original in 1969. That first conference and its attendant political dynamics (see chapter 4) led to major expansions in the food stamp and school-meals programs, the creation of the WIC program, and better nutrition labeling on processed food products. Its 2022 namesake, the White House declared, "will galvanize action by anti-hunger and nutrition advocates; food companies; the health care community; local, state, territorial and Tribal governments; people with lived experiences; and all Americans, and it will launch a national plan outlining how we achieve this goal."[65]

It is far too soon to know what effects the 2022 conference will have—if any—but not too soon to ponder the seemingly intractable condition its participants confronted: tens of millions of Americans still seem unable to afford or gain regular access to sufficient healthy food in a nation literally awash in the stuff.[66] The "paradox of want amidst plenty," again. You are Joseph Biden or his successor. What are your options?

The Charitable Box: Food Banks and Food Pantries

Every Wednesday and Friday around 1:00 p.m., rain, shine, or snow, a line forms on the sidewalk outside the community health center in my Boston neighborhood, which, amid its stately Victorian houses and iconic early twentieth-century New England triple-decker apartment buildings, has its fair share of low-income residents, group homes, and transitional housing for those undergoing drug and alcohol rehab. At 2:30 sharp a door opens and center staff start to hand out boxes of free food to anyone in line, until the food runs out—which is often, leaving those at the end of the line frustrated at their bad luck. If the weather is good, some will gather on the other side of the street and swap foods according to their tastes, dietary issues, and cultural familiarity. Some will grumble to one another about what's in The Box that week—*three loaves of white bread and ten pounds of potatoes!*—but never to the center's staff, who try to provide a variety of fresh and shelf-stable products. Some in line are faces I see on the subway. They see me, but we never acknowledge it, not even in nodding acquaintance. It would be embarrassing. My neighborhood food pantry, in a nutshell, is why the charitable box is the *least* desirable form of food assistance. Don't get me wrong: I admire the center for running its pantry, just as I admire the herculean efforts of everyone in the "emergency" food system—from the Greater Boston Food Bank, which processes and distributes nearly two million pounds of food each week to hundreds of food pantries and social-services agencies in eastern Massachusetts, to the young idealists at Lovin' Spoonfuls who "rescue" surplus fruits and vegetables from the region's produce wholesalers and supermarkets for distribution to partner food pantries. But, despite all the hard work and best intentions, The Box should not be the foundation of how a wealthy nation feeds those who need food.[67]

For one thing The Box can only fill gaps left by government food programs, SNAP in particular, as became abundantly clear during the COVID-19 pandemic.[68] In fact, those in the emergency food system talk routinely about one version of the "SNAP Gap," in this case that time of the month after program benefits are exhausted and before they kick in the next month, with some estimates that over 50 percent of those visiting food pantries are SNAP enrollees.[69] Everyone in the emergency food system also is well aware that without SNAP and other government programs, the nation's food banks and food pantries would be overwhelmed, as they nearly were during the pandemic.[70] Despite the workplace food drives and variations on Project Bread's Walk for Hunger, and acknowledging the sector's heroics during COVID, the charitable model is not sustainable without government support.[71] *It never was.* While the Feeding America network of food banks generates donations from millions of Americans who care about preventing hunger, much of the food it distributes comes from the federal government, through either Section 32 surplus-commodity buyouts or The Emergency Food Assistance Program (TEFAP), which also provides hundreds of millions each year to enable food banks to purchase foods in wholesale markets. Don't forget: Reagan's "government cheese" begat TEFAP and an emergency food system that has only grown since, but on a bedrock of government support.[72]

Most important, what is in The Box is what is available, whether as a result of direct donation (through a church's Thanksgiving canned-food drive, for example) or what a food pantry can get from the regional food bank, which for its part needs to cover its costs to obtain, store, and distribute surplus and purchased foods. There is no way that The Box comes close to providing even the "low-cost nutritious diet" supported by SNAP's Thrifty Food Plan, which, as James Ohls and Harold Beebout once pointed out, tries not to depart "drastically from the typical food buying habits of low-income Americans."[73] If the Thrifty Food Plan is not exactly living "high on the hog," as the saying goes, The Box doesn't get you much beyond the hind quarters.

Finally, standing in line for The Box is demeaning, no matter the sensitivity and solicitude of those handing it out. It was so for the desperate souls in the breadlines of the Great Depression, it was so for unemployed coal miners in the hollows of Appalachia who lined up for monthly surplus-commodity allotments under Eisenhower's Needy Families program, it was so for newly laid-off steelworkers in Youngstown awaiting blocks of "government cheese," it was so for the marginally "middle class" out of work because of COVID and in their cars at "pop up" food-distribution sites, and it is no less so today. My neighbors who queue up each

FIGURE 19. Sign outside the local food pantry, Boston, May 29, 2022. Source: Photo by the author.

week for The Box are proud people. Some are coming off of time in jail for drug offenses or are immigrants of varied legal status working low-wage jobs, populations largely ineligible for most forms of federal and state aid. Others are trying to fill the gap left after SNAP benefits run out, a condition especially typical among larger low-income households. Unlike at many food pantries, nobody at the health center asks those in line if they are "eligible," demands to see an identification card, or requires that they sit through a sermon before getting food. But they're still standing in line. Are they "deserving"? Do they really need food? Ask yourself: Would *you* stand in the summer heat on a public sidewalk where your neighbors can see you to pick up a box of food you and your family did *not* need?

The Government Box: Commodity Distribution

While the Trump-era Harvest Box idea on which this book opened met with widespread derision, its lineage can be traced back to the surplus-commodity schemes of the Depression. Those direct-distribution programs largely disappeared in the early 1940s, to be revived a decade later when farm surpluses again bedeviled policy makers. In fact, as we recall, criticism of the variety and nutritional inadequacy of foods in Eisenhower's Needy Families allotments led to the modern Food Stamp Program, which by the 1970s had supplanted commodity distribution except on sparsely populated tribal lands and other places with few retail options. It came back, in limited form, with government cheese in the 1980s, but in most instances the federal government has since contented itself with moving bulk commodities through the now well-established network of food banks under TEFAP and Section 32 buyouts, such as those that offset surpluses generated by Trump's trade wars.

Putting history aside, what about the merits of having the USDA assemble and distribute its own food parcels, per Sonny Perdue's Harvest Box? Hearkening back as far as the first surplus wheat-disposal effort under the Hoover administration, the flaws in such direct-distribution schemes should be apparent by now. However, if we need reminding, we have some recent experience from the Farmers to Families pandemic food-box program.

While the Trump administration promoted Farmers to Families as a way to feed the suddenly food insecure, the program was designed as much to bail out the thousands of farmers and food producers stuck with excess perishable stock with the abrupt closure of cruise ships, hotels, restaurants, schools, and thousands of businesses of all types.[74] The nation again confronted a misalignment between supply and demand, with millions having less money to purchase food while crops rotted in fields and animals were euthanized due to the lack of markets. An obvious solution, at least in the view of the administration, was for the federal government to buy up surplus foods for distribution to those in need. A lot of surplus stocks already were being shipped to food banks through an expanded TEFAP, helping to meet much of the initial surge in demand. The Farmers to Families program, enabled by broad congressional authority to provide pandemic food relief and supported by $3 billion from the first round of stimulus funding, was designed to get food to those who needed it as quickly as possible by having private contractors assemble "family sized" food parcels according to USDA nutritional guidelines, after which they would be shipped to food banks, "faith-based" organizations, and other agencies for final distribution. Secretary Perdue, channeling his inner Henry Wallace (okay, maybe Ezra Taft Benson), made the connections: "During this time of national crisis, President Trump and USDA are standing with our farmers, ranchers, and all citizens to make sure they are taken care of. . . . This program will not only provide immediate relief for our farmers and ranchers, but it will also allow for the purchase and distribution of our agricultural abundance to help our fellow Americans in need."[75]

Farmers to Families had its successes. From May 2020 through January 2021, program contractors moved over one hundred million boxes of surplus and purchased foods to those who needed assistance, provided producers with critical income, and prevented some perishable foods from going to waste.[76] And the program enabled contractors to employ workers to process and package food instead of dumping unsorted product on already overburdened food banks. In short Farmers to Families did some good.

This being said, the program encountered problems typical of commodity distribution generally, bringing to mind the "Rube Goldberg" jibe about The Box by its critics at the start of this book. First, and admitting that no massive government program rushed to implementation is ever perfect, the contractors hired had widely varied experience in food processing, packaging, and delivery—some none at all—leading to criticisms that the USDA ignored established food-industry processing and supply chains, much to the frustration of the companies left in the lurch. For example, while a Texas wedding planner with no food aggregation and delivery experience got a $40 million contract, major food distributors like Sysco and USFoods were left out, in part because the USDA originally prioritized lowest-cost bidders, some whose proposals betrayed inexperience and led to poor performance. Some areas of the country, notably the Northeast, were underserved in proportion to their population and the severity of the pandemic's impacts, raising questions about how contracts were awarded.[77] Despite USDA guidelines, this variability in contractor expertise and experience also affected the range and nutritional quality of foods put into The Box, leading even those being helped to complain about what they got.[78]

Second, it was bureaucratically cumbersome, and many operators struggled to navigate complex and shifting government contracting rules, much less standard federal and state health and safety regulations governing food preparation, packaging, and storage. Rules requiring that packages contain a combination of foods based on USDA nutritional guidelines—the stated rationale behind The Box—caused delivery and distribution problems for food banks accustomed to tailoring distribution to their diverse clienteles and in many instances led to greater food waste as recipients discarded foods they could not eat for religious or dietary reasons or which they simply did not like.

Then there was politics. A food parcel put together and delivered by the government or its contractors always is open to political manipulation, reminiscent of the discriminatory aspects of the old commodity-distribution programs. With Farmers to Families, concerns about politicization were raised the moment the USDA announced that The Box would contain a letter signed by President Trump in which he took credit for feeding the hungry. The letter was inserted apparently at the instigation of Trump's daughter and adviser, Ivanka. While "credit claiming" is the stuff of politics, 2020 was a presidential election year, and the letter caused considerable consternation among many otherwise nonpolitical food banks and food pantries. Some took pains to remove the letter before distributing The Box to their clients. Claims that contractors were picked for political ties to the administration or the Trump reelection campaign were common enough that some hired a lobbyist to shape their response.[79] Images of President and Ivanka Trump posing with stacks of Farmers to Families boxes just before the 2020 Republican National Convention caused no small stir, especially after Secretary of Agriculture Perdue broke federal ethics rules by using the formally nonpartisan event to openly urge the president's reelection.[80] Finally, as with the charitable model, those getting The Box still had to stand in line, still subject to the element of shame that comes with being seen to need help.[81]

FIGURE 20. President Donald Trump arriving to speak about the Farmers to Families Food Box Program at Flavor First Growers and Packers, in Mills River, North Carolina, August 24, 2020. Source: Photo by Nell Redmond. Stock Image ID: 10754317h, Associated Press/Shutterstock.

OK, so why not ship The Box directly? Let's take Sonny Perdue at his word and figure out a way to deliver a prescribed mix of foods once or twice a month to the homes of food-insecure families. Maybe even toss in recipe cards, à la Blue Apron (or at least SNAP-Ed). While this approach reduces the "shaming" element, since recipients do not need to stand in line, it does not eliminate other objections, chief among them the limited array of foods provided. *The Box does not allow choice.* Moreover, however delivered, The Box assumes a household's capacity to store and use everything in it. (Direct shipping also requires an address to which The Box can delivered, an assumption one should not make for people struggling with poverty and unstable housing arrangements.)

Also, to be blunt, such a plan is a straight subsidy to Amazon and Walmart, which dominate the online food-delivery business. While one could make the same argument about recent USDA initiatives to enable SNAP enrollees to use their EBT cards to purchase food online, there at least households retain freedom of choice, like any other consumer.[82]

The Biden administration ended Farmers to Families in May 2021, by which time it had delivered over 175 million boxes of food at a cost of over $5 billion, or roughly twenty-nine dollars per box—a unit cost critics argued was higher than what consumers often paid at retail for the same items.[83] In its place the new USDA leadership expanded TEFAP and Section 32 surplus programs, provided grants to build food-bank capacity to process bulk commodities, boosted funding to enable more food-bank sourcing from local farmers, and expanded SNAP benefits so that more Americans could buy more food in the retail marketplace.[84]

In the end, whether it is put together by charities or by the government, whether it is motivated by altruism or the imperative to use up surplus commodities, *The Box is still The Box*. While it can plug gaps in the food-security safety net, it should never be at the center.

Provide Cash Assistance

Economists seem clear that providing the poor with cash is the simplest and most effective way to improve their lives. Even Richard Nixon, not exactly a liberal, thought so when proposing his ill-fated Family Assistance Plan. But, this being America, providing the poor with cash is "welfare" and thus politically problematic. The Senate's failure in 2022 to renew pandemic supplemental child-support benefits because some senators wanted benefits tied to work requirements (for the parents, one presumes) or felt that the poor might not spend the additional money wisely suggests that any effort to get more cash to the poor is doomed in the current political environment.[85] That might change, but one cannot imagine an expansion of cash support not being wrapped in rules that ultimately make it hard for anyone eligible to obtain benefits.

And, to be honest about it, there are no guarantees that enrollees will use the extra cash on food, a point that has shaped debate over cash versus "in-kind" benefits as far back as the original Food Stamp Plan. Put simply, cash is fungible and can be used for *anything*. SNAP benefits, on the other hand, *must* be used for food. While critics are correct that SNAP dollars free up cash for other purposes—even, heaven forbid, a day with the kids at the local amusement park—its restrictions ensure that program funds are used for the intended purpose: food. Yes, it's a fiction, but one we all agree to live with.

Not Worth Considering

Other ideas don't merit deeper discussion. For example, few would take seriously proposals to bring back government-run soup kitchens in the absence of a major disaster, in which case the Federal Emergency Management Administration pays contractors to set up relief operations. The federal government could incentivize retailers to offer food at a discount to those in need, reminiscent of Henry Wallace's "two price" plan, but one doubts such an idea would get far, even in this day of EBT cards, and for many of the same reasons as back then. Besides, just adding more money to EBT cards has essentially the same discounting effect. What about more WIC-like food vouchers? We may as well talk about food stamps.

Put Funds into a Debit Card to Purchase Food at Any Retailer

Welcome to SNAP. QED.

Okay, that's a bit flippant. I end this book with a mostly unqualified praise of the Supplemental Nutrition Assistance Program. SNAP could be better.[86] For starters, we make it too hard for those eligible to obtain and keep benefits. While some do not enroll because of a lack of knowledge, age and infirmity, language and immigration status, or a sense of shame about needing "charity," a major factor in what some call the "SNAP Gap" is the program's complexity.[87] Because Congress, through PRWORA, gave the states a fair bit of leeway in how to administer food stamps, states vary in how easy or hard they make it on technically eligible households to enroll and stay enrolled, even though the federal government fully funds all SNAP benefits. Some states require in-person interviews, while others allow for online application; some require enrollees to renew every three months, others every six; some states require fingerprinting or drug tests, and others do not. You get the point. Scholars of public administration call such rules "administrative burdens" insofar that they make it harder for technically eligible households to obtain or keep benefits.[88] Such burdens may align with prevailing attitudes about the poor, especially able-bodied men, but they make little sense if the goal is to feed people. We should make it easier to apply for and retain benefits, and we should make the rules more consistent and equitable regardless of residence. Our fealty to federalism should not mean that where you live determines your ability to have a decent diet. In this regard Puerto Rico should be brought back into the SNAP system. Puerto Ricans living on the island, as opposed to Orlando or Philadelphia, are US citizens too, last we checked.[89]

While SNAP benefits are adjusted for inflation, the program's antipoverty impacts would be improved if benefits also were adjusted more to account for variations in food prices *across* regions and between urban and rural areas. At present the maximum benefit level, intended to ensure a nutritionally adequate diet, is uniform across the continental United States, which may be a good deal for residents of comparatively low-cost areas but harder on those in higher-cost locales.[90] Benefit levels also do not take into account pertinent household characteristics, such as the age of any children, in the process underfunding households with voracious teenagers compared to those with toddlers.

SNAP rules also could adjust to how most Americans actually shop and eat. Regardless of income, most of us now buy more prepared hot foods—Costco's famous $4.99 rotisserie chicken is not a "luxury" food for budget and time-pressed families—and most of us spend less time to prepare and eat food at home. Yet SNAP's rules, even with recent adjustments in the Thrifty Food Plan, still assume that Mom is in the kitchen, cooking from scratch. More likely, whoever prepares dinner probably just came from work and is just trying to cobble together something decent in short order.[91] (Did someone say Cheetos Cheesy Jalapeño Mac 'n Cheese?) US representative Bobby Rush, Democrat from Illinois, was blunt about current restrictions: "The fact that you can use SNAP to purchase a frozen, breaded chicken, but not a hot rotisserie chicken or a salad from a grocery store salad bar, frankly makes no sense."[92] While there are myriad reasons for the long-term trends in how Americans shop and eat, all beyond the scope of this book, it is illogical to treat SNAP households as if they were not subject to the same time pressures besetting many (if not most) US households. Food is food, right? Then don't decide that some food is "luxury" simply because someone else prepared it.

These are suggestions for improving the program. Otherwise, *SNAP works*. It leverages the "normal channels of trade" to supplement the diets of those who need food, enabling enrollees to obtain food like any other consumer—no colored coupons and no standing in line for The Box. Despite media-fueled claims to the contrary, the program is remarkably free of fraud and error, particularly since the advent of the EBT card, and its benefits formula, while open to critique, is comparatively immune to political manipulation. You qualify based on net household income, not because of who you are, who you know, or what you believe. No mandatory sermons await in checkout lanes. SNAP also supplements income in ways that withstand the usual critiques about welfare, and its benefits structure makes it more responsive to swings in household income than other assistance programs. And it has broad political legitimacy. As Teihan, Jolliffe, and Smeeding put it, "SNAP conforms to many of the key demands conservatives and liberals have for safety net programs, such as engaging the private sector . . . and allowing participants a high degree of choice in the food they buy."[93]

Engaging the private sector. Giving consumers a choice. What could be more American? The genius behind the original Food Stamp Plan is no less apparent today and brings to mind that point Milo Perkins made so many decades ago: "Good times are likely to be followed by bad times, however, and a mechanism like the Stamp Plan can serve the general welfare if it is contracted to a mere skeleton in times of great prosperity, but kept alive so that it can be expanded in times of depression to help cushion the shock."[94]

Yes, the Supplemental Nutrition Assistance Program can be better. But without it millions of Americans would be far worse off. And if that sounds like faint praise, so be it. The "paradox of want amidst plenty" has not disappeared. Short of a systemic solution to poverty—the root cause of food insecurity—and in a land of so much food, often bordering on the obscene, SNAP at least ensures that all Americans get a better chance at a decent diet, a minimum element for a decent life, without sacrificing all personal autonomy and pride. We can debate SNAP's rules. There is no debating the moral imperative for keeping what works.

APPENDIX

TABLE 1 Supplemental Nutrition Assistance Program participation and costs, 1961–2022

Fiscal year	Average participation (thousands)	Total costs[1] ($ millions)
1961	50	0.4
1962	140	13.2
1963	335	18.6
1964	360	28.6
1965	632	32.5
1966	1,218	64.8
1967	1,831	105.5
1968	2,419	173.1
1969	2,878	250.5
1970	4,340	576.9
1971	9,368	1,575.9
1972	11,109	1,866.7
1973	12,166	2,207.4
1974	12,862	2,837.5
1975	17,064	4,618.7
1976	18,549	5,685.5
1977	17,077	5,461.0
1978	16,001	5,519.7
1979	17,653	6,939.8
1980	21,082	9,206.5
1981	22,430	11,225.2

TABLE 1 *(Continued)*

Fiscal year	Average participation (thousands)	Total costs ($ millions)
1982[2]	21,717	10,836.7
1983	21,625	11,847.1
1984	20,854	11,578.8
1985	19,899	11,703.2
1986	19,429	11,638.4
1987	19,113	11,604.2
1988	18,645	12,316.8
1989	18,806	12,901.6
1990	20,049	15,447.3
1991	22,625	18,747.3
1992	25,407	22,462.3
1993	26,987	23,653.0
1994	27,474	24,493.5
1995	26,619	24,620.4
1996	25,543	24,331.0
1997	22,858	21,507.6
1998	19,791	18,988.3
1999	18,183	17,820.9
2000	17,194	17,054.0
2001	17,318	17,789.4
2002	19,096	20,637.0
2003	21,250	23,816.3
2004	23,811	27,099.0
2005	25,628	31,072.0
2006	26,549	32,903.1
2007	26,316	33,173.5
2008	28,223	37,639.6
2009	33,490	53,619.9
2010	40,302	68,283.5
2011	44,709	75,686.5
2012	46,609	78,411.1
2013	47,636	79,859.0
2014	46,664	74,060.3
2015	45,767	73,946.8

2016	44,220	70,912.1
2017	42,317	68,175.0
2018	40,776	65,448.8
2019	35,702	60,387.1
2020	39,875	79,255.9
2021	41,558	113,857.7
2022	41,207	119,242.2

Source: Food and Nutrition Service, US Department of Agriculture, February 20, 2023, https://fns-prod.azureedge.us/pd/supplemental-nutrition-assistance-program-snap

[1]Total costs include the federal share of state administrative expenses, nutrition education, and employment and training programs, plus other federal costs.

[2]Puerto Rico participated in the Food Stamp Program from FY1975 through June FY1982. A separate Nutrition Assistance Grant began in July 1982

Chronology

Key Moments in Food Stamps and the Supplemental
Nutrition Assistance Program

1939   The USDA uses authority under Section 32 of the Agricultural
Adjustment Act of 1935 to initiate the first Food Stamp Plan.

1943   The USDA terminates the Food Stamp Plan as wartime demand
eliminates most surpluses.

1959   Amendments to the Agricultural Trade Development and
Assistance Act of 1954 (PL 86-341) authorize the USDA to run a
food stamp pilot program through 1962; the authority was never
utilized.

1961   John F. Kennedy uses Section 32 authority to initiate food stamp
pilot programs.

1964   The Food Stamp Act (PL 88-525) establishes a permanent Food
Stamp Program.

1971   Food Stamp Act amendments of 1970 (PL 91-671, enacted in
January 1971) establish uniform national standards for eligibility
and work-registration requirements, adjust monthly allotments,
limit purchase requirements to 30 percent of net household
income, and extend the program to Guam, Puerto Rico, and the
US Virgin Islands.

1973   The Agriculture and Consumer Protection Act (PL 93-86)
requires states to offer food stamps in all jurisdictions and
expands eligibility to those in drug and alcohol treatment.

1974   The Food Stamp Program begins operating nationwide; Congress
authorizes the USDA to pay 50 percent of state administrative
costs (PL 93-347).

1977   Food Stamp Act amendments, as contained within the Food and
        Agriculture Act (PL 93–86), eliminate purchase requirements,
        establish income-eligibility guidelines and new deductions,
        restrict eligibility for students and noncitizens, establish new
        job-search requirements, and eliminate categorical eligibility for
        those enrolled in Aid to Families with Dependent Children and
        Supplemental Security Income programs.

1981   The Omnibus Budget Reconciliation Act reduces Food Stamp
        Program spending by approximately 15 percent through narrower
        eligibility rules, reduced deductions for living expenses, delays in
        adjusting benefits to cost of living, tighter administrative
        regulations, and prohibitions on using federal funds for program
        outreach; it also shifts Puerto Rico to a nutrition-assistance block
        grant.

1985   The Food Stamp Act (PL 99–198) eliminates sales tax on food
        stamp purchases, reinstates categorical eligibility for AFDC and
        SSI enrollees, and requires states to implement employment and
        training programs.

1988   The Hunger Prevention Act (PL 100–435) authorizes pilot
        projects on the use of electronic benefits-delivery systems.

1990   The Mickey Leland Memorial Domestic Hunger Relief Act (PL
        101–624) authorizes the use of Electronic Benefits Transfer
        systems.

1993   The Mickey Leland Childhood Hunger Relief Act (PL 103–66)
        eliminates the shelter-deduction cap and adjusts other deduc-
        tions to increase benefits for households with children.

1996   The Federal Agricultural Improvement and Reform Act (PL
        104–127) imposes some restrictions in food stamp eligibility,
        more work requirements, and new caps on program spending
        over the next two fiscal years.

        The Personal Responsibility and Work Opportunity Reconcili-
        ation Act (PL 104–193) eliminates eligibility for most legal
        immigrants and anyone convicted of a drug felony, imposes work
        requirements and time limits for able-bodied adults without
        dependents, gives states greater flexibility in administering

program rules, eliminates categorical eligibility for enrollees in the Transitional Assistance for Needy Families welfare program, and mandates that states implement EBT systems before October 1, 2002.

2002 The Farm Security and Rural Investment Act (PL 107–171) reverses some PRWORA restrictions, restores eligibility to legal immigrants, and allows group homes to redeem EBT benefits directly.

2008 The Food, Conservation, and Energy Act (PL 110–234) expands benefits, simplifies rules, and changes the name of the Food Stamp Act to the Food and Nutrition Act and of the Food Stamp Program to the Supplemental Nutrition Assistance Program.

2009 The American Recovery and Reinvestment Act (PL 111–5) increases monthly SNAP benefit levels through 2013.

2014 The Agricultural Act (PL 113–79) expands the range of eligible retailers, enables home delivery for vulnerable populations, authorizes healthy-incentives programs, and pilot programs to move enrollees into work or higher-paying jobs.

2018 The Agricultural Act (PL 115–334) increases funding for employment and training programs.

2020–22 Pandemic stimulus packages temporarily increase SNAP-benefit levels through February 2023.

2021 The USDA recalibrates the Thrifty Food Plan for first time since 2006, increasing benefits by approximately 20 percent.

Notes

1. Tales at the Intersection of Want and Plenty

1. Quoted in Julie Kosterlitz, "Beefing Up Food Stamps," *National Journal*, February 17, 1990, 391.

2. Helena Bottemiller Evich, "Trump Pitches Plan to Replace Food Stamps with Food Boxes," *Politico*, February 12, 2018.

3. Caitlin Dewey, "Trump Wants to Slash Food Stamps and Replace Them with a 'Blue Apron'-Type Program," *Washington Post*, February 12, 2018.

4. Tracy Jan et al., "Trump Wants to Overhaul America's Safety Net with Giant Cuts to Housing, Food Stamps, and Health Care," *Washington Post*, February 12, 2018.

5. It's a ripping saga, to be sure. See Christopher Bosso, *Framing the Farm Bill: Ideology, Interests, and the Agricultural Act of 2014* (Lawrence: University Press of Kansas, 2017); and Jonathan Coppess, *The Fault Lines of Farm Policy: A Legislative and Political History of the Farm Bill* (Lincoln: University of Nebraska Press, 2018).

6. Helena Bottemiller Evich and Catherine Boudreau, "The Food Stamp Fight That Could Kill the Farm Bill," *Politico*, March 3, 2018.

7. Steve Burak, Kathy Baylis, and Jonathan Coppess, "US Agriculture Often Bears the Cost of Trade Disputes," *farmdoc daily* 7 (2017): 181, Department of Agricultural and Consumer Economics, University of Illinois at Urbana-Champaign.

8. Binyamin Appelbaum, "Their Soybeans Piling Up, Farmers Hope Trade War Ends before Beans Rot," *New York Times*, November 6, 2018, A1; Tom

Polansek et al., "Hog Industry Worldwide Getting Slaughtered in Trade War," *Reuters,* December 28, 2018.

9. Eduardo Porter and Karl Russell, "Firing Back at Trump in the Trade War with Tariffs Aimed at His Base," *New York Times,* October 3, 2018; Associated Press, "American Whiskey Exports Starting to Rebound," *U.S. News,* March 4, 2022.

10. Committee on Economic and Environmental Impacts of Increasing Biofuels Production, National Research Council, *Renewable Fuel Standard: Potential Economic and Environmental Effects of U.S. Biofuel Policy* (Washington, DC: National Academies Press, 2011); Paul Wescott, "U.S. Ethanol Expansion Driving Changes throughout the Agricultural Sector," *Amber Waves,* September 3, 2007.

11. "USDA Launches Trade Mitigation Programs," press release 0172.18, US Department of Agriculture, September 4, 2018, www.usda.gov/media /press-releases/2018/09/04/usda-launches-trade-mitigation-programs; Kara Clifford Billings, *The Emergency Food Assistance Program (TEFAP): Background and Funding,* report no. R45408, Congressional Research Service, June 15, 2022, https://crsreports.congress.gov/product/pdf/R/R45408, 21.

12. Helena Bottemiller Evich, "Food Stamp Spending Jumped Nearly 50 Percent in 2020," *Politico,* January 27, 2021.

13. H. Clare Brown, "Farmers Will Destroy One in Four Cranberries This Year," *Counter,* November 23, 2018.

14. This point is made by Peter Eisinger, *Toward an End to Hunger in America* (Washington, DC: Brookings, 1997).

15. The "paradox of want amidst plenty" is attributed to Secretary Henry Wallace, who used it in his book, *New Frontiers* (New York: Reynal and Hitchcock, 1934), but it likely originated in a speech by journalist Walter Lippman: "Poverty and Plenty," in *Proceedings of the National Conference of Social Work* (Chicago: University of Chicago Press, 1932), 234–35; see also Janet Poppendieck, *Breadlines Knee-Deep in Wheat: Food Assistance in the Great Depression,* 2nd ed. (Berkeley: University of California Press, 2014), xvi; and Ray F. Harvey, *Want in the Midst of Plenty: The Genesis of the Food Stamp Plan* (Washington, DC: American Council on Public Affairs, 1941), 4.

16. On the origins of US food-assistance policy, see Poppendieck, *Breadlines Knee-Deep in Wheat.*

17. Jamaica ran a food stamp program in the 1980s in response to the devaluation of its currency but later replaced it with cash assistance. See Dan Levy

and Jim Ohls, "Evaluation of Jamaica's PASTH Conditional Cash Transfer Program," *Journal of Development Effectiveness* 2, no. 4 (2008): 421–41. In 2020 Argentina rolled out a debit card–based Tarjeta Alimentar program in response to rising food costs and child hunger, but its scope was comparatively modest. See "Argentine Government Struggling to Reduce Poverty and Debt," *Business Times,* February 7, 2020.

18. Paul Pierson, "Increasing Returns, Path Dependence, and the Study of Politics," *American Political Science Review* 94, no. 2 (2000): 251–67; Matthew Gritter asked some of the same questions in *The Policy and Politics of Food Stamps and SNAP* (New York: Palgrave, 2015).

19. I use the term "food stamps" when referring to the program before 2008, "SNAP" after.

20. Laura Tiehan, *The Food Assistance Landscape: Fiscal Year 2019 Annual Report,* EIB-218 (Washington, DC: Economic Research Service, US Department of Agriculture, 2020).

21. Parke Wilde, *Food Policy in the United States: An Introduction* (New York: Routledge, 2013), 174; for an overview of how that definition evolved, see Eisinger, *Toward an End.*

22. Craig Gunderson and James Ziliak, "Food Insecurity Research in the United States: Where We Have Been and Where We Need to Go," *Applied Economic Perspectives* 40, no. 1 (2018): 119–35.

23. Alisha Coleman-Jensen et al., *Household Food Security in the United States in 2020,* ERR-299 (Washington, DC: Economic Research Service, US Department of Agriculture, 2021).

24. The federal government's fiscal year runs October 1 through September 30. *Additional Information about the Updated Budget and Economic Outlook: 2021 to 2031,* Congressional Budget Office, July 2021, www.cbo.gov/publication/57373, 11; Jordan Jones, Saied Toossi, and Leslie Hodges, *The Food and Nutrition Assistance Landscape: Fiscal Year 2021 Annual Report,* EIB-237 (Washington, DC: Economic Research Service, US Department of Agriculture, 2022).

25. On "entitlements," see Ronald F. King, *Budgeting Entitlements: The Politics of Food Stamps* (Washington, DC: Georgetown University Press, 2000), 17–25; for a useful overview, see Dianne Whitmore Schanzenbach, "Exploring Options to Improve the Supplemental Nutrition Assistance Program (SNAP)," *Annals of the American Academy of Political and Social Sciences* 686 (2019): 204–29.

26. King, *Budgeting Entitlements,* esp. chap. 10.

27. Jason DeParle, "Biden Administration Prompts Largest Permanent Increase in Food Stamps," *New York Times,* August 16, 2021, A1; on how SNAP benefits are determined, see Hilary Hoynes, Leslie Granahan, and Diane Schanzenbach, "SNAP and Food Consumption," in *SNAP Matters: How Food Stamps Affect Health and Well-Being,* ed. Judith Bartfeld et al. (Stanford, CA: Stanford University Press, 2015): 107–33; and Jones, Toossi, and Hodges, *Food and Nutrition Assistance Landscape,* 6.

28. Higher thresholds apply in Alaska and Hawai'i. "2021 Poverty Guidelines," US Department of Health and Human Services, accessed February 15, 2023, https://aspe.hhs.gov/topics/poverty-economic-mobility/poverty-guidelines/prior-hhs-poverty-guidelines-federal-register-references; "2023 Poverty Guidelines," US Department of Health and Human Services, accessed February 17, 2023, https://aspe.hhs.gov/topics/poverty-economic-mobility/poverty-guidelines.

29. Jamie Lutz and Caitlin Welsh, "Solving Food Insecurity among U.S. Veterans and Military Families," Center for Strategic and International Studies, June 2022, www.csis.org/analysis/solving-food-insecurity-among-us-veterans-and-military-families.

30. USDA data, cited in "SNAP—It Ain't Just for Cities," American Farm Bureau Federation, August 14, 2017, www.fb.org/market-intel/snap-it-aint-just-for-cities; Mark Rank and Thomas Hirschl, "Likelihood of Using Food Stamps during the Adulthood Years," *Journal of Nutrition Education and Behavior* 32, no. 3 (2005): 137–46.

31. Kathryn Cronquist, *Characteristics of Supplemental Nutrition Assistance Program Households: Fiscal Year 2018,* report SNAP-19-CHAR, Office of Policy Support (Washington, DC: US Department of Agriculture, 2019).

32. Jason DeParle, "As Schools Shut Down, a New Federal Program Eased Child Hunger, Study Finds," *New York Times,* July 21, 2020, A17.

33. Alisha Coleman-Jensen et al., *Household Food Security in the United States in 2021,* ERR-309 (Washington, DC: Economic Research Service, US Department of Agriculture, 2022).

34. Jacob Klerman and Caroline Danielson, "The Transformation of the Supplemental Nutrition Assistance Program," *Journal of Policy Analysis and Management* 30, no. 4 (2011): 863–88; see also Pamela Herd and Donald

Moynihan, *Administrative Burden: Policymaking by Other Means* (New York: Sage, 2018): 191–214.

35. SNAP also is available in the District of Columbia, the US Virgin Islands, and Guam. While the DC program works similarly to the fifty states, program rules vary for the territories. Puerto Rico operates its own version under a federal food-assistance block grant (see chapter 5).

36. See Herd and Moynihan, *Administrative Burden*, 143–64; Kara Newby and Xi Chen, "Decisions That Matter: State Supplemental Nutrition Assistance Program Policy Restrictiveness Limits SNAP Participation Rate," *Social Science Quarterly* 103, no. 4 (2022): 868–82.

37. "SNAP Participation Rates, by State, All Eligible People, Fiscal Year 2019," US Department of Agriculture, Food and Nutrition Service, accessed February 18, 2023, www.fns.usda.gov/usamap/2019.

38. Tiehan, *Food Assistance Landscape*, 18–19; Dottie Rosenbaum and Brynne Keith-Jennings, *SNAP Costs and Caseloads Declining: Trends Expected to Continue* (Washington, DC: Center for Budget Priorities and Policy, 2016).

39. Heather Haddon and Jesse Newman, "Retailers Worry Food-Stamp Overhaul Will Hit Them Hard," *Wall Street Journal*, April 6, 2018.

40. Andrew Fisher, *Big Hunger: The Unholy Alliance between Corporate America and Anti-hunger Groups* (Cambridge, MA: MIT Press, 2017).

41. Michael Katz, *The Undeserving Poor: From the War on Poverty to the War on Welfare* (New York: Pantheon, 1980).

42. See Christopher Howard, *The Welfare State Nobody Knows: Debunking Myths about U.S. Social Policy* (Princeton, NJ: Princeton University Press, 2007); and Douglas Arnold, *Fixing Social Security: The Politics of Reform in a Polarized Age* (Princeton, NJ: Princeton University Press, 2022).

43. Eli Rosenberg, "Walmart and McDonald's Have the Most Workers on Food Stamps and Medicaid, New Study Shows," *Washington Post*, November 18, 2020.

2. "To Encourage Domestic Consumption"

1. Quoted in Ray F. Harvey, *Want in the Midst of Plenty: The Genesis of the Food Stamp Plan* (Washington, DC: American Council on Public Affairs, 1941), 3.

2. Janet Poppendieck, *Breadlines Knee-Deep in Wheat: Food Assistance in the Great Depression*, 2nd ed. (Berkeley: University of California Press, 2014), chap. 7. The USDA at the same time authorized the plowing under of ten million acres of surplus cotton, but the pig slaughter got the headlines.

3. Jonathan Coppess, *The Fault Lines of Farm Policy: A Legislative and Political History of the Farm Bill* (Lincoln: University of Nebraska Press, 2018); Bruce Gardner, *American Agriculture in the Twentieth Century: How It Flourished and What It Cost* (Cambridge, MA: Harvard University Press, 2002); Adam Sheingate, *The Rise of the Agricultural Welfare State: Institutions and Interest Group Power in the United States, France, and Japan* (Princeton, NJ: Princeton University Press, 2001); David Danbom, *The Resisted Revolution: Urban America and the Industrialization of Agriculture, 1900–1930* (Ames: Iowa State University Press, 1979); Sarah Phillips, *This Land, This Nation: Conservation, Rural America, and the New Deal* (New York: Cambridge University Press, 2007).

4. Poppendieck, *Breadlines Knee-Deep in Wheat*, 114.

5. Quoted in Van Perkins, *Crisis in Agriculture: The Agricultural Adjustment Administration and the New Deal, 1933* (Berkeley: University of California Press, 1969); see also Coppess, *Fault Lines*, 27.

6. Harvey, *Want in the Midst*, 4; Poppendieck, *Breadlines Knee-Deep in Wheat*, 123–25.

7. Coppess, *Fault Lines*, 14–19.

8. Sheingate, *Agricultural Welfare State*, 122; also, Kenneth Finegold, "Agriculture and the Politics of U.S. Social Provision: Social Insurance and Food Stamps," in *The Politics of Social Policy in the United States*, ed. Margaret Weir, Ann Shola Orloff, and Theda Skocpol (Princeton, NJ: Princeton University Press, 1988), 199–234; for data on aggregate farm income, see National Bureau of Economic Research, "Net Income of Farm Operators from Farming for United States," FRED, Federal Reserve Bank of St. Louis, August 17, 2012, https://fred.stlouisfed.org/series/A08158USA144NNBR.

9. See Poppendieck, *Breadlines Knee-Deep in Wheat*, xvi; and Harvey, *Want in the Midst*, 4.

10. Norman Thomas, *After the New Deal, What?* (New York: Macmillan, 1936), 33, quoted in Poppendieck, *Breadlines Knee-Deep in Wheat*, 127.

11. Milo Perkins, *Report of the Associate Administrator of the Agricultural Adjustment, in Charge of the Division of Marketing and Marketing Agreements,*

and the President of the Federal Surplus Marketing Commodities Corporation, 1939–1940 (Washington, DC: US Government Printing Office, 1939); John Mark Hansen, Gaining Access: Congress and the Farm Lobby, 1919–1981 (Chicago: University of Chicago Press, 1991); Coppess, Fault Lines, 24.

12. Henry A. Wallace, Anniversary Statement on the Food Stamp Plan (Washington, DC: US Department of Agriculture, 1940).

13. Agricultural Adjustment Act of 1935, Pub. L. No. 320, Sec. 32, 70th Cong. (1935). For a detailed analysis of the FSCC's legal authority under Section 32, see Samuel Herman, "The Food Stamp Plan: A Study in Law and Economics," Journal of Business of the University of Chicago 13, no. 4 (1940): 331–59; 14, no. 1 (1941): 11–35.

14. See Harvey, Want in the Midst, 25.

15. Megan Stubbs, The Commodity Credit Corporation, report no. R44606, Congressional Research Service, January 14, 2021, https://crsreports.congress .gov/product/pdf/R/R44606.

16. Herman, "Food Stamp Plan" (1940), 344.

17. Harvey, Want in the Midst, 10.

18. Janet Poppendieck, Free for All: Fixing School Food in America (Berkeley: University of California Press, 2010), chap. 2.

19. Poppendieck, Breadlines Knee-Deep in Wheat, 239 (emphasis added).

20. Rachel L. Moran, "Consuming Relief: Food Stamps and the New Welfare of the New Deal," Journal of American History 97, no. 4 (2011): 1005–6. And, yes, I like kohlrabi.

21. Moran, 1007.

22. Harvey, Want in the Midst, 13–14; Poppendieck, Breadlines Knee-Deep in Wheat, 63.

23. Harvey, Want in the Midst, 24.

24. On US notions of "deservedness" see, among others, Michael Katz, The Underserving Poor: From the War on Poverty to the War on Welfare (New York: Pantheon, 1980); Theda Skocpol, Protecting Soldiers and Mothers: The Political Origins of Social Policy in the United States (Cambridge, MA: Harvard University Press, 1992).

25. Committee on Agriculture, US House of Representatives, "A History of the Origins of the Food Stamp Program," Food Stamp Act of 1976: Report Together with Supplemental Views, Dissenting Views, and Including

the Congressional Budget Office Estimates on H.R. 13613, 94th Cong., 2d Sess. (1976), 393.

26. Josephine Brown, *Public Relief, 1929-1939* (New York: Holt, 1940).

27. Herman, "Food Stamp Plan" (1940), 338-39.

28. "Two-Price Plan," *Time*, November 14, 1938, 63, quoted in Moran, "Consuming Relief," 1007.

29. Harvey, *Want in the Midst*, 30.

30. Eva Bertram, "The Institutional Origins of 'Workfarist' Social Policy," *Studies in American Political Development* 21, no. 3 (2007): 208; Winifred Bell, *Aid to Dependent Children* (New York: Columbia University Press, 1965), 107; on the role of race in the shape of New Deal social-welfare policy, see Jill Quadagno, *The Transformation of Old Age Security: Class and Politics in the American Welfare State* (Chicago: University of Chicago Press, 1988), and Ira Katznelson, *Fear Itself: The New Deal and the Origins of Our Time* (New York: Liveright, 2013).

31. Poppendieck, *Breadlines Knee-Deep in* Wheat, 167-68, 230; William Leuchtenburg, *Franklin Roosevelt and the New Deal, 1932-1940* (New York: Harper and Row, 1963); James Agee and Walker Evans, *Let Us Now Praise Famous Men* (Boston: Houghton Mifflin, 1940).

32. Katznelson, *Fear Itself*; Finegold, "Agriculture and the Politics," 206-7; Frances Fox Piven and Richard Cloward, *Regulating the Poor: The Functions of Public Welfare* (New York: Pantheon, 1971), chap. 3; Nick Kotz, *Let Them Eat Promises: The Politics of Hunger in America* (Englewood Cliffs, NJ: Prentice-Hall, 1989), 21-43.

33. Poppendieck, *Breadlines Knee-Deep in Wheat*, 163.

34. "Disposal of Surplus Commodities," *Agricultural Department Appropriation Bill for 1941, Hearings before the United States House Committee on Appropriations, Subcommittee on Agriculture Department Appropriations*, 76th Cong., 3d Sess. (1939) (statement of Milo Perkins), 837-38; Finegold, "Agriculture and the Politics," 203-4.

35. Milo Perkins, *Report of the Administrative Official in Charge of Surplus Removal and Marketing Agreement Programs* (Washington, DC: Surplus Marketing Administration, US Department of Agriculture, 1940).

36. Milo Perkins, "Eating the Surplus" (address, National Association of Retail Grocers, Kansas City, MO, June 21, 1939).

37. Wallace, quoted in Frederick Barkley, "Stamp Food–Sales Test Watched in Rochester: Distribution of Surpluses to the Needy Expected to Provide Key to a National Relief Program," *New York Times,* May 21, 1939, E6.

38. Harvey, *Want in the Midst,* 15.

39. Leuchtenburg, *Franklin Roosevelt;* Theodore Lowi, *The End of Liberalism: Ideology, Policy, and the Crisis of Public Authority* (New York: Norton, 1969); Edwin Amenta, *Bold Relief: Institutional Politics and the Origins of Modern American Social Policy* (Princeton, NJ: Princeton University Press, 1998).

40. Perkins, "Eating the Surplus," also quoted in Committee on Agriculture, "History of the Origins," 394.

41. Committee on Agriculture, "History of the Origins," 398.

42. "Grocers Approve Plan to Aid Needy: Department of Agriculture to Start Distributing Excess Farm Produce Soon," *New York Times,* March 14, 1939, 32.

43. An observation made by Kotz in *Let Them Eat Promises.*

44. Harvey, *Want in the Midst,* 15; on the power of southern members of Congress, see Katznelson, *Fear Itself.*

45. Finegold, "Agriculture and the Politics," 205.

46. Norman Gold et al., *Economic Analysis of the Food Stamp Plan* (Washington, DC: Bureau of Agricultural Economics and Surplus Marketing Administration, US Department of Agriculture, 1940), 10; Samuel Herman, "The Food Stamp Plan: Termination," *Journal of Business of the University of Chicago* 16, no. 3 (1943): 184–85.

47. Perkins, "Eating the Surplus," 1.

48. Gold et al., *Economic Analysis,* 2–3.

49. Herman, "Food Stamp Plan" (1940), 339.

50. "Food Stamps," *Compass* 21, no. 1 (1939): 3.

51. J. Frank Grimes, "Expanding Consumption of Agricultural Products: The Government Must Take a Hand," speech before the Chamber of Commerce of the United States, Washington, DC, May 2, 1939, printed in *Vital Speeches of the Day* 5, no. 17 (1939): 537.

52. Committee on Agriculture, "History of the Origins," 406; Moran, "Consuming Relief," 1022, 1003.

53. Herman, "Food Stamp Plan" (1943), 177.

54. Joseph Coppock, "The Food Stamp Plan: Moving Surplus Commodities with Special Purpose Money," *Transactions of the American Philosophical*

Society 37, no. 2 (1947): 140n4; Jerry Bruce Thomas, *An Appalachian New Deal: West Virginia in the Great Depression* (Lexington: University Press of Kentucky, 1998).

55. Herman, "Food Stamp Plan" (1943), 173; Poppendieck, *Free for All,* chap. 2.

56. Perkins, *Administrative Official,* 5.

57. Gold et al., *Economic Analysis,* 10; Harvey, *Want in the Midst,* 20.

58. Dorothy Chausse, "The Food Stamp Plan Comes to Chicago," *Social Science Review* 14, no. 3 (1940): 561.

59. Harvey, *Want in the Midst,* 16.

60. Perkins, *Administrative Official,* 14; Moran, "Consuming Relief," 1010–12n19.

61. Harvey, *Want in the Midst,* 29.

62. Herman, "Food Stamp Plan" (1943), 185.

63. Perkins, *Administrative Official,* 13–14; Committee on Agriculture, "History of the Origins," 417.

64. Milo Perkins, "Thirty Million Customers for the Surplus," in *Yearbook of Agriculture, 1940* (Washington, DC: US Department of Agriculture, 1941), 653–55.

65. Coppock, "Food Stamp Plan," 134.

66. "Food Stamps as a Subsidy for Low Wages," editorial, *Social Service Review* 13, no. 4 (1939): 687.

67. Chausse, "Food Stamp Plan Comes," 561; Herman, "Food Stamp Plan" (1943), 189.

68. Coppock, "Food Stamp Plan," 137–38.

69. Herman, "Food Stamp Plan" (1943), 191.

70. Moran, "Consuming Relief," 1016–17.

71. Bessie Garrod to Eleanor Roosevelt, March 10, 1941, quoted in Moran, "Consuming Relief," 1017.

72. *Agricultural Department Appropriations Bill, 1944, Hearings before the Subcommittee on Agriculture Department Appropriations,* US House of Representatives, 78th Cong., 1st Sess. (1943) (statement of Roy Hendrickson, Director, Food Distribution Administration), 1112–13.

73. Herman, "Food Stamp Plan" (1943), 178.

74. Coppock, "Food Stamp Plan," 188.

75. Harvey, *Want in the Midst,* 8; Finegold, "Agriculture and the Politics," 205.

76. Herman, "Food Stamp Plan" (1943), 173.

77. Coppock, "Food Stamp Plan," 133.

78. Frederick V. Waugh, "Programs for Using Agricultural Surpluses to Reduce Malnutrition and to Benefit Farmers," *Journal of Farm Economics* 22, no. 1 (1940): 329; the USDA was meticulous in tracking the use of food stamps to purchase surplus commodities. See, for example, Economic Analysis Section, *Use of Blue Stamps under the Food Stamp Plan, May 1939-1940* (Washington, DC: Surplus Marketing Administration, US Department of Agriculture, 1940).

79. Gold et al., *Economic Analysis,* 66.

80. Harvey, *Want in the Midst,* 33.

81. Coppock, "Food Stamp Plan," 158-61.

82. Gold et al., *Economic Analysis,* 3.

83. Coppock, "Food Stamp Plan," 176-77.

84. Viviana A. Zelizer, *The Social Meaning of Money: Pin Money, Paychecks, Poor Relief, and Other Currencies* (Princeton, NJ: Princeton University Press, 1997, cited in Moran, "Consuming Relief," 1019.

85. Coppock, "Food Stamp Plan," 186; see also Moran, "Consuming Relief," 1015.

86. Moran, "Consuming Relief," 1001-22; on the food retail marketplace of the 1930s, see chapter 2 in Benjamin Davison, "Farm to Table: The Supermarket Industry and American Society, 1920-1990" (PhD diss., University of Virginia, 2018).

87. Committee on Agriculture, "History of the Origins," 413-14.

88. Herman, "Food Stamp Plan" (1943), 192.

89. Coppock, "Food Stamp Plan," 152.

90. Committee on Agriculture, "History of the Origins," 413.

91. Herman, "Food Stamp Plan" (1943), 182; Coppock, "Food Stamp Plan," 134.

92. Moran, "Consuming Relief," 1014.

93. Harvey, *Want in the Midst,* 22.

94. Coppock, "Food Stamp Plan," 154.

95. "Food Stamps," 3.

96. Katznelson, *Fear Itself;* Finegold, "Agriculture and the Politics."

3. The Paradox Anew

1. Milo Perkins, "Agricultural Aspects of Food Stamp Plan Operations," summary of statement at the Sixth Annual Meeting of the National Association of Food Chains, Chicago, October 10, 1939.

2. Jeffrey Berry, *Feeding Hungry People: Rulemaking in the Food Stamp Program* (New Brunswick, NJ: Rutgers University Press, 1984).

3. See Marjorie DeVault and James Pitts, "Surplus and Security: Hunger and the Origins of the Food Stamp Program," *Social Problems* 31, no. 5 (1984): 545–57.

4. Committee on Agriculture, US House of Representatives, "A History of the Origins of the Food Stamp Program," *Food Stamp Act of 1976: Report Together with Supplemental Views, Dissenting Views, and Including the Congressional Budget Office Estimates on H.R. 13613*, 94th Cong., 2d Sess. (1976), 412.

5. The committee also shared jurisdiction with the Senate Committee on Agriculture over farm credit and farm security until the Legislative Reorganization Act of 1948.

6. *National Food Allotment Plan, Hearings before a Subcommittee of the Committee on Agriculture and Forestry*, US Senate, 78th Cong. (1944), 9.

7. Martin Abel, "Frederick V. Waugh: A Profile of Relevance," *Choices* 3, no. 4 (1988), 42–44.

8. Abel, 117–18.

9. *National Food Allotment Plan*; Janet Poppendieck, *Breadlines Knee-Deep in Wheat: Food Assistance in the Great Depression*, 2nd ed. (Berkeley: University of California Press, 2014), 242–43; Committee on Agriculture, "History of the Origins," 444.

10. Kenneth Finegold, "Agriculture and the Politics of U.S. Social Provision: Social Insurance and Food Stamps," in *The Politics of Social Policy in the United States*, ed. Margaret Weir, Ann Shola Orloff, and Theda Skocpol (Princeton, NJ: Princeton University Press, 1988), 221; Cong. Rec., 78th Cong., 2d Sess. (1944), 90, pt. 2, p. 1613.

11. *Agriculture Department Appropriations Bill for 1947, Hearings before the Subcommittee of the Committee on Appropriations Committee*, House of Representatives, 79th Cong., 2d Sess. (1946) (statement of Clinton Anderson, Secretary of Agriculture), 2–4.

12. Committee on Agriculture, "History of the Origins," 445.

13. Quoted in Berry, *Feeding Hungry People*, 23.

14. See Bruce Gardner, *American Agriculture in the Twentieth Century: How It Flourished and What It Cost* (Cambridge, MA: Harvard University Press, 2002), esp. chap. 2.

15. Agricultural Stabilization and Conservation Service, *History of CCC Bin Storage Program, 1933–1975* (Washington, DC: US Department of Agriculture, 1975), 9.

16. See Edward Shapsmeir and Frederick Shapsmeir, "Eisenhower and Agricultural Reform: Ike's Farm Policy Legacy Appraised," *American Journal of Economics and Sociology* 51, no. 2 (1992): 147–49; Jonathan Coppess, *The Fault Lines of Farm Policy: A Legislative and Political History of the Farm Bill* (Lincoln: University of Nebraska Press, 2018), esp. 73–94.

17. *History of CCC Bin Storage*, 5.

18. See Janet Poppendieck, *Free for All: Fixing School Food in America* (Berkeley: University of California Press, 2010).

19. Committee on Agriculture, "History of the Origins," 445.

20. "Post-Marshall Plan Aid Already Being Devised," *Barron's National Business and Financial Weekly*, February 13, 1950, 8; Virgil Dean, "Charles F. Brannan and the Rise and Fall of Truman's 'Fair Deal' for Farmers" *Agricultural History* 69, no. 1 (1995): 28–53; on postwar agricultural-policy debates more broadly, see Adam Sheingate, *The Rise of the Agricultural Welfare State: Institutions and Interest Group Power in the United States, France, and Japan* (Princeton, NJ: Princeton University Press, 2001), 128–39.

21. Calculated from the US Bureau of Labor Statistics, "Unemployment Rate," FRED, Federal Reserve Bank of St. Louis, December 2022, https://fred .stlouisfed.org/series/UNRATE.

22. Coppess, *Fault Lines of Farm Policy*, 74.

23. See *Committee on Agriculture and Forestry*, US Senate, 83rd Cong., 1st Sess. (1953) (statement of Ezra Taft Benson, Secretary of Agriculture-Designate).

24. For a deep analysis of party and crop alignments in the House Agriculture Committee during this period, see Charles O. Jones, "The Role of the Congressional Subcommittee," *Midwest Journal of Political Science* 6, no. 4 (1962): 327–44.

25. It's much more complicated than that, of course. On the divisions between corn, wheat, and cotton, see Coppess, *Fault Lines of Farm Policy*.

26. Committee on Agriculture, "History of the Origins," 447.

27. Poppendieck, *Breadlines Knee-Deep in Wheat*, 244.

28. "Food Distribution Programs," *Hearings before a Subcommittee of the Committee on Agriculture and Forestry*, US Senate, 86th Cong., 1st Sess. (1959), esp. 28.

29. See Ardeth Maney, *Still Hungry after All These Years: Food Assistance Policy from Kennedy to Reagan* (Boulder, CO: Greenwood, 1989), 21.

30. See John Ferejohn, "Logrolling in an Institutional Context: A Case Study of Food Stamp Legislation," in *Congress and Policy Change*, ed. Gerald C. Wright Jr., Leroy N. Rieselbach, and Lawrence C. Dodd (New York: Agathon, 1986), 229.

31. Quoted in Randall Ripley, "Legislative Bargaining and the Food Stamp Act, 1964," in *Congress and Urban Problems: A Casebook on the Legislative Process*, ed. Frederic Cleaveland (Washington, DC: Brookings Institution, 1969), 282.

32. Poppendieck, *Breadlines Knee-Deep in Wheat*, 245.

33. For a useful history, see Norwood Allen Kerr, "The Evolution of USDA Surplus Disposal Programs," *National Food Review*, July–September 1988, 25–28.

34. Committee on Agriculture, "History of the Origins," 447.

35. Committee on Agriculture, 453.

36. "1956 Democratic Party Platform," American Presidency Project, August 13, 1956, www.presidency.ucsb.edu/documents/1956-democratic-party-platform; "Republican Party Platform of 1956," American Presidency Project, August 20, 1956, www.presidency.ucsb.edu/documents/republican-party-platform-1956.

37. "Food Stamp Program," *Hearings before the Subcommittee on Consumers Study of the Committee on Agriculture*, US House of Representatives, 85th Cong., 2d Sess. (1958), 34.

38. "Food Distribution Programs," esp. 20–44.

39. See Coppess, *Fault Lines of Farm Policy*, 104–10; and Christopher Bosso, *Framing the Farm Bill: Ideology, Interests, and the Agricultural Act of 2014* (Lawrence: University Press of Kansas, 2017).

40. US Department of Agriculture, "An Analysis of Food Stamp Plans," January 3, 1957, in Committee on Agriculture, "History of the Origins," 462–71; Maney, *Still Hungry*, 26.

41. Committee on Agriculture, "History of the Origins," 471.

42. Bureau of the Budget, "Fiscal Year Ending June 30, 1960," in *Budget of the United States Government* (Washington, DC: Bureau of the Budget, 1959), 317.

43. "Food Stamp Plan: Disposal of Surplus Commodities," *Hearing before the Committee on Agriculture,* US House of Representatives, 84th Cong., 1st Sess. (1955), esp. 45–66.

44. On the origins of Public Law 480, see chapter 9 in Barry Riley, *The Political History of American Food Aid: An Uneasy Benevolence* (New York: Oxford University Press, 2017).

45. "Food Stamps Defeated: House Bars Plan to Distribute Farm Surplus to Needy," *New York Times,* August 19, 1958, 20.

46. See Jones, "Congressional Subcommittee," 330.

47. "Food Stamp Program" (1958).

48. Committee on Agriculture, "History of the Origins," 474; Coppess, *Fault Lines of Farm Policy,* 114–15.

49. Committee on Agriculture, "History of the Origins," 474.

50. "Food Stamp Plan Tabled," *New York Times,* August 7, 1958, 26.

51. Ripley, "Legislative Bargaining," 285.

52. "Democrats Sweep 1958 Elections; Will Have 64 Senators, 283 Representatives, 35 Governors," *CQ Almanac,* 14th ed., 1958, https://library.cqpress.com/cqalmanac/document.php?id=cqal58-1340275.

53. Ripley, "Legislative Bargaining," 287.

54. Committee on Agriculture, "History of the Origins," 478.

55. Quoted in Berry, *Feeding Hungry People,* 23.

56. An Act to Amend the Agricultural Trade Development and Assistance Act of 1954, and for Other Purposes, Pub. L. No. 86–341, 73 Stat 606 (1959), sec. 306; United Press International, "Senate Vote Approves Experimental Surplus Relief Food Stamp Project," *Washington Post,* September 8, 1959, A15; Ripley, "Legislative Bargaining," 287.

57. Committee on Agriculture, "History of the Origins," 480.

58. Poppendieck, *Breadlines Knee-Deep in Wheat,* 243.

59. "Remarks of Senator John F. Kennedy at Charleston, West Virginia, April 11, 1960," John F. Kennedy Presidential Library, accessed February 16, 2023, www.jfklibrary.org/archives/other-resources/john-f-kennedy-speeches/charleston-wv-19600411.

60. Homer Bigart, "Depression Rivaling '30s Grips Kentucky-Virginia Coal Area," *New York Times,* January 11, 1959, 1.

61. Richard Johnston, "Kennedy Pledges West Virginia Aid," *New York Times,* April 26, 1960, 28.

62. See Robert Rupp, *The Primary That Made a President: John F. Kennedy and West Virginia* (Knoxville: University of Tennessee Press, 2020).

63. "Food Distribution Programs," esp. 20–44; Maney, *Still Hungry,* 23–25.

64. See Michael Harrington, *The Other America: Poverty in the United States* (New York: Macmillan, 1962); and Nick Kotz, *Let Them Eat Promises: The Politics of Hunger in America* (Englewood Cliffs, NJ: Prentice-Hall, 1969).

65. See, for example, Anthony Downs, "Up and Down with Ecology: The Issue-Attention Cycle," *Public Interest* 28 (1972): 38–50; and Roger W. Cobb and Charles D. Elder, *Participation in American Politics: The Dynamics of Agenda Building* (Boston: Allyn and Bacon, 1972).

66. See David Mayhew, "The Long 1950s as a Policy Era," in *The Politics of Major Policy Reform in Postwar America,* ed. Jeffery Jenkins and Sydney Milkus (New York: Cambridge University Press, 2014), 27–47.

67. Orville L. Freeman, "Freeman Weighs the Farm Surplus," *New York Times,* September 24, 1961, SM36.

68. Carolyn Dimitri, Anne Effland, and Neilson Conklin, *The 20th Century Transformation of U.S. Agricultural and Farm Policy* (Washington, DC: Economic Research Service, US Department of Agriculture, 2005), 5.

69. Democratic Advisory Committee, "Policy Statement for 1960," *New York Times,* December 7, 1959, 38.

70. "Republican Party Platform of 1960," American Presidency Project, July 25, 1960, www.presidency.ucsb.edu/documents/republican-party-platform-1960.

71. Leonor Sullivan, interview, September 2, 1976, Katie Louchheim Oral Histories, 1974–76, Schlesinger Library, Harvard University, quoted in Sam Rosenfeld, "Fed by Reform: Congressional Politics, Partisan Change, and the Food Stamp Program, 1961–1981," *Journal of Policy History* 22, no. 4 (2020): 478.

72. Charles Lindblom, "The Science of Muddling Through," *Public Administration Review* 19, no. 2 (1969): 79–88.

73. On keeping policy solutions in play, see John Kingdon, *Agendas, Alternatives, and Public Policies* (Boston: Little, Brown, 1984); and Frederick V.

Waugh, "Programs for Using Agricultural Surpluses to Reduce Malnutrition and to Benefit Farmers," *Journal of Farm Economics* 22, no. 1 (1940): 324–34.

74. See Don Paarlberg, *Subsidized Food Consumption* (Washington, DC: American Enterprise Institute, 1963).

75. Freeman, "Freeman Weighs."

76. "Food Distribution Programs," 50.

77. *Food Stamp Act of 1964, Hearings before the Committee on Agriculture and Forestry*, US Senate, 88th Cong., 2d Sess. (1964) (statement of Orville L. Freeman, Secretary of Agriculture), 9.

78. *Food Stamp Plans, Hearings before the House Committee on Agriculture*, US Senate, 65th Cong., 1st Sess. (1959), 14, cited in Berry, *Feeding Hungry People*, 24.

79. John F. Kennedy, "Special Message to Congress, Program for Economic Recovery and Growth," American Presidency Project, February 2, 1961, www.presidency.ucsb.edu/documents/special-message-the-congress-program-for-economic-recovery-and-growth.

80. Ripley, "Legislative Bargaining," 289.

81. Marguerite Joutz, "Overlooked No More: Isabelle Kelley, Who Developed a Food Stamp Program to Feed Millions," *New York Times,* June 21, 2019, B6.

82. See Berry, *Feeding Hungry People,* 24–28; and Maney, *Still Hungry,* 26–31.

83. See DeVault and Pitts, "Surplus and Scarcity," 548.

84. See Kotz, *Let Them Eat Promises,* 46.

85. See Maney, *Still Hungry,* 159–60nn6–7.

86. Committee on Agriculture, "History of the Origins," 482.

87. Rick Hampson, "When W. Va. Lost Its Voice: JFK's Death Still Resonates," *USA Today,* October 29, 2013.

88. Committee on Agriculture, "History of the Origins," 482.

89. "The Food Stamp Program: An Initial Evaluation of the Pilot Projects," US Department of Agriculture, April 1962, https://naldc.nal.usda.gov/download/7263455/pdf; Robert Reese and Sadye Adelson, "Food Consumption and Dietary Levels under the Pilot Food Stamp Program: Detroit, Michigan, and Fayette County, Pennsylvania," US Department of Agriculture, 1962, https://naldc.nal.usda.gov/download/CAT87201906/pdf.

90. Maney, *Still Hungry,* 30.

91. Committee on Agriculture, "History of the Origins," 485, 494; see also "Food Stamp Program" (1962).

92. Maurice MacDonald, "Food Stamps: An Analytical History," *Social Service Review* 51, no. 4 (1977): 646.

93. Berry, *Feeding Hungry People*, 30.

94. See Paarlberg, *Subsidized Food Consumption.*

95. Berry, *Feeding Hungry People*, 490–91.

96. Ripley, "Legislative Bargaining," 292; MacDonald, "Food Stamps," 646.

97. Ripley, "Legislative Bargaining," 290.

98. Berry, *Feeding Hungry People*, 32.

99. MacDonald, "Food Stamps," citing G. William Hoagland, *Federal Aid for Food Assistance* (Washington, DC: Congressional Budget Office), 1976, 12.

4. Farm Programs + Food Programs

1. Timothy A. Huelskamp, "Congressional Change: Committees on Agriculture in the U.S. Congress" (PhD diss., American University, 1995), 192.

2. With apologies to the immortal Sam Cooke, for the use of "A Change Is Gonna Come."

3. John R. Williams, "Aspects of the American Presidential Election of 1960," *Australian Quarterly* 33, no. 1 (1961): 25–36.

4. John Mark Hansen, *Gaining Access: Congress and the Farm Lobby, 1919–1981* (Chicago: University of Chicago Press, 1991); William P. Browne et al., *Sacred Cows and Hot Potatoes: Agrarian Myths in Agricultural Policy* (Boulder, CO: Westview, 1992).

5. Douglass Cater, *Power in Washington: A Critical Look at Today's Struggle to Govern in the Nation's Capital* (New York: Random House, 1964); on changes in agricultural politics, see Adam Sheingate, *The Rise of the Agricultural Welfare State: Institutions and Interest Group Power in the United States, France, and Japan* (Princeton, NJ: Princeton University Press, 2001).

6. Sheingate, *Agricultural Welfare State;* William P. Browne, *Private Interests, Public Policy, and American Agriculture* (Lawrence: University Press of Kansas, 1988); Parke Wilde, *Food Policy in the United States: An Introduction* (New York: Routledge, 2013); Bruce Gardner, *American Agriculture in the Twen-*

tieth Century: How It Flourished and What It Cost (Cambridge, MA: Harvard University Press, 2002).

7. Noted in Hansen, *Gaining Access,* 167.

8. See Sam Rosenfeld, "Fed by Reform: Congressional Politics, Partisan Change, and the Food Stamp Program, 1961–1981," *Journal of Policy History* 22, no. 4 (2020): 474–507.

9. Food Stamp Act of 1964, Pub. L. No. 88–525, 88th Cong., H.R. 10222 (1964).

10. Richard F. Fenno, *Power of the Purse: Appropriations Politics in Congress* (Boston: Little, Brown, 1965). On Whitten's hold over the USDA, see Nick Kotz, *Let Them Eat Promises: The Politics of Hunger in America* (Englewood Cliffs, NJ: Prentice-Hall, 1969), 84–102; and Bobby J. Smith II, "Mississippi's War against the War on Poverty: Food Power, Hunger, and White Supremacy," Study the South, July 1, 2019, https://southernstudies.olemiss.edu/study-the-south/ms-war-against-war-on-poverty/.

11. Charles O. Jones, "Joseph G. Cannon and Howard W. Smith: An Essay on the Limits of Leadership in the House of Representatives," *Journal of Politics* 30, no. 3 (1968): 617–46.

12. Julius Duscha, "Congress Gets Request to Expand Stamp Plan," *Washington Post,* April 23, 1963, A6; Ardith Maney, *Still Hungry after All These Years: Food Assistance Policy from Kennedy to Reagan* (Boulder, CO: Greenwood, 1989), 41–42.

13. *The Food Stamp Plan, Hearings before the Committee on Agriculture,* US House of Representatives, 88th Cong., 1st Sess. (1963) (statement of Orville L. Freeman, Secretary of Agriculture, on H.R. 5733), 8, 14.

14. Randall B. Ripley, "Legislative Bargaining and the Food Stamp Act, 1964," in *Congress and Urban Problems: A Casebook on the Legislative Process,* ed. Frederic C. Cleaveland (Washington, DC: Brookings Institution, 1969): 279–310; John Ferejohn, "Logrolling in an Institutional Context: A Case Study of Food Stamp Legislation," in *Congress and Policy Change,* ed. Gerald C. Wright Jr., Leroy N. Rieselbach, and Lawrence C. Dodd (New York: Agathon, 1986), 223–54.

15. *Food Stamp Plan,* 21.

16. Ripley, "Legislative Bargaining," 301.

17. H.R. 5733, Sec. 10 (d), as published in *Food Stamp Plan,* 4.

18. Maney, *Still Hungry,* 42.

19. Julius Duscha, "Food Stamps Opposed by Rural Congressmen," *Washington Post,* August 17, 1963, A2.

20. Rosenfeld, "Fed by Reform," 502n18; on the 1962 farm bill, see Jonathan Coppess, *The Fault Lines of Farm Policy: A Legislative and Political History of the Farm Bill* (Lincoln: University of Nebraska Press, 2018), esp. 117–19.

21. Ripley, "Legislative Bargaining," 297.

22. Associated Press, "House Unit Votes Down Tobacco Research Bill," *Washington Post,* February 28, 1963, A10.

23. Ripley, "Legislative Bargaining," 298.

24. Associated Press, "Wheat-Cotton Bill Goes to Rules; Backers Hope for Action Today," *Washington Post,* March 10, 1963, A2; Coppess, *Fault Lines,* 124–25; Sheingate, *Agricultural Welfare State,* 142.

25. Ripley, "Legislative Bargaining," 299.

26. Associated Press, "Sudden Approval to Wheat Measure," *Washington Post,* March 11, 1963, A2.

27. Hansen, *Gaining Access,* 172; Richard Lyons, "Farm Bill Logjam Broken as Leaders Delay House Action," *Washington Post,* March 25, 1964, A2; C. P. Trussell, "Johnson Phone Effort Credited with House Victory on Farm Bill," *New York Times,* April 10, 1964, 15.

28. Ripley, "Legislative Bargaining," 301.

29. Quoted in Jeffrey Berry, *Feeding Hungry People: Rulemaking in the Food Stamp Program* (New Brunswick, NJ: Rutgers University Press, 1984), 34.

30. C. P. Trussell, "House Rules Unit Clears Food Bill: But Date for Floor Action on Stamps Is Uncertain," *New York Times,* March 20, 1964, 13; Julius Duscha, "Wheat Bill Maneuvers Bring GOP Outburst," *Washington Post,* March 26, 1964, A4.

31. "H.R. 10222. Passage," Govtrack, April 8, 1964, www.govtrack.us /congress/votes/88-1964/h149.

32. Ripley, "Legislative Bargaining," 305.

33. Trussell, "Johnson Phone Effort Credited," 15.

34. Ferejohn, "Logrolling," 223–53. Explaining the timber-industry origins of the term "logroll" would take up too much space. Google it.

35. Ripley, "Legislative Bargaining," 293.

36. Huelskamp, "Congressional Change," 164.

37. Ripley, "Legislative Bargaining," 306.

38. David Binder, "Jamie Whitten, Who Served 53 Years in House, Dies at 85," *New York Times*, September 10, 1995, D13; Rep. John Dingell of Michigan would serve just over fifty-nine years (1955–2015).

39. On party realignment in the United States, see Walter Dean Burnham, *Critical Elections and the Mainsprings of American Politics* (New York: Norton, 1970); and James Sundquist, *Dynamics of the Party System: Alignment and Realignment of Political Parties in the United States* (Washington, DC: Brookings Institution Press, 1983).

40. William Blair, "House Votes Farm Funds, Rejects Curbs on Red Sales," *New York Times*, May 21, 1964, 1.

41. On Johnson's legendary capacity to persuade, see Robert Caro, *Master of the Senate: The Years of Lyndon Johnson* (New York: Knopf, 2002).

42. *Food Stamp Plan*, 99–112; *Food Stamp Act of 1964, Hearings before the Committee on Agriculture and Forestry*, US Senate, 88th Cong., 2d Sess. (1964), 53–65, 81–82.

43. C.P. Trussell, "Senate Votes Permanent Food-Stamp Program to Improve Diet of the Needy," *New York Times*, July 1, 1964, 13.

44. Ripley, "Legislative Bargaining," 308.

45. Berry, *Feeding Hungry People*, 35.

46. Janet Poppendieck, *Breadlines Knee-Deep in Wheat: Food Assistance in the Great Depression*, 2nd ed. (Berkeley: University of California Press, 2014), 252; Ronald F. King, *Budgeting Entitlements: The Politics of Food Stamps* (Washington, DC: Georgetown University Press, 2000), 46.

47. Maurice MacDonald, "Food Stamps: An Analytical History," *Social Service Review* 51, no. 4 (1977): 648.

48. James C. Ohls and Harold Beebout, *The Food Stamp Program: Design Tradeoffs, Policy, and Impacts* (Washington, DC: Urban Institute Press, 1993), 14.

49. Earl Caldwell, "Abernathy Seeks Poverty Explanation," *New York Times*, June 22, 1968, 23.

50. Jeffrey Pressman and Aaron Wildavsky, *Implementation: How Great Expectations in Washington Are Dashed in Oakland; or, Why It's Amazing That Federal Programs Work at All* (Berkeley: University of California Press, 1973).

51. Maney, *Still Hungry*, 46–47; Gilbert C. Fite, "Mechanization of Cotton Production since World War II," *Agricultural History* 54, no. 1 (1980): 190–207;

on the effects in northern cities, see Frances Fox Piven and Richard Cloward, *Regulating the Poor: The Functions of Public Welfare* (New York: Pantheon, 1971), chaps. 6-8.

52. Maney, *Still Hungry*, 69-82; Marjorie DeVault and James Pitts, "Surplus and Scarcity: Hunger and the Origins of the Food Stamp Program," *Social Problems* 31 no. 5 (1984): 549.

53. Kotz, *Let Them Eat Promises*, 53.

54. See Don Paarlberg, *Subsidized Food Consumption* (Washington, DC: American Enterprise Institute, 1963); and Berry, *Feeding Hungry People*, 42-50.

55. Kotz, *Let Them Eat Promises*, 55.

56. MacDonald, "Food Stamps," 648.

57. DeVault and Pitts, "Surplus and Scarcity," 546-48.

58. In addition to Kotz, *Let Them Eat Promises*, see Berry, *Feeding Hungry People*; Maney, *Still Hungry*; and Judith A. Segal, *Food for the Hungry: The Reluctant Society* (Baltimore: Johns Hopkins University Press, 1970).

59. Citizens Board of Inquiry into Hunger and Malnutrition in the United States, *Hunger U.S.A.* (Boston: Beacon, 1968).

60. CBS Reports, *Hunger in America* (New York: Columbia Broadcasting System, 1968); See Kotz, *Let Them Eat Promises*, 181-82; and Berry, *Feeding Hungry People*, 43-45.

61. Kotz, *Let Them Eat Promises*, 163-74; Maney, *Still Hungry*, 83-98.

62. Smith, "Mississippi's War."

63. Berry, *Feeding Hungry People*, 48-49; Ferejohn, "Logrolling," 234-35; Coppess, *Fault Lines*, 129-30.

64. Cong. Rec. 41,985 (1970), as quoted in Peter Eisinger, *Toward an End to Hunger in America* (Washington, DC: Brookings, 1997), 44.

65. Norwood A. Kerr, "Drafted into the War on Poverty: USDA Food and Nutrition Programs, 1961-1969," *Agricultural History* 64, no. 2 (1990): 154-66.

66. Berry, *Feeding Hungry People*, 51.

67. Maney, *Still Hungry*; Kotz, *Let Them Eat Promises*, 69; Bureau of the Census, *Current Population Reports* P-60, no. 62 (1969): 1.

68. Kotz, *Let Them Eat Promises*, 71; Maney, *Still Hungry*, 107-9.

69. Orville Freeman, interview 4 (IV) by Michael L. Gillette, oral history transcript, LBJ Library Oral Histories, LBJ Presidential Library, Austin, TX, www.discoverlbj.org/item/oh-freemano-19881117-4-06-13.

70. Rosenfeld, "Fed by Reform," 482–83; Eisinger, *Toward an End,* 78–84.

71. Kotz, *Let Them Eat Promises,* 152–53.

72. Robert Sam Anson, *McGovern: A Biography* (New York: Holt, Rinehart and Winston, 1972); on Dole, see Richard Ben Cramer, *What It Takes: The Way to the White House* (New York: Random House, 1992); and Jerry Hagstrom, "Dole's Legacy of Fighting Hunger," *National Journal Daily,* December 9, 2021, 5.

73. Berry, *Feeding Hungry People,* 50; see also "Who's Who in Capital's Farm Power Structure," *New York Times,* April 5, 1970, 57.

74. Quoted in Kotz, *Let Them Eat Promises,* 207

75. Kotz, 194.

76. Kotz, 195–204; Homer Bigart, "Hunger in America: Stark Deprivation Haunts a Land of Plenty," *New York Times,* February 16, 1969, 1; Warren Weaver, "Hunger: It Jolts a Senate Coalition," *New York Times,* February 23, 1969, E6.

77. "McGovern to Fight Hunger Study Cut," *New York Times,* February 15, 1969, 14.

78. Maney, *Still Hungry,* 114; Robert Sherrill, "Why Can't We Just Give Them Food?," *New York Times,* March 22, 1970, 233.

79. Kotz, *Let Them Eat Promises,* 206–7.

80. See Matthew Gritter, *Republican Presidents and the Safety Net: From Moderation to Backlash* (Washington, DC: Lexington Books, 2018).

81. See, for example, Charles O. Jones, *Clear Air: The Policies and Politics of Pollution Control* (Pittsburgh: University of Pittsburgh Press, 1975).

82. Rosenfeld, "Fed by Reform," 484.

83. Kotz, *Let Them Eat Promises,* 223; Walter Rugabear, "Nixon Proposes $1-Billion Drive to Fight Hunger," *New York Times,* May 7, 1969, 1; "Attacking Hunger—Next Year," editorial, *New York Times,* May 9, 1969, 46

84. Richard Nixon, "Special Message to Congress Recommending a Program to End Hunger in America," May 6, 1969, Nixon Presidential Papers, Richard Nixon Presidential Library and Museum, Yorba Linda, CA; William Blair, "Plan Would Force States to Take Part in Food Programs," *New York Times,* June 7, 1969, 1.

85. James Naughton, "Free Food Stamps Voted by Senate," *New York Times,* September 25, 1969, 21; "Food Stamps for All Poor Called Unlikely of Passage,"

New York Times, September 6, 1969, 22; Associated Press, "House Panel Bars Food Stamp Program Gains," *New York Times,* December 11, 1969, 1.

86. Chisholm initially saw assignment to the House Committee on Agriculture as an insult but apparently was convinced by a local rabbi that she could use the seat to advocate for hungry constituents. See Joseph Telushkin, *Rebbe: The Life and Teachings of Menachem M. Schneerson, the Most Influential Rabbi in Modern History* (New York: HarperCollins, 2014), 13–14.

87. Coppess, *Fault Lines,* 129.

88. See Hansen, *Gaining Access,* 203–8.

89. DeVault and Pitts, "Surplus and Scarcity," 554; on the politics of the conference, see Jack Rosenthal, "Much Angry Talk, Some Action, on Hunger," *New York Times,* December 7, 1969, sec. 4, p. 2; and Sherrill, "Why Can't We?"

90. King, *Budgeting Entitlements,* 53.

91. MacDonald, "Food Stamps," 652.

92. Berry, *Feeding Hungry People,* 64–68.

93. MacDonald, "Food Stamps," 651; Marjorie Hunter, "To End Hunger: Nixon Aides Back Use of Cash over Stamps in Hunger Drive," *New York Times,* May 8, 1969, 1; James Naughton, "Nixon Aide Denies Relief Plan Ends U.S. Food Stamps," *New York Times,* August 20, 1969, 1; Vincent J. Burke and Vee Burke, *Nixon's Good Deed: Welfare Reform* (New York: Columbia University Press, 1974), 120–23.

94. Hansen, *Gaining Access,* 207.

95. See Daniel Patrick Moynihan, *The Politics of a Guaranteed Income: The Nixon Administration and the Family Assistance Plan* (New York: Random House, 1973).

96. Berry, *Feeding Hungry People,* 68; see also Richard P. Nathan, "Food Stamps and Welfare Reform," *Policy Analysis* 2, no. 1 (1976): 61–70.

97. See Eva Bertram, "The Institutional Origins of 'Workfarist' Social Policy," *Studies in American Political Development* 21, no. 3 (2007): 203–29.

98. Marjorie Hunter, "House Unit Votes Food Stamp Bill," *New York Times,* December 2, 1970, 11; Hunter, "Food Stamp Compromise Is Approved by Conferees," *New York Times,* December 23, 1970, 1; "Food Stamps: Fresh Skirmishes in the Politics of Hunger," *New York Times,* December 27, 1970, sec. 4, p. 2; "Washington: For the Record," *New York Times,* January 1, 1971, 12.

99. Julius Duscha, "Up, Up, Up—Butz Makes Hay Down on the Farm," *New York Times,* April 16, 1972, sec. SM, p. 34; William Robbins, "Nixon Farm Proposals Stir Old Democratic Fears," *New York Times,* February 18, 1973, 3.

100. See Coppess, *Fault Lines,* 138–46.

101. Gardner, *American Agriculture,* 237–40; Charles Schultze, *The Distribution of Farm Subsidies* (Washington, DC: Brookings Institution, 1971).

102. Berry, *Feeding Hungry People,* 61; William Robbins, "Farm Aid Voted by Senate Panel," *New York Times,* May 10, 1973, 23.

103. Hansen, *Gaining Access,* 210; see also Ferejohn, "Logrolling," 237–40; and Michael Lyons and Marcia Whicker Taylor, "Farm Politics in Transition: The House Agriculture Committee," *Agricultural History* 55, no. 2 (1981): 128–46.

104. King, *Budgeting Entitlements,* 57–58.

105. Martin Tolchin, "Urban-Rural Coalition Successful on Farm and Food Stamp Measure," *New York Times,* July 29, 1977, 14.

106. Berry, *Feeding Hungry People,* 90–92; King, *Budgeting Entitlements,* 68–69; Nancy Hicks, "March 1 Rise in Cost of Food Stamps Opposed in Suit," *New York Times,* January 23, 1975, 17.

107. MacDonald, "Food Stamps," 655.

108. *An Act to Suspend Increases in the Costs of Coupons to Food Stamp Recipients as a Result of Recent Administrative Actions,* Pub. L. No. 94-4 (1975); on the emergence of greater legislative oversight of the Food Stamp Program in the 1970s, see Berry, *Feeding Hungry People,* 105–26.

109. Richard Lyons, "House Democrats Oust 3 Chairmen," *New York Times,* January 23, 1975, 1; on the centrality of the House Committee on Agriculture in the politics of congressional reform, see Rosenfeld, "Fed by Reform."

110. Lyons and Taylor, "Farm Politics in Transition," 134–35; on Foley's views, see Sherrill, "Why Can't We?"

111. "Dole, McGovern, Introduce Major Food Stamp Reform Legislation," press release, October 5, 1975, Office of Senator Robert Dole, courtesy of the Dole Archives, University of Kansas, Lawrence.

112. Berry, *Feeding Hungry People,* 80–84; King, *Budgeting Entitlements,* 75; "Food Stamp Furor," *Newsweek,* October 20, 1975, 35–36; Michael Katz, *The Underserving Poor: From the War on Poverty to the War on Welfare* (New York: Pantheon, 1980).

113. *Options for Reforming the Food Stamp Program, Hearings before the Select Committee on Nutrition and Human Needs,* US Senate, 94th Cong., 1st Sess. (1975).

114. King, *Budgeting Entitlements,* 70–71; Maney, *Still Hungry,* 122–27; Berry, *Feeding Hungry People,* 86–89; Ferejohn, "Logrolling," 241–42; Nancy Hicks, "Food Stamp Shift Barred in Senate," *New York Times,* May 8, 1975, 42; "Food Stamp Curbs Urged by Buckley," *New York Times,* October 9, 1975, 44.

115. Berry, *Feeding Hungry People,* 127–36, 94–96; "Butz Has Kind Words on Bergland's Choice," *New York Times,* December 27, 1976, 21; see also Rosenfeld, "Fed by Reform," 495–96; Maney, *Still Hungry,* 129–30; and Coppess, *Fault Lines,* 147–49.

116. William Robins, "Government Weighs a Proposal to Make Food Stamps Free," *New York Times,* March 30, 1977, 38; "Talmadge Gives Food Stamp Plan," *New York Times,* April 8, 1977, 19.

117. "Senate Passes 5-Year Farm Bill Exceeding Carter's Support Level," *New York Times,* May 25, 1977, 14.

118. Linda Demkovich, "The 'Odd Couple' Is Whipping Up a New Dish on Food Stamps," *National Journal,* March 19, 1977, 428–29.

119. Martin Tolchin, "House Backs Carter's Plan for Free Food Stamps," *New York Times,* July 26, 1977, 40.

120. Joe Richardson, *A Concise History of the Food Stamps Program,* report no. 79-244, Congressional Research Service, 1979, in University of North Texas Library, accessed March 22, 2023, https://digital.library.unt.edu /ark:/67531/metacrs8857/m1/1/high_res_d/79-244EPW_1979Nov16.pdf, 3–4; Seth King, "$4 Billion Farm Aid Voted by Congress," *New York Times,* September 17, 1977, 48; "President Signs Farm Bill with Food Stamp Reform," *New York Times,* September 30, 1977, 94.

121. See Eisinger, *Toward an End,* 36–56.

122. King, *Budgeting Entitlements,* 80–82.

123. Barbara Claffey and Thomas Stucker, "The Food Stamp Program," *Proceedings of the Academy of Political Science* 34, no. 3 (1982): 46; King, *Budgeting Entitlements,* 63–114.

124. Sheingate, *Agricultural Welfare State,* 149.

125. Judith Parris, "The Senate Reorganizes Its Committees, 1977," *Political Science Quarterly* 94, no. 2 (1979): 319–37; "Requiem for the Hunger Committee," editorial, *New York Times,* November 16, 1977, 28.

126. Ohls and Beebout, *Food Stamp Program*, 17.

127. John G. Peters, "The 1977 Farm Bill: Coalitions in Congress," in *The New Politics of Food*, ed. Don F. Hadwiger and William P. Browne (Lexington, MA: Heath, 1978), 25.

128. Theodore J. Lowi, "Four Systems of Policy, Politics, and Choice," *Public Administration Review* 32, no. 298 (1972): 299–300.

129. Huelskamp, "Congressional Change," 95.

130. Ira Katznelson, *Fear Itself: The New Deal and the Origins of Our Time* (New York: Liveright, 2013), 25; Maney, *Still Hungry*, 111–12.

5. Welfare Politics

1. 141 Cong. Rec. S13336, as quoted in Ronald F. King, *Budgeting Entitlements: The Politics of Food Stamps* (Washington, DC: Georgetown University Press, 2000), 207.

2. Matthew Levendusky, *The Partisan Sort: How Liberals Became Democrats and Conservatives Became Republicans* (Chicago: University of Chicago Press, 2009).

3. King, *Budgeting Entitlements*, 65; Michael Katz, *The Undeserving Poor: From the War on Poverty to the War on Welfare* (New York: Pantheon, 1980).

4. Sam Rosenfeld, "Fed by Reform: Congressional Politics, Partisan Change, and the Food Stamp Program, 1961–1981," *Journal of Policy History* 22, no. 4 (2020): 499.

5. Matthew Gritter addressed similar issues in *The Policy and Politics of Food Stamps and SNAP* (New York: Palgrave, 2015).

6. Ronald Reagan, "Address before a Joint Session of Congress on the Program for Economic Recovery," American Presidency Project, February 18, 1981. www.presidency.ucsb.edu/documents/address-before-joint-session-the-congress-the-program-for-economic-recovery-0.

7. Among others, see Paul Pierson, *Dismantling the Welfare State? Reagan, Thatcher, and the Politics of Retrenchment* (Cambridge: Cambridge University Press, 1994).

8. Ardith Maney, *Still Hungry after All These Years: Food Assistance Policy from Kennedy to Reagan* (Boulder, CO: Greenwood, 1989), 134.

9. Katz, *Undeserving Poor;* William Crafton, "The Incremental Revolution: Ronald Reagan and Welfare Reform in the 1970s," *Journal of Policy History* 26,

no. 1 (2014): 27–47; on dynamics of problem definition, see David Rochefort and Roger Cobb, eds., *The Politics of Problem Definition: Shaping the Public Agenda* (Lawrence: University Press of Kansas, 1994).

10. Jeffrey Berry, *Feeding Hungry People: Rulemaking in the Food Stamp Program* (New Brunswick, NJ: Rutgers University Press, 1984), 98.

11. Steven Roberts, "Food Stamps Program: How It Grew and How Reagan Wants to Cut It Back," *New York Times*, April 4, 1981; Maney, *Still Hungry*, 134–35.

12. Berry, *Feeding Hungry People*, 97.

13. John Ferejohn, "Logrolling in an Institutional Context: A Case Study of Food Stamp Legislation," in *Congress and Policy Change*, ed. Gerald C. Wright Jr., Leroy N. Rieselbach, and Lawrence C. Dodd (New York: Agathon, 1986), 246.

14. King, *Budgeting Entitlements*, 115–38.

15. See Aaron Wildavsky, *The Politics of the Budgetary Process*, 4th ed. (Boston: Little, Brown, 1984).

16. Kenneth Finegold, "Agriculture and the Politics of U.S. Social Provision: Social Insurance and Food Stamps," in *The Politics of Social Policy in the United States*, ed. Margaret Weir, Ann Shola Orloff, and Theda Skocpol (Princeton, NJ: Princeton University Press, 1988), 229.

17. James Ellwood, "Congress Cuts the Budget: The Omnibus Reconciliation Act of 1981," *Public Budgeting and Finance* 2, no. 1 (1982): 50–64.

18. Berry, *Feeding Hungry People*, 97–98; Maney, *Still Hungry*, 134–37.

19. See King, *Budgeting Entitlements*, 118–22.

20. Berry, *Feeding Hungry People*, 146.

21. Carlton David and Benjamin Senauer, "Needed Directions in Domestic Food Assistance Policies and Programs," *American Journal of Agricultural Economics* 68, no. 5 (1986): 1254.

22. For a thorough review, see Betsy Thorn et al., *Update to Feasibility Study of Implementing SNAP in Puerto Rico: Final Report*, Insight Policy Research (Washington, DC: US Department of Agriculture, 2022).

23. Jonathan Coppess, *The Fault Lines of Farm Policy: A Legislative and Political History of the Farm Bill* (Lincoln: University of Nebraska Press, 2018), 151–57.

24. Ferejohn, "Logrolling," 248.

25. Ferejohn, 250.

26. Ronald Reagan, "Statement about Distribution of the Cheese Inventory of the Commodity Credit Corporation," American Presidency Project, December 22, 1981, www.presidency.ucsb.edu/node/246355.

27. Maney, *Still Hungry*, 136; Berry, *Feeding Hungry People*, 149–50; Barry Bluestone and Russell Harrison, *The Deindustrialization of America: Plant Closings, Community Abandonment, and the Dismantling of Basic Industry* (New York: Basic Books, 1982); on economic uncertainty and food insecurity, see Dean Jolliffe and James Ziliak, eds., *Income Volatility and Food Assistance in the United States* (Kalamazoo, MI: Upjohn Institute for Employment Research, 2008).

28. Berry, *Feeding Hungry People*, 149–50.

29. Ward Sinclair, "Cheese Giveaway Churning," *Washington Post*, December 5, 1981.

30. Finegold, "Agriculture and the Politics," 219; "Surplus Cheese Goes to Poor as President Signs Farm Bill," *New York Times*, December 23, 1981, A12.

31. Kristen Lucas and Patrice Buzzanell, "It's the Cheese: Collective Memory of Hard Times during Deindustrialization," in *Food as Communication/Communication as Food*, ed. Janet Cramer et al. (New York: Lang, 2011), 95–113; for a more sardonic approach, see Russell Baker, "Study in Cheese," *New York Times*, January 20, 1982, A27.

32. Maney, *Still Hungry*, 140–42; Robert Pear, "U.S. Hunger on Rise Despite Swelling of Food Surpluses," *New York Times*, July 19, 1983, A1.

33. Janet Poppendieck, *Sweet Charity: Emergency Food and the End of Entitlement* (New York: Viking, 1998), 101.

34. Kara Clifford Billings, *The Emergency Food Assistance Program (TEFAP): Background and Funding*, report no. R45408, Congressional Research Service, June 15, 2022, https://crsreports.congress.gov/product/pdf/R/R45408, 21.

35. See Poppendieck, *Sweet Charity*; for a more critical take two decades later, see Andrew Fisher, *Big Hunger: The Unholy Alliance between Corporate America and Anti-hunger Groups* (Cambridge, MA: MIT Press, 2017).

36. "The 104th Congress: The Republican Leader; Excerpts from Gingrich's Speech on the Party's Agenda for the 104th Congress," *New York Times*, January 5, 1005, A23.

37. Coppess, *Fault Lines*, 159–66.

38. David Super, "The Quiet 'Welfare' Revolution: Resurrecting the Food Stamp Program in the Wake of the 1996 Welfare Law," *New York University Law Review* 71 (2004): 1280n36.

39. Peter Eisinger, *Toward an End to Hunger in America* (Washington, DC: Brookings Institution, 1997), 40, 53; James C. Ohls and Harold Beebout, *The*

Food Stamp Program: Design Tradeoffs, Policy, and Impacts (Washington, DC: Urban Institute Press, 1993), 130–45.

40. Eisinger, *Toward an End*, 84–89; Kenneth Cooper, "Four House Select Committees Expire as Symbols of Reform," *Washington Post*, April 1, 1993.

41. Coppess, *Fault Lines*, 176–81.

42. On the late Reagan and Bush years, see King, *Budgeting Entitlements*, 139–74; on program budgets, see 245–46.

43. King, *Budgeting Entitlements*, 175–83.

44. James Ziliak, "Why Are So Many Americans on Food Stamps?," in *SNAP Matters: How Food Stamps Affect Health and Well-Being*, ed. Judith Bartfeld et al. (Stanford, CA: Stanford University Press, 2015), 22.

45. R. Kent Weaver, *Ending Welfare as We Know it* (Washington, DC: Brookings Institution, 2000); on food stamps and PRWORA, see Gritter, *Policy and Politics*, 23–36.

46. Super, "Quiet 'Welfare' Revolution," 1290–94; for a conservative critique, see Martin Anderson, *Welfare: The Political Economy of Welfare Reform in the United* States (Palo Alto, CA: Hoover Institution Press, 1978).

47. Katz, *Undeserving Poor;* Frances Fox Piven and Richard Cloward, *Regulating the Poor: The Functions of Public Welfare* (New York: Pantheon, 1971); Eva Bertram, "The Institutional Origins of 'Workfarist' Social Policy," *Studies in American Political Development* 21, no. 3 (2007): 203–29.

48. Super, "Quiet 'Welfare' Revolution," 1295n85.

49. King, *Budgeting Entitlements*, 190; Robert Pear, "Lump-Sum Grants for Nutrition Aid Proposed by G.O.P.," *New York Times*, February 18, 1995, A1.

50. King, *Budgeting Entitlements*, 197–205.

51. Ronald King, "Welfare Reform, Block Grants, Expenditure Caps, and the Paradox of the Food Stamp Program," *Political Science Quarterly* 114, no. 3 (1999): 359–85.

52. 141 Cong. Rec. S13336, quoted in King, *Budgeting Entitlements*, 203.

53. Super, "Quiet 'Welfare' Revolution," 1297n90, 1271–397.

54. Super, 1281; Weaver, *Ending Welfare*, 54–101; Peter Edelman, *Searching for America's Heart: RFK and the Renewal of Hope* (Boston: Houghton Mifflin, 2001), chap. 4, pp. 119–43.

55. Robert Pear, "G.O.P. Finds It Difficult to Deflect Attacks on the School Lunch Proposals," *New York Times*, April 9, 1995, A18; Pear, "2 Nutrition Pro-

grams Win Crucial Backing in the Senate," *New York Times,* June 10, 1995, A8; Coppess, *Fault Lines,* 185–88.

56. King, *Budgeting Entitlements,* 206–10.

57. Jerry Hagstrom, "Farm Team Goes to Bat for Food Stamps," *National Journal,* March 11, 1995, 623.

58. William J. Clinton, "Statement on Signing the Federal Agricultural Improvement and Reform Act of 1996," American Presidency Project, April 4, 1996, www.presidency.ucsb.edu/node/223005.

59. Including, it seems, paying a former football star to give inspirational talks. See Cindy Boren, "Brett Favre Sued by the State of Mississippi over Welfare Misspending," *Washington Post,* May 10, 2022.

60. Gene Falk and Patrick Landers, *Temporary Assistance to Needy Families (TANF) Block Grant: Responses to Frequently Asked Questions,* report no. RL32760, version 208, Congressional Research Service, December 7, 2022, https://crsreports.congress.gov/product/pdf/RL/RL32760/208.

61. Pamela Herd and Donald Moynihan, *Administrative Burden: Policymaking by Other Means* (New York: Sage, 2018), 191–214.

62. William J. Clinton, "Remarks on Signing the Personal Responsibility and Work Opportunity Reconciliation Act of 1996 and an Exchange with Reporters," American Presidency Project, accessed February 16, 2023, www.presidency.ucsb.edu/node/222681.

63. Peter Edelman, "The Worst Thing Bill Clinton Has Done," *Atlantic,* March 1997.

64. Poppendieck, *Sweet Charity,* 158–59; on the "geographic maldistribution" of food pantries, see Eisinger, *Toward an End,* 119–20.

65. Super, "Quiet 'Welfare' Revolution," 1395; Eisinger, *Toward an End,* 127.

66. Catherine Boudreau and Helena Bottemiller Evich, "Conway's Crusade: Getting to 'Yes' on a Budget to Save the Farm Bill," *Politico,* July 19, 2017.

67. Super, "Quiet 'Welfare' Revolution," 1308–9, 1321–22; on the "make work pay" framing, see Pierson, *Dismantling the Welfare State?,* 122–25.

68. Jerry Hagstrom, "Proposal to Split Farm Bill Divides Congress," *National Journal Daily,* July 8, 2013.

69. Christopher Bosso, *Framing the Farm Bill: Ideology, Interests, and the Agricultural Act of 2014* (Lawrence: University Press of Kansas, 2017), chap. 3; on food stamps and the 2002 farm bill, see Gritter, *Policy and Politics,* 37–52; on

regional battles over commodity programs in the first decade of the 2000s, see Coppess, *Fault Lines,* 205–36.

70. "President Promotes Compassionate Conservatism," Office of the Press Secretary, April 30, 2002, https://georgewbush-whitehouse.archives .gov/news/releases/2002/04/20020430-5.html.

71. George W. Bush, "Remarks on Signing the Farm Security and Rural Investment Act of 2002," May 13, 2002, *Public Papers of the President* (Washington, DC: Government Printing Office, 2002), 782, quoted in Gritter, *Policy and Politics,* 47.

72. Two vetoes, actually: the second came after a clerical error required passing the bill a second time. No substantive changes were made in the corrected bill.

73. Ziliak, "So Many Americans," 18–49.

74. Gabriella Morrongiello, "California Surfer Uses Food Stamps to Buy Sushi and Won't Work," *Washington Examiner,* April 13, 2013;r Beth Reinhard, "The Return of the Welfare Queen," *National Journal,* December 12, 2013.

75. Vanessa Williamson, Theda Skocpol, and John Coggin, "The Tea Party and the Remaking of Republican Conservatism," *Perspectives on Politics* 9, no. 1 (2011): 25–43; Anthony DiMaggio, *The Rise of the Tea Party: Political Discontent and Corporate Media in the Age of Obama* (New York: Monthly Review, 2011).

76. Michael Barone and Chuck McCutcheon, *The Almanac of American Politics, 2014* (Chicago: University of Chicago Press, 2013), 2–3.

77. Tim Fernholz, "GOP Freshmen: 'Full Steam Ahead,'" *National Journal,* January 21, 2011.

78. Norman Ornstein, "Four Really Dumb Ideas That Should Be Avoided, *Roll Call,* January 26, 2011.

79. See Bosso, *Framing the Farm Bill;* and Coppess, *Fault Lines,* 237–84.

80. Jennifer Steinhauer, "Enduring Drought, Farmers Draw the Line at Congress," *New York Times,* August 12, 2012.

81. Humberto Sanchez, "Kristi Noem Not Happy about Farm Bill's Fate," *Roll Call,* September 12, 2012 (emphasis in original).

82. Jerry Hagstrom, "Food Stamps Are Key Component to Getting Farm Bill Passed," *National Journal,* April 10, 2013.

83. Ron Nixon, "Split among House Republicans over How Deeply to Cut May Delay Farm Bill," *New York Times,* July 13, 2012, A13.

84. Charles Abbott, "Senate Passes Farm Bill; Food Stamp Fight Looms in House," *Reuters*, June 10, 2013, www.reuters.com/article/us-usa-agriculture-farm-bill-idUSBRE95915T20130611.

85. David Rogers, "Tom Vilsack Urges House to Plow Ahead on Farm Bill," *Politico*, June 12, 2013. Note: Representative McGovern is not related to the late George McGovern but did serve as an intern to the senator in the 1970s.

86. Coppess, *Fault Lines*, 262.

87. Billy Chase, "House Farm Bill Suffers Stunning Defeat as Finger Pointing Begins," *National Journal*, June 20, 2013; David Rogers, "How the Farm Bill Failed," *Politico*, June 23, 2013.

88. Michael McAuliffe, Arthur Delaney, and Sabrina Saddiqui, "Food Stamp Cuts Derail Farm Bill," *Huffington Post*, June 22, 2013.

89. Hagstrom, "Proposal to Split."

90. Tal Kopan, "Obama Threatens Veto on Farm Bill," *Politico*, July 11, 2013.

91. David Rogers, "House Approves Plan to Cut Food Stamps," *Politico*, September 19, 2013.

92. Jill Lawrence, "Profiles in Negotiation: The 2014 Farm and Food Stamp Deal," Center for Effective Public Management at Brookings, October 2015, www.brookings.edu/wp-content/uploads/2016/06/CEPMLawrence FarmBill.pdf, 12.

93. Ron Nixon, "Farm Bill Compromise Will Reduce Spending and Change Programs," *New York Times*, January 27, 2014.

94. David Rogers, "Farm Bill Agreement Heading to Floor," *Politico*, January 27, 2014.

95. Ron Nixon, "House Approves Farm Bill, Ending a 2-Year Impasse," *New York Times*, January 30, 2014, A14.

96. Jerry Hagstrom, "Why Is the Farm Bill Finally Ripe for Passage?," *National Journal*, February 2, 2014.

97. Ron Nixon and Derek Willis, "No Help for Farm Bill from Miffed Kansans in the House," *New York Times*, January 31, 2014.

98. Eric Wasson, "House Passes $956B Farm Bill," *Hill*, January 29, 2014.

99. David Rogers, "Congress Approves 5-Year Farm Bill," *Politico*, February 4, 2014; Ron Nixon, "Senate Passes Long-Stalled Farm Bill," *New York Times*, February 4, 2014.

100. No, I'm not forgetting Keith Sibelius (1969–81) or Jerry Moran (1997–2011), who represented the First District in between Dole, Roberts, and Huelskamp. Neither were as active in agriculture and nutrition-program politics.

101. Tracy Jan et al., "Trump Wants to Overhaul America's Safety Net with Giant Cuts to Housing, Food Stamps, and Health Care," *Washington Post*, February 12, 2018; Heather Haddon and Jacob Bunge, "Agriculture Secretary Perdue Favors Food Stamp Restrictions," *Wall Street Journal*, October 11, 2017.

102. Glenn Thrush and Thomas Kaplan, "House Farm Bill Collapses amid Republican Disarray," *New York Times,* May 19, 2018, A1; Ellyn Ferguson, "Fight over Food Stamps among Big Hurdles Facing Farm Bill," *Roll Call,* June 19, 2018.

103. Thomas Kaplan and Nicholas Fandos, "Stubborn Divide as a Hard-Line Bill Fails and a Compromise Is Delayed, *New York Times,* June 22, 2018, A12.

104. Emily Cochrane, "Battle over Wall Risks Shutdown as Lawmakers Scramble to Fund Government," *New York Times,* November 16, 2018, A15.

105. Catie Edmonson, "Senate, Rejecting Curbs on Food Stamps, Passes Compromise Farm Bill," *New York Times,* December 12, 2018, A18; Juliegrace Brufke, "House Passes $867 Billion Farm Bill, Sending It to Trump," *Hill,* December 12, 2018.

106. Katie Rogers and Catie Edmonson, "Trump Administration Moves to Restrict Food Stamp Access the Farm Bill Protected," *New York Times,* December 21, 2018, A18; Spencer Hsu, "Federal Judge Strikes Down Trump Plan to Slash Food Stamps for 700,000 Unemployed Americans," *Washington Post,* October 18, 2020; Rebecca Beitsch, "DHS Unwinds Trump-Era Public Charge Restrictions," *Hill,* September 8, 2022.

6. Let Us Now Praise the Food Stamp Plan

1. Richard P. Nathan, *The Role of the Food Stamp Program,* testimony before the Senate Select Committee on Nutrition and Human Needs, 94th Cong., 1st Sess. (1975) (Washington, DC: Government Printing Office, 1975), 109.

2. Peter Eisinger, *Toward an End to Hunger in America* (Washington, DC: Brookings, 1997).

3. Matthew Gritter, *The Policy and Politics of Food Stamps and SNAP* (New York: Palgrave, 2015), 4.

4. Gritter, 53–70.

5. Burdett Loomis, "The Politics of Vouchers," in *Vouchers and the Provision of Social Services,* ed. C. Eugene Sterle et al. (Washington, DC: Brookings Institution Press, 2000), 92–115; more broadly, see Christopher Howard, *The Welfare State Nobody Knows: Debunking Myths about U.S. Social Policy* (Princeton, NJ: Princeton University Press, 2007).

6. See Pamela Herd and Donald Moynihan, *Administrative Burden: Policymaking by Other Means* (New York: Sage, 2018).

7. David Super, "The Quiet 'Welfare' Revolution: Resurrecting the Food Stamp Program in the Wake of the 1996 Welfare Law," *New York University Law Review* 71 (2004): 1279n35.

8. See Adam Sheingate, "Policy Regime Decay," *Policy Studies Journal* 50, no. 1 (2022): 65–89; Jonathan Coppess, *The Fault Lines of Farm Policy: A Legislative and Political History of the Farm Bill* (Lincoln: University of Nebraska Press, 2018), 269–84.

9. John Ferejohn, "Logrolling in an Institutional Context: A Case Study of Food Stamp Legislation," in *Congress and Policy Change,* ed. Gerald C. Wright Jr., Leroy N. Rieselbach, and Lawrence C. Dodd (New York: Agathon, 1986), 251.

10. Kenneth Finegold, "Agriculture and the Politics of U.S. Social Provision: Social Insurance and Food Stamps," in *The Politics of Social Policy in the United States,* ed. Margaret Weir, Ann Shola Orloff, and Theda Skocpol (Princeton, NJ: Princeton University Press, 1988), 230.

11. See Super, "Quiet 'Welfare' Revolution," 1285n50; and Eisinger, *Toward an End,* 91–106; on welfare-program vulnerability more broadly, see Paul Pierson, *Dismantling the Welfare State? Reagan, Thatcher, and the Politics of Retrenchment* (Cambridge: Cambridge University Press, 1994).

12. Tracy Roof, "Interest Groups and Food Stamps Program: Issues in Reauthorizing SNAP" (paper presented at the 2016 Annual Meeting of the Southern Political Science Association, San Juan, January 9, 2016).

13. Heather Haddon and Jesse Newman, "Retailers Worry Food-Stamp Overhaul Will Hit Them Hard," *Wall Street Journal,* April 6, 2018; for a broader view on the new shape of agribusiness lobbying in Congress, see Clare Brock, "Partisan Polarization and Corporate Lobbying: Information, Demand, and Conflict," *Interest Groups and Advocacy* 10, no. 2 (2021): 95–113.

14. Molly Ball, "How Republicans Lost the Farm," *Atlantic*, January 27, 2014, www.theatlantic.com/politics/archive/2014/01/how-republicans-lost-the-farm/283349/.

15. This critique is made by Andrew Fisher, in *Big Hunger: The Unholy Alliance between Corporate America and Anti-hunger Groups* (Cambridge, MA: MIT Press, 2017).

16. See Pierson, *Dismantling the Welfare State?*, 166–69.

17. Food Stamp Act of 1964, Pub. L. No. 88–525, 88th Cong., H.R. 10222 (1964).

18. For an accessible overview, see chapter 10 in Parke Wilde, *Food Policy in the United States: An Introduction*, 2nd ed. (New York: Routledge, 2018); Craig Gunderson and James Ziliak, "Food Insecurity Research in the United States: Where We Have Been and Where We Need to Go," *Applied Economic Perspectives and Policy* 40, no. 1 (2018): 119–35; and Diane Whitmore Schanzenbach, "Exploring Options to Improve the Supplemental Nutrition Assistance Program (SNAP)," *Annals of the American Academy of Political and Social Sciences* 686 (2019): 204–29.

19. Children in male-headed households also qualify. "WIC Food Packages: Maximum Monthly Allowances," Food and Nutrition Service, US Department of Agriculture, September 9, 2022, www.fns.usda.gov/wic/wic-food-packages-maximum-monthly-allowances; on the WIC program's history and politics, see Eisinger, *Toward an End*, 58–63.

20. Barry Popkin, "The Challenge in Improving the Diets of Supplemental Nutrition Assistance Program Recipients: A Historical Commentary," in "The Supplemental Nutrition Assistance Program's Role in Addressing Nutrition-Related Health Issues," special issue, *American Journal of Preventive Medicine 5*, no. 2 (2017): S106–S114.

21. Charles Lane, "How Liberals Undermine the Food Stamp Program," *Washington Post*, February 15, 2017.

22. Robert Moffit, "Multiple Program Participation and the SNAP Program," in *SNAP Matters: How Food Stamps Affect Health and Well-Being*, ed. Judith Bartfeld et al. (Stanford, CA: Stanford University Press, 2015), 213–43.

23. Hilary Hoynes, Leslie Granahan, and Diane Schanzenbach, "SNAP and Food Consumption," in Bartfeld et al., *SNAP Matters*, 107–33.

24. Amanda Bitler, "The Health and Nutrition Effects of SNAP: Selection into the Program and a Review of the Literature on Its Effects," in Bartfeld et

al., *SNAP Matters*, 134–60; Alison Jacknowitz et al., "Exploring the Challenges and Coping Strategies in Households Relying on SNAP and Food Pantries," *Journal of Hunger and Environmental Nutrition* 14, nos. 1–2 (2019): 281–95.

25. Christian Gregory, Matthew Rabbit, and David Ribar, "The Supplemental Nutrition Assistance Program and Food Insecurity," in Bartfeld et al., *SNAP Matters*, 74–106; Colleen Hefflen et al., "Hypertension, Diabetes, and Medication Adherence among the Older Supplemental Nutrition Assistance Program Population," *Journal of Applied Gerontology* 41, no. 3 (2022): 780–87; Christian Gregory and Alisha Coleman-Jensen, "Adults in Households with More Severe Food Insecurity Are More Likely to Have a Chronic Disease," *Amber Waves*, Economic Research Service, US Department of Agriculture, October 2017, 1–4, www.ers.usda.gov/amber-waves/2017/october/adults-in-households-with-more-severe-food-insecurity-are-more-likely-to-have-a-chronic-disease/.

26. Steven Garansky et al., "Foods Typically Purchased by Supplemental Nutrition Assistance Program (SNAP) Households," Food and Nutrition Service, US Department of Agriculture, November 18, 2016, www.fns.usda.gov /snap/foods-typically-purchased-supplemental-nutrition-assistance-program-snap-households; Jay Zagorsky and Patricia Smith, "The Association between Socioeconomic Status and Adult Fast-Food Consumption in the U.S.," *Economics and Human Biology* 27 (2017): 12–25; Bhagyashree Katare, James Binkley, and Kaiyen Chen, "Nutrition and Diet Quality of Food at Home by Supplemental Nutrition Assistance Program (SNAP) Status," *Food Policy* 105 (2021): 102165.

27. Ji Young Lee et al., "Time Use and Eating Patterns of SNAP Participants over the Benefit Month," *Food Policy* 106 (2022): 102168; Katare, Binkley, and Chen, "Nutrition and Diet Quality"; Sabrina Young and Hayden Stewart, "U.S. Fruit and Vegetable Affordability on the Thrifty Food Plan Depends on Purchasing Power and Safety Net Supports," *International Journal of Environmental Research and Public Health* 19, no. 5 (2022): 2772–84.

28. Popkin, "Challenge of Improving"; Bee Wilson, *The Way We Eat Now: How the Food Revolution Has Transformed Our Lives, Our Bodies, and Our World* (New York: Basic Books, 2019); Michael Moss, *Salt, Sugar, Fat: How the Food Giants Hooked Us* (New York: Random House, 2013).

29. Laura Castner and Juliette Henke, *Benefit Redemption Patterns in the Supplemental Nutrition Assistance Program*, Mathematica Policy Research Reports, 2011, https://ideas.repec.org/p/mpr/mprres/b746c9a56cb34547b47

5799386b0182a.html, 20–22; Tim Carmen, "Spray Cheese, Beef Jerky and Stuffed Olives to Be Counted as Staples under Trump Administration Food Stamp Proposal," *Washington Post*, May 30, 2019; on criteria for becoming a SNAP retailer, see "Is My Store Eligible?," Food and Nutrition Service, US Department of Agriculture, accessed February 17, 2023, www.fns.usda.gov /snap/retailer/eligible.

30. Carmen Heredia Rodriguez, "Advocacy Group Pushes for Changes in U.S. Food Assistance Programs," *Kaiser Health News,* January 19, 2017.

31. Marion Nestle, *Soda Politics: Taking on Big Soda (and Winning)* (New York: Oxford University Press, 2015).

32. Michael Moss, "While Warning about Fat, U.S. Pushes Cheese Sales," *New York Times,* November 7, 2010, A1.

33. See, for example, Marion Nestle, *Food Politics: How the Food Industry Influences Nutrition and Health* (Berkeley: University of California Press, 2002).

34. Susan Levine, *School Lunch Politics* (Princeton, NJ: Princeton University Press, 2008); Janet Poppendieck, *Free for All: Fixing School Food in America* (Berkeley: University of California Press, 2010); Clare Brock, "Framing Child Nutrition Programs: The Impact of Party and District Characteristics on Elite Framing." *Social Science Quarterly* 98, no. 2 (2017): 628–43.

35. Anahad O'Connor, "In the Shopping Cart of a Food Stamp Household: Lots of Soda," *New York Times,* January 13, 2017.

36. Diane Whitmore Schanzenbach, *Pros and Cons of Restricting SNAP Purchases,* testimony before the House Committee on Agriculture, February 16, 2017, www.govinfo.gov/content/pkg/CHRG-115hhrg24325/html/CHRG-115hhrg24325.htm, 6; see also Hoynes, Granahan, and Schanzenbach, "SNAP and Food Consumption."

37. Kirsten Leng et al., "How Does the Gus Schumacher Nutrition Incentive Program Work? A Theory of Change," *Nutrients* 14, no. 10 (2022): 2022–45.

38. Susan Bartlett et al., *Evaluation of the Healthy Incentives Pilot (HIP): Final Report* (Washington, DC: US Department of Agriculture, 2014); Lauren Olsho et al., "Financial Incentives Increase Fruit and Vegetable Intake among Supplemental Nutrition Assistance Program Participants: A Randomized Controlled Trial of the USDA Healthy Incentives Pilot," *American Journal of Clinical Nutrition* 104, no. 2 (2016): 423–35; Darius Mozaffarian et al., "Cost Effectiveness of Financial Incentives and Disincentives for Improving Food

Purchases and Health through the U.S. Supplemental Nutrition Assistance Program (SNAP): A Microsimulation Study," *PLoS Med* 15, no. 10 (2018): e1002661.

39. Schanzenbach, "Exploring Options," 217; Castner and Henke, *Benefit Redemption Patterns,* 4-5.

40. See Ann Schneider and Helen Ingram, *Policy Design for Democracy* (Lawrence: University Press of Kansas, 1997); for a more famous work, see Richard Thaler and Cass Sunstein, *Nudge: Improving Decisions about Health, Wealth, and Happiness* (New York, Penguin Books: 2009).

41. Joshua Benning and John Hogan, "Estimating the Impact of Education on Household Fruit and Vegetable Purchases," *Applied Economic Perspectives and Policy* 36, no. 3 (2013): 460-78.

42. Gunderson and Ziliak, "Food Insecurity Research"; Caroline Ratcliffe, Signe-Mary McKernan, and Sisi Zhang, "How Much Does the Supplemental Nutrition Assistance Program Reduce Food Insecurity?," *American Journal of Agricultural Economics* 93, no. 4 (2011): 1082-98; Parke Wilde and Mark Nord, "The Effect of Food Stamps on Food Security: A Panel Data Approach," *Review of Agricultural Economics* 27, no. 3 (2005): 425-32; Craig Gunderson and Hilary Seligman, "How Can We Fully Realize SNAP's Health Benefits?" *New England Journal of Medicine* 386, no. 15 (2022): 1389-91.

43. Finegold, "Agriculture and the Politics," 231.

44. See Howard, *Welfare State Nobody Knows.*

45. Marjorie DeVault and James Pitts, "Surplus and Scarcity: Hunger and the Origins of the Food Stamp Program," *Social Problems* 31 no. 5 (1984): 556.

46. "2023 Poverty Guidelines," US Department of Health and Human Services, accessed February 17, 2023, https://aspe.hhs.gov/topics/poverty-economic-mobility/poverty-guidelines.

47. Laura Tiehen, Dean Jolliffe, and Timothy Smeeding, "The Effect of SNAP on Poverty," in Bartfeld et al., *SNAP Matters,* 49-73.

48. James Ziliak, "Why Are So Many Americans on Food Stamps?," in Bartfeld et al., *SNAP Matters,* 27.

49. Tiehen, Jolliffe, and Smeeding, "Effect of SNAP," 52.

50. Karina Piser, "In Puerto Rico, 40 Percent Suffer Food Insecurity with No End in Sight," *AG Insider,* Food and Environmental Network, December 7, 2020, https://thefern.org/ag_insider/in-puerto-rico-40-percent-suffer-food-insecurity-with-no-end-in-sight/.

51. Judith Bartfeld et al., "Conclusions," in Bartfeld et al., *SNAP Matters*, 245.

52. Tiehen, Jolliffe, and Smeeding, "Effect of SNAP," 68.

53. Hilary Hoynes, Diane Schanzenbach, and Douglas Almond, "Long-Run Impacts of Childhood Access to the Safety Net," *American Economic Review* 106, no. 4 (2016): 903–34.

54. Crystal Yang, "Does Public Assistance Reduce Recidivism?" *American Economic Review* 107, no. 5 (2017): 551–55.

55. Joseph Coppock, "The Food Stamp Plan: Moving Surplus Commodities with Special Purpose Money," *Transactions of the American Philosophical Society* 37, no. 2 (1947): 186.

56. For example, see James Morone, "American Ways of Welfare," *Perspectives on Politics* 1, no. 1 (2003): 137–46; on the "make work pay" debate, see Paul Pierson, *Dismantling the Welfare State?*, 122–25.

57. Schanzenbach, "Exploring Options"; Jeehoon Han, "The Impact of SNAP Work Requirements on Labor Supply," *Labour Economics* 74 (2022): 10289; Joel Cuffey et al., "Work Effort and Work Requirements for Food Assistance among U.S. Adults," *American Journal of Agricultural Economics* 104 (2022): 294–317.

58. Tiehen, Jolliffe, and Smeeding, "Effect of SNAP," 66.

59. Ed Bolen and Stacy Dean, "Waivers Add Key State Flexibility to SNAP's Three-Month Time Limit," Center on Budget and Policy Priorities, February 6, 2018, www.cbpp.org/research/food-assistance/waivers-add-key-state-flexibility-to-snaps-three-month-time-limit; *FNS Controls over SNAP Benefits for Able-Bodied Adults without Dependents*, audit report 27601-0002-31, Office of Inspector General, US Department of Agriculture, September 2016, www.usda.gov/sites/default/files/27601-0002-31.pdf.

60. James C. Ohls and Harold Beebout, *The Food Stamp Program: Design Tradeoffs, Policy, and Impacts* (Washington, DC: Urban Institute Press, 1993), 11.

61. Jordan Jones, Saied Toossi, and Leslie Hodges, *The Food and Nutrition Assistance Landscape: Fiscal Year 2021 Annual Report*, EIB-237, Economic Research Service, US Department of Agriculture, June 2022, www.ers.usda.gov/publications/pub-details/?pubid=104145, 6.

62. Sanford Schram, Richard Fording, and Joe Soss, "Do Work Requirements for Federal Assistance Help People Escape Poverty? No. Here's What Really Happens," *Washington Post*, August 13, 2018.

63. On the pattern of doubling down on work requirements despite their suboptimal effectiveness, see Eva Bertram, "The Institutional Origins of 'Workfarist' Social Policy," *Studies in American Political Development* 21, no. 3 (2007): 203–29.

64. Quoted in Kate Sullivan, "White House Will Host First Food Insecurity Conference in 50 Years," CNN Politics, May 4, 2022, www.cnn.com/2022 /05/04/politics/white-house-conference-food-insecurity-jose-andres/index .html. Note: Representative McGovern was a key driver in convening the 2022 conference.

65. "White House Announces Conference on Hunger, Nutrition and Health in September," White House, May 5, 2022, www.whitehouse.gov /briefing-room/statements-releases/2022/05/04/white-house-announces-conference-on-hunger-nutrition-and-health-in-september/.

66. Adrian Nicole LeBlanc, "How Hunger Persists in a Rich Country Like America," *New York Times,* September 2, 2020; for one postconference assessment, see Ximena Bustello, "Key Takeaways from Biden's Conference on Hunger and Nutrition in America," National Public Radio, September 28, 2022, www.npr.org/2022/09/28/1125575122/biden-hunger-america-conference.

67. See Eisinger, *Toward an End,* 107–21; on the Greater Boston Food Bank, see "Mission and Values," accessed February 17, 2023, www.gbfb.org/who-we-are/about-us/; on Lovin' Spoonfuls, see "What We Do," accessed February 17, 2023, https://lovinspoonfulsinc.org/food-rescue/what-we-do/.

68. Jason DeParle, "Amid a Deadly Virus and Crippled Economy, One Form of Aid Has Proved Reliable: Food Stamps," *New York Times,* August 15, 2021, A1.

69. Anne Byrne and David Just, "The Other Half: An Examination of Monthly Food Pantry Cycles in the Context of SNAP Benefits," *Applied Economic Perspectives and Policy* 43, no. 2 (2021): 716–31; Castner and Henke, *Benefit Redemption Patterns,* 31–42. Another "SNAP Gap" is the difference between those technically eligible and those who actually enroll in the program.

70. Nina Lakhani, "'A Perfect Storm': US Facing Hunger Crisis as Demand for Food Banks Soars," *Guardian,* April 2, 2020; Helena Bottemiller Evich, "'There's Only So Much We Can Do': Food Banks Plead for Help," *Politico,* June 8, 2020; Sharon Cohen, "Millions of Hungry Americans Turn to Food Banks for 1st Time," *Associated Press News,* December 7, 2020; see also James Ziliak, "Food Hardship during the COVID-19 Pandemic and the Great Recession," *Applied Economic Perspectives and Policy* 43, no. 1 (2021): 132–52.

71. Kyle Swenson, "A Food Pantry's Closure Means More Than Lost Meals for Hundreds of Families," *Washington Post*, April 28, 2022.

72. For critiques of the "emergency" food system, and of the US food-bank model in particular, see Fisher, *Big Hunger*; and Joel Berg and Angela Gibson, "Why the World Should Not Follow the Failed United States Model of Fighting Domestic Hunger," *International Journal of Environmental Research and Public Health* 19 (2022): 814–28.

73. Ohls and Beebout, *Food Stamp Program*, 37; for more on the Thrifty Food Plan, see Angela Babb, "A Brief Genealogy of the Thrifty Food Plan," *Food, Culture, and Society* 25 (2022): 1–28.

74. Laura Reiley, "Full Fields, Empty Fridges: Farmers Plow Their Unused Produce Back into the Field. Food Banks Struggle to Feed Millions of New Unemployed. A Federal Plan Will Play Matchmaker," *Washington Post*, April 23, 2020.

75. "USDA Announces Coronavirus Food Assistance Program," press release 0222.20, April 27, 2020, www.usda.gov/media/press-releases/2020/04/17/usda-announces-coronavirus-food-assistance-program.

76. For a balanced analysis, see Emily Broad Lieb et al., *An Evaluation of the Farmers to Families Food Box Program*, Harvard Law School Food Law and Policy Clinic and National Sustainable Agriculture Coalition, February 2021, https://chlpi.org/wp-content/uploads/2013/12/F2F-Food-Box-ES-Online-Final1.pdf; for a decidedly partisan take, see Select Subcommittee on the Coronavirus Crisis, *Farmers to Families? An Investigation into the Trump Administration's Food Box Program*, US House of Representatives, October 2021, https://coronavirus.house.gov/sites/democrats.coronavirus.house.gov/files/SSCC_Staff_Report-Farmers_to_Families_Food_Box_Program.pdf.

77. Courtney Weaver, "Food Aid Effort Faulted for Neglecting New York and US North East," *Financial Times*, May 27, 2020; Laura Rolley, "Trump's Signature Effort to Direct Farm Surplus to Needy Families Abruptly Withdraws Large Contract amidst Criticism of Rollout," *Washington Post*, May 22, 2020.

78. Mackensy Lunsford, "Million Dollar Hot Dogs: Farmers to Families Food Boxes Promised Nutrition, Came Packed with Processed Meat," *Asheville Citizen Times*, October 28, 2020.

79. Isaac Arnsdorf, "Contractors for Trump's Controversial $3 Billion Food Aid Program Have Hired a Longtime Lobbyist to Tout Their Work," *Propublica*, June 2, 2020.

80. *Farmers to Families,* 40–43.

81. Andrew Coe, "Free Food, with a Side of Shaming," *New York Times,* June 26, 2020, A27.

82. "USDA to Invest in Expanding SNAP online shopping," press release FNS-0008-22, Food and Nutrition Service, US Department of Agriculture, July 7, 2022, www.fns.usda.gov/news-item/fns-0008.22.

83. Jones, Toossi, and Hodges, *Food and Nutrition Assistance,* 4.

84. "USDA to Invest $1 Billion to Purchase Healthy Food for Food Insecure Americans and Build Food Bank Capacity," press release 0123.21, US Department of Agriculture, June 4, 2021, www.usda.gov/media/press-releases/2021/06/04/usda-invest-1-billion-purchase-healthy-food-food-insecure-americans; Jason DeParle, "Many Need Food, Energizing Push to Expand Relief," *New York Times,* April 5, 2021, A1.

85. Ben Casselman, "Child Tax Credit's Extra Help Ends, Just as Covid Surges Anew," *New York Times,* January 2, 2022, A1.

86. For a still-useful analysis of the trade-offs, see Ohls and Beebout, *Food Stamp Program;* for a more recent work, see Gunderson and Seligman, "SNAP's Health Benefits?"; on the experience of enrollees trying to navigate the system, see Maggie Dickinson, *Feeding the Crisis: Care and Abandonment in America's Food Safety Net* (Berkeley: University of California Press, 2019).

87. See Amy Finkelstein and Matthew Notowidigdo, *Take-Up and Targeting: Experimental Evidence from SNAP* (Cambridge, MA: National Bureau of Economic Research, 2018).

88. Herd and Moynihan, *Administrative Burden,* esp. 191–214; Dickinson, *Feeding the Crisis;* Carolyn Barnes, "'It Takes a While to Get Used To': The Costs of Redeeming Public Benefits," *Journal of Public Administration Research and Theory* 31, no. 2 (2021): 295–310; Kara Newby and Xi Chen, "Decisions That Matter: State Supplemental Nutrition Assistance Program Policy Restrictiveness Limits SNAP Participation Rate," *Social Science Quarterly* 103, no. 4 (2022): 868–82.

89. For a recent analysis, see Betsy Thorn et al., *Update to Feasibility Study of Implementing SNAP in Puerto Rico: Final Report,* Food and Nutrition Service, US Department of Agriculture, July 2022, https://fns-prod.azureedge.us/sites/default/files/resource-files/PRSNAP-Feasibility-Report.pdf.

90. Tiehen, Jolliffe, and Smeeding, "Effect of SNAP," 63; Young and Stewart, "U.S. Fruit and Vegetable" 2781.

91. Lee et al., "Time Use."

92. Maeve Sheehey, "Rotisserie Chicken with Food Stamps? Lift the Ban, Lawmakers Say," Bloomberg Government, May 19, 2022, https://about.bgov.com/news/rotisserie-chicken-with-food-stamps-lift-the-ban-lawmakers-say/.

93. Tiehen, Jolliffe, and Smeeding, "Effect of SNAP," 69.

94. Milo Perkins, "Agricultural Aspects of Food Stamp Plan Operations," summary of statement at the Sixth Annual Meeting of the National Association of Food Chains, Chicago, October 10, 1939.

Suggested Reading

Amenta, Edwin. *Bold Relief: Institutional Politics and the Origins of Modern American Social Policy*. Princeton, NJ: Princeton University Press, 1998.

Bell, Winifred. *Aid to Dependent Children*. New York: Columbia University Press, 1965.

Berry, Jeffrey. *Feeding Hungry People: Rulemaking in the Food Stamp Program*. New Brunswick, NJ: Rutgers University Press, 1984.

Bosso, Christopher. *Framing the Farm Bill: Ideology, Interests, and the Agricultural Act of 2014*. Lawrence: University Press of Kansas, 2017.

Browne, William. *Private Interests, Public Policy, and American Agriculture*. Lawrence: University Press of Kansas, 1988.

Coppess, Jonathan. *The Fault Lines of Farm Policy: A Legislative and Political History of the Farm Bill*. Lincoln: University of Nebraska Press, 2018.

Danbom, David. *The Resisted Revolution: Urban America and the Industrialization of Agriculture, 1900–1930*. Ames: Iowa State University Press, 1979.

Dickinson, Maggie. *Feeding the Crisis: Care and Abandonment in America's Food Safety Net*. Berkeley: University of California Press, 2019.

DiMaggio, Anthony. *The Rise of the Tea Party: Political Discontent and Corporate Media in the Age of Obama*. New York: Monthly Review, 2011.

Edelman, Peter. *Searching for America's Heart: RFK and the Renewal of Hope*. Boston: Houghton Mifflin, 2001.

Eisinger, Peter. *Toward an End to Hunger in America*. Washington, DC: Brookings, 1997.

Fisher, Andrew. *Big Hunger: The Unholy Alliance between Corporate America and Anti-hunger Groups*. Cambridge, MA: MIT Press, 2017.

Gardner, Bruce. *American Agriculture in the Twentieth Century: How It Flourished and What It Cost*. Cambridge, MA: Harvard University Press, 2002.

Gritter, Matthew. *The Policy and Politics of Food Stamps and SNAP*. New York: Palgrave, 2015.

Hansen, John Mark. *Gaining Access: Congress and the Farm Lobby, 1919–1981*. Chicago: University of Chicago Press, 1991.

Harrington, Michael. *The Other America: Poverty in the United States*. New York: Macmillan, 1962.

Herd, Pamela, and Donald Moynihan. *Administrative Burden: Policymaking by Other Means*. New York: Sage, 2018.

Howard, Christopher. *The Welfare State Nobody Knows: Debunking Myths about U.S. Social Policy*. Princeton, NJ: Princeton University Press, 2007.

Katz, Michael. *The Underserving Poor: From the War on Poverty to the War on Welfare*. New York: Pantheon, 1980.

Katznelson, Ira. *Fear Itself: The New Deal and the Origins of Our Time*. New York: Liveright, 2013.

King, Ronald F. *Budgeting Entitlements: The Politics of Food Stamps*. Washington, DC: Georgetown University Press, 2000.

Kotz, Nick. *Let Them Eat Promises: The Politics of Hunger in America*. Englewood Cliffs, NJ: Prentice-Hall, 1989.

Leuchtenburg, William. *Franklin Roosevelt and the New Deal, 1932–1940*. New York: Harper and Row, 1963.

Levendusky, Matthew. *The Partisan Sort: How Liberals Became Democrats and Conservatives Became Republicans*. Chicago: University of Chicago Press, 2009.

Levine, Susan. *School Lunch Politics*. Princeton, NJ: Princeton University Press, 2008.

Maney, Ardeth. *Still Hungry after All These Years: Food Assistance Policy from Kennedy to Reagan*. Boulder, CO: Greenwood, 1989.

Moynihan, Daniel Patrick. *The Politics of a Guaranteed Income: The Nixon Administration and the Family Assistance Plan*. New York: Random House, 1973.

Nestle, Marion. *Food Politics: How the Food Industry Influences Nutrition and Health*. Berkeley: University of California Press, 2002.

———. *Soda Politics: Taking on Big Soda (and Winning)*. New York: Oxford University Press, 2015.

Ohls, James C., and Harold Beebout. *The Food Stamp Program: Design Tradeoffs, Policy, and Impacts*. Washington, DC: Urban Institute Press, 1993.

Perkins, Van. *Crisis in Agriculture: The Agricultural Adjustment Administration and the New Deal, 1933*. Berkeley: University of California Press, 1969.

Phillips, Sarah. *This Land, This Nation: Conservation, Rural America, and the New Deal*. New York: Cambridge University Press, 2007.

Pierson, Paul. *Dismantling the Welfare State? Reagan, Thatcher, and the Politics of Retrenchment*. Cambridge: Cambridge University Press, 1994.

Piven, Frances Fox, and Richard Cloward. *Regulating the Poor: The Functions of Public Welfare*. New York: Pantheon, 1971.

Poppendieck, Janet. *Breadlines Knee-Deep in Wheat: Food Assistance in the Great Depression*. 2nd ed. Berkeley: University of California Press, 2014.

———. *Free for All: Fixing School Food in America*. Berkeley: University of California Press, 2010.

———. *Sweet Charity: Emergency Food and the End of Entitlement*. New York: Viking, 1998.

Quadagno, Jill. *The Transformation of Old Age Security: Class and Politics in the American Welfare State*. Chicago: University of Chicago Press, 1988.

Riley, Barry. *The Political History of American Food Aid: An Uneasy Benevolence*. New York: Oxford University Press, 2017.

Segal, Judith A. *Food for the Hungry: The Reluctant Society*. Baltimore: Johns Hopkins University Press, 1970.

Sheingate, Adam. *The Rise of the Agricultural Welfare State: Institutions and Interest Group Power in the United States, France, and Japan*. Princeton, NJ: Princeton University Press, 2001.

Skocpol, Theda. *Protecting Soldiers and Mothers: The Political Origins of Social Policy in the United States*. Cambridge, MA: Harvard University Press, 1992.

Wilde, Parke. *Food Policy in the United States: An Introduction*. New York: Routledge, 2013.

Index

ABAWDs. *See* able-bodied adults without dependents

Abernathy, Ralph, 90, 93

able-bodied adults without dependents (ABAWDs), 4, 163–165

abuse. *See* fraud and abuse

administrative burdens, 133, 149, 177

AFDC. *See* Aid to Families with Dependent Children

Affordable Care Act of 2010, 137

Agricultural Act of 1956, 58–59

Agricultural Act of 1958, 61

Agricultural Act of 1970, 102

Agricultural Adjustment Act of 1933, 24

Agricultural Adjustment Act of 1935, 24. *See also* Section 32

agricultural commodities. *See* commodities

Agricultural Improvement Act of 2018, 145

Agricultural Marketing Service (AMS), 72–77

agricultural mindset, 48, 67, 79, 150

agricultural policy: food assistance as byproduct of, 49, 54; vs. food policy, tensions in, 7–8; postwar demographic shift and, 78–79; after World War II, 47, 53–54

agricultural production. *See* production

agricultural trade. *See* trade

Agricultural Trade Development and Assistance Act of 1954 (Public Law 480), 60, 62–66

Agriculture and Consumer Protection Act of 1973, 103

Agriculture and Food Act of 1981, 119–120

agriculture committees. *See* House Committee on Agriculture; Senate Committee on Agriculture, Nutrition, and Forestry

Agriculture Department, US. *See* US Department of Agriculture

Aid to Dependent Children program, 29

Aid to Families with Dependent Children (AFDC) program: under

Block, John, 117
block grants: proposals to convert federal programs into, 129–132, 149; to Puerto Rico, 118–119, 162, 193n35; TANF, 132–133, 162
Blue Apron, 2, 174
blue stamps, 16, 34*fig.*, 73. *See also* Food Stamp Plan
Boll Weevil Democrats, 116
bonus bucks programs, 158
bourbon, 5, 6
Brannan, Charles, 53
Brazil, 5
breadlines, 3, 15, 67
breakfast programs, school, 11. *See also* school meal programs
budget, federal: under Bush (George W.), 135; under Clinton, 127–128; debt ceiling in, 138; deficits in, 122, 127; discretionary spending in, 117, 137, 150; under Reagan, 113–120; reconciliation process for, 117, 127–128, 130, 137; surpluses in, 135
budget, food stamp, 10–11; under Bush (George H. W.), 127; under Carter, 109–110, 114; under Clinton, 127, 129, 133; congressional role in, 12, 89–90; during COVID-19 pandemic, 12, 145; Food Stamp Act on, 89; during Food Stamp Plan era, 38, 42, 43–44; under Johnson, 95; under Nixon, 98, 100, 103–104; under Obama, 137, 141–143; under Reagan, 113–120, 125; state contributions to, 14, 89–90, 103; under Trump, 2, 11, 144–145; by year, 1961–2022, 181–183*table*

budget, USDA: for agricultural vs. nutrition programs, 110; Whitten's hold on, 81. *See also specific programs*
Bush, George H. W., 127
Bush, George W., 135–136, 220n72
Butz, Earl, 102–103

capitalism, 15, 23, 46, 68
Carter, Jimmy, 107–110, 114
cash assistance: direct, 9, 29; end of, 132, 149; during Great Depression, 29, 37, 40; vs. in-kind benefits, 2, 100, 148–149, 176; as modern alternative to food stamps, 175–176; in other countries, 9, 190n17; vs. pilot food stamp program, 76. *See also specific programs*
categorical eligibility, 109, 125, 133
CBS, 93
CCC. *See* Commodity Credit Corporation
Chamber of Commerce, US, 36, 39, 88
charity, food distribution as, 3, 16, 28
cheese: "government," 121–124, 168, 170; imported, 154
Chicago, 27
China, 5, 7
chiseling, 44–45
Chisholm, Shirley, 99, 212n86
chronology of SNAP, 185–187
cities. *See* urban areas
citizens, birthright, 13
Citizens Board of Inquiry into Hunger and Malnutrition in the United States, 93

economic depression, in rural areas in 1960s, 68–69. *See also* Great Depression

economic recessions. *See* recessions

education, nutritional, 159

Eisenhower, Dwight, 57–66; Agricultural Act of 1956 vetoed by, 58–59; in election of 1956, 57; Kennedy's criticism of policies of, 66, 78–79; Needy Families program under, 57, 168, 170; Public Law 480 signed by, 64; Republican continuation of policies of, 69; resistance to food stamps, 17, 58–59, 61, 62; surplus strategies under, 53, 71

elections, federal oversight of, 79. *See also* congressional elections; presidential elections

Electronic Benefits Transfer. *See* EBT

eligibility, food stamp: automatic/categorical, 109, 125, 133; under Bush (George W.), 135; under Clinton, 133; during COVID-19 pandemic, 14; establishment of national standards for, 98; in Food Stamp Plan, 33, 45; under Ford, 105–107; of immigrants, 13, 133, 135–136, 144; under Nixon, 98, 101; in pilot food stamp program, 75; under Reagan, 114, 126; states' role in determining, 83, 89, 92; under Trump, 144; in welfare "reform," 133; of working poor, 101, 134

Ellender, Allen, 87–88, 96

Emerson, Bill, 1, 126

employment. *See* unemployment; work requirements

Energy Policy Act of 2005, 5–6

enrollees, food stamp: cost of stamps to (*See* purchase requirements); demographics of, 13, 161; food pantries visited by, 167; malnutrition in, 155; nutritional outcomes for, 19–20, 147, 153–159; poverty rates for, 13, 161; states' role in approving, 14

enrollees, number of: under Carter, 110; under Nixon, 104; under Reagan, 114, 117–118; under Trump, 11, 145; by year, 1961–2022, 181–183*table*

ethanol, plant-based, 5–6

European Union, 5

executive orders, 70–71

FAIR. *See* Federal Agricultural Improvement and Reform Act

Families First Coronavirus Response Act of 2020, 165

Family Assistance Plan, 100–101, 108, 175

farm bills: definition of, 4; first omnibus version of, 61; reauthorization of Food Stamp Act in, 78, 99–104, 135; in resilience of food stamps, 150–151. *See also specific laws*

farm bills, attempts to remove food stamps from, 134–145; in 1981, 119–120, 131; in 1996, 131; in 2012, 140–141; in 2014, 113, 141–143; in 2018, 113, 143–145

farmers: commodity distribution as program for, 39, 43; food stamps as taking money of, 81, 89, 95; foreign food aid as program for, 63; paid not to produce, 24; perverse incentives for, 5–6, 23; trade mitigation payments to, 6; views on commodity distribution, 39; views on Food Stamp Plan, 39–40; views on supply management, 30; welfare for, 126

Farmers to Families Food Box Program, 3*fig.*, 7, 170–175, 174*fig.*

farms, reduction in number and consolidation of, 68–69

Farm Security and Rural Investment Act of 2002, 135

Federal Agricultural Improvement and Reform Act (FAIR) of 1996, 131–132

federal budget. *See* budget, federal

Federal Emergency Management Administration (FEMA), 176

Federal Emergency Relief Administration, 29

federal government shutdowns, 145

Federal Surplus Commodities Corporation (FSCC): and cash assistance, 29; in Food Stamp Plan, 31, 33; integration into USDA, 42; in purchase and distribution of surplus food, 25–26; Surplus Marketing Corporation as successor to, 35

Federal Surplus Relief Corporation. *See* Federal Surplus Commodities Corporation

Feeding America, 124, 167–168

FEMA, 176

feminist critique of Food Stamp Plan, 44

Ferejohn, John, 119, 120, 150

financial crisis of 1998, Asian, 135

Finegold, Kenneth, 117, 160

Foley, Thomas, 105, 107–108

Food, Conservation, and Energy Act of 2008, 136, 220n72

food-allotment bills, 50–51, 54, 56, 66

Food and Agriculture Act of 1977, 109, 122

Food and Nutrition Service, USDA, 99, 107, 155

food assistance: as byproduct of agricultural policy, 49, 54; vs. food production, in USDA mission, 11; to foreign countries, 60, 63–65, 68, 71; origins and development of programs for, 9; SNAP as percentage of spending on, 11; spending on, under Nixon, 98; spending on, under Reagan, 120; USDA's role in administration of, 11. *See also specific programs*

food banks, 6, 124, 166–170

food boxes. *See* Farmers to Families; Harvest Box

food consumption. *See* consumption

Food Distribution Administration, 42

food drives, 168

Food for Peace program, 65, 68, 71, 85, 95

food industry, in resilience of food stamps, 20, 151–152

food insecurity: in COVID-19 pandemic, 7, 11–12, 14; definition of, 11; impact of SNAP on, 159 food pantries, 6, 124, 166–170, 169*fig.*

food policy, vs. agricultural policy, tensions in, 7–8

food production. *See* production

Food Research and Action Center (FRAC), 3, 105

food reserve, strategic, 69

food restrictions: on "bad" foods, 154–158; in Food Stamp Act, 88, 154; in Food Stamp Plan, 34–35, 40–41, 44–45; on "luxury" foods, 88, 154, 178–179; in pilot food stamp program, 73, 75; recommendations on changes to, 178–179; in SNAP, 12, 153–159; in WIC, 153–157

Food Security Act of 1985, 109, 125

Food Stamp Act of 1964, 18, 79–90; amendments of 1970–1971 to, 98–99, 102; amendments of 1973 to, 103, 105; amendments of 1974 to, 106; amendments of 1977 to, 108–110, 112, 125; Contract with America on repeal of, 129; costs and funding sources for, 81–82, 89; in farm bills (*See* farm bills); food restrictions in, 88, 154; Johnson's signing of, 80*fig.*, 88–89; movement of bill through Congress, 77, 79–88; origins of SNAP in, 12; postwar shift in rural vs. urban political power in, 79; preamble to, text of, 80, 153; requirement for reauthorization of, 89; significance of passage of, 89–90. *See also* Food Stamp Program

food stamp budget. *See* budget

Food Stamp Division, USDA, 72

food stamp enrollees. *See* enrollees

Food Stamp Plan (1939–1943), 31–47; analysis of effectiveness of, 43–47; authorship of, 31; business support for, 33, 36, 37*fig.*, 39–40; chronology of key moments in, 185; critics of, 40–41; duration of, 38; eligibility for, 33, 45; enrollees' opinion of, 41; expansion and reach of, 33, 38, 45; legal authority under Section 32 for, 35, 38, 44, 72; lessons learned from, in pilot food stamp program, 72–73, 82; mechanisms of, 33–36; name of, 33; number of enrollees in, 38, 45; orange and blue stamps in, 16, 34–35, 34*fig.*, 73; origins and development of, 31–33, 38; promotion of, 32*fig.*; public support for, 39–40; restrictions on purchases in, 34–35, 40–41, 44–45; rollout in Rochester, 16, 33; spending on, 38, 42, 43–44; termination of, 41–42, 46, 48

Food Stamp Program (FSP, 1964–2008), 88–146; chronology of key moments in, 185–187; costs for enrollees (*See* purchase requirements); eligibility for (*See* eligibility); expansion of, 89, 95, 100, 103–104; vs. Family Assistance Plan, 100–101; hunger as unintended consequence of, 90–96; as official name until 2008, 10, 136; participation rates in, 92, 104; passage of law establishing, 88–90 (*See also* Food

Stamp Act); reauthorization of, 89, 94, 99-104, 135; spending on, 95, 97, 98, 100, 103; states opting out of, 89, 92; states' role in, 89-90, 92, 103. *See also* SNAP; *specific politicians*

food stamps, 34*fig.*, 121*fig.*; authorship of concept of, 31; chronology of key moments in, 185-187; as form of commodity, 103, 109, 111, 120; as form of guaranteed annual income, 101; impacts on nutrition, 19-20, 147, 153-159; impacts on poverty, 14-16, 159-165, 178; as income supplement (*See* income supplement); as in-kind benefit, 2, 100, 130, 148-149, 176; paradox of want amidst plenty in origins of, 7-8, 21-25; in political party platforms, 57; primer on, 10-16; reasons for resilience of, 19, 113, 147-153; recommendations for improving, 177-179; vs. SNAP, use of terms, 2, 10, 191n19; as welfare (*See* welfare). *See also* Food Stamp Plan; Food Stamp Program; SNAP

food stamps, alternatives to. *See* alternatives

food stamps, postwar revival of, 17-18, 48-77; Agricultural Marketing Service in, 72-77; business opposition to, 58; congressional bills in 1940s proposing, 48-51; congressional bills in 1950s proposing, 57-65; eligibility for, 75; Kennedy's pilot programs in, 71-76, 74*fig.*, 81-83;

rediscovery of hunger in, 65-70; Sullivan's demonstration projects in, 62-64; USDA lack of interest in, 48-49, 53-57; USDA report on feasibility of, 59

Ford, Gerald, 105-107

FRAC. *See* Food Research and Action Center

fraud and abuse of food stamps: under Clinton, 134; under Ford, 106-107; media coverage of, 106; under Reagan, 114-115, 118, 122

Freedom Caucus, 144

Freeman, Orville: and funding for food stamps, 82, 95, 97; and hunger, 93; on Needy Families program, 71; in passage of Food Stamp Act, 77, 82, 84, 92; in pilot food stamp program, 72, 74, 76, 77; on surpluses, 68

FSCC. *See* Federal Surplus Commodities Corporation

FSP. *See* Food Stamp Program

Gallup, George, 39

General Accounting Office, 33

"generational dependence," 128

Gingrich, Newt: in attempts to remove food stamps from farm bills, 131; and block grants, 130, 149; in Contract with America, 127; in election of 1994, 127; and Freedom Caucus, 144; and Tea Party, 137; on welfare reform, 125

"government cheese," 121-124, 168, 170

government shutdowns, 145

Nathan, Richard, 147
National American Wholesale
Grocers Association, 28, 31
National Corn-Hog Committee of
Twenty-Five, 21
National Council of Farmer
Cooperatives, 50–51, 54
National Dairy Council, 154
National Farmers Union, 24, 58, 88
National Food Allotment Plan. *See*
allotment bills
National Food and Grocery
Conference Committee, 33
National Milk Producers Federation,
154
National Nutrition Council, 49
National Nutrition Survey, 94,
97–98
National Retail Dry Goods Associa-
tion, 29
National Retail Merchants Associa-
tion, 28
National School Lunch Program,
11, 53. *See also* school meal
programs
Needy Families program, 57, 71, 168,
170. *See also* TANF
New Deal: Chamber of Commerce
on, 39; and distribution of
surplus food, 24, 30; Keynesian
economics in, 37. *See also specific*
programs
New York, 16, 33
New York Times (newspaper), 65
Nixon, Richard, 97–104; in election
of 1960, 78; in election of 1968,
97; Family Assistance Plan of,
100–101, 108, 175; Food Stamp

Program under, 98–104; on
hunger, 97–98; White House
Conference on Food, Nutrition,
and Health under, 99, 101, 165
North American Free Trade
Agreement of 1992, 5
nutrition: analysis of SNAP's impact
on, 19–20, 147, 153–159; in Food
Stamp Plan, 43; in Harvest Box,
2–3, 154; in healthy incentives
programs, 158–159; and military
draft, 30, 49; in pilot food stamp
program, 74; Reagan's budget cuts
and, 117; SNAP as percentage of
federal spending on, 11; USDA
spending on agricultural programs
vs., 110; in WIC, 153–157; during
World War II, 30, 49, 50. *See also*
malnutrition
Nutrition Incentives Program, 158
Nutrition Reform and Work
Opportunity Act of 2013, 141

Obama, Barack, 137–142
obesity, 154
OBRA. *See* Omnibus Budget
Reconciliation Act
Office of Management and Budget,
2–3, 117
Ohio, 27, 77
Ohls, James, 168
Okies, 24
Omnibus Budget Reconciliation Act
(OBRA) of 1981, 117–120, 126
orange stamps, 16, 34*fig.*, 73. *See also*
Food Stamp Plan
Oregon, 14
outreach efforts, 105, 117, 126

production-management programs: Democratic views on, 54–55, 68–69, 103; in Great Depression, 24, 30; postwar, 53–55; Republican views on, 54–55, 62

Project Bread, 167

prunes, 34–35

PRWORA. *See* Personal Responsibility and Work Opportunity Reconciliation Act

Public Law 88-525. *See* Food Stamp Act of 1964

Public Law 480. *See* Agricultural Trade Development and Assistance Act of 1954

public opinion: on Aid to Families with Dependent Children, 128–129; on Food Stamp Plan, 39–40; of pilot food stamp program, 76; on stamps used for "luxury" foods, 106; on welfare, 113

Puerto Rico: food-assistance block grant to, 118–119, 162, 193n35; Food Stamp Plan in, 38; Food Stamp Program in, 102; and pilot food stamp program, 73; recommendations on return to SNAP, 178

purchase requirements: in Food Stamp Act, 88, 98; in Food Stamp Plan, 36, 38, 40–41, 45–46; in pilot food stamp program, 73, 76

purchase requirements, in Food Stamp Program: attempts to reinstate, 119; as barrier to use, 91; end of, 104–110; reductions in, 95, 98–101

purchase restrictions. *See* food restrictions

racial discrimination, and Kennedy's food stamp bill, 83–84

racial segregation, 83

Rayburn, Sam, 63

Reagan, Ronald, 113–126, 116*fig.*; block grants to Puerto Rico under, 118–119, 162; budget cuts under, 113–120, 125; budget reconciliation under, 117, 127; cheese surplus under, 121–124; in election of 1980, 114; eligibility for food stamps under, 114, 126; fraud and abuse under, 114–115, 118, 122

recessions: of 1938, 30; in 1970s, 104; in 1980s, 120–121, 125; in 1990s, 127; of 2007–9, 137, 161

recipients, food stamp. *See* enrollees

reconciliation, budget, 117, 127–128, 130, 137

relief agencies: food distribution through, 3, 27, 53; on Food Stamp Act, 88; in Food Stamp Plan, 35, 37, 39; on pilot food stamp program, 76

Republican members of Congress: in Contract with America, 127, 129, 137; on converting federal programs into block grants, 129–132; in elections (*See* congressional elections); on food stamps as welfare, 83, 112–113; Freedom Caucus of, 144; midwestern, views on surpluses, 54–55; in passage of Food Stamp Act, 81, 83–86; in Pledge to

Republican members of Congress
(continued)
America, 137; on production
management, 54–55, 62; in
Reagan's budget cuts, 115–116,
119; on shrinking of safety net,
112–113; on strategic food reserve,
69; Tea Party in, 137, 144. *See also
specific members*
Republican Party: food stamps and
surpluses in platform of, 39, 57;
National Convention of 2020, 173
Richmond, Fred, 104, 108–109
Ripley, Randall, 85–87
Roberts, Pat, 130–132, 143
Rochester, 16, 33
Roosevelt, Eleanor, 22, 41
Roosevelt, Franklin, 22–24, 49
rural areas: depression in 1960s in,
68–69; Food Stamp Plan in, 34, 39;
pilot food stamp program in, 83;
postwar political power of, vs.
urban areas, 78–79
rural Democrats: in coalition with
urban Democrats, 104, 108–109,
120, 125; in elections of 1974, 105;
on foreign food aid, 63; opposition
to food stamps, 61–63; in passage
of Food Stamp Act, 85
Rush, Bobby, 178
Rust Belt, 121

safety net: need for, 112; Reagan's
cuts to, 114, 118; Republican
efforts to shrink, 112–113; role of
food stamps in, 113, 148, 153
sales taxes, 38
Schanzenbach, Diane, 158, 162–163

school meal programs: challenges of
food distribution to, 27; current
spending on SNAP vs., 11;
Kennedy's executive orders on,
71; postwar food distribution to,
53; Reagan's cuts to, 118
Schumacher, Gus, 158
"Scrooge stamps," 91
Second Harvest, 124
Section 32 of Agricultural Adjustment Act: cash assistance under,
29; on domestic consumption,
25–26, 29; Food Stamp Plan under,
35, 38, 44, 72; and Food Stamp
Program, 95; Kennedy's food
stamp pilot program under, 72;
Kennedy's proposed bill under,
80–81; purchase and distribution
of food under, 25–26, 29; source of
funding for, 25; underspent funds
under Benson, 56–57
Senate, US: bipartisan conservative
coalition in, 79, 81; elections for
(*See* congressional elections);
hearings on hunger in, 95–96;
political power of rural vs. urban
areas in, 79; in Reagan's budget
cuts, 117; reorganization of
committee system of, 110. *See also*
Democratic members; Republican
members; *specific laws and
members*
Senate Committee on Agriculture,
Nutrition, and Forestry: on
allotment bills, 50; changes after
elections of 1974, 106; changes
after elections of 1980, 115–116;
Food Stamp Act in, 87–88; Food

Stamp Act reauthorizations in, 103, 135; jurisdiction shared with House Committee on Banking and Currency, 200n5; midwestern Republicans vs. southern Democrats in, 55; postwar shift in political power and, 79; on purchase requirements, 108; Reagan's budget cuts in, 119; reorganization and renaming of, 110; resistance to food stamps in, 49, 58; in Select Committee on Nutrition and Human Needs, 95. *See also specific laws and members*

Senate Committee on Labor and Public Welfare, 95

Senate Finance Committee, 58

Senate Select Committee on Nutrition and Human Needs, 95–98, 110

Senate Subcommittee on Nutrition, 110, 116, 119, 126

Senate Subcommittee on Poverty, 92

sharecroppers, 29, 37, 81, 90

shutdowns, government, 145

Sibelius, Keith, 222n100

single mothers, 127–128

Smeeding, Timothy, 162, 164, 179

Smith, Howard, 81, 86, 87

SNAP (2008–present): chronology of key moments in, 185–187; vs. food stamps, use of terms, 2, 10, 191n19; impacts on nutrition, 19–20, 147, 153–159; impacts on poverty, 14–16, 159–165, 178; as largest food-assistance program, 10–11; logo of, 10*fig.*; primer on, 10–16; reasons for resilience of,

19, 113, 147–153; recommendations for improving, 177–179. *See also* food stamps

SNAP-Ed program, 159, 174

SNAP Gap, 155, 167, 169, 177

Social Security Act of 1935, 29

Social Security Amendments of 1956, 58

Social Security benefits, 13

social-welfare agencies and organizations: on Family Assistance Plan, 100; on Food Stamp Act, 88; in Food Stamp Plan, 33, 46; on postwar revival of food stamps, 58; on Reagan's budget cuts, 118

social workers, 28, 37, 40

soda, 154, 156–158

soup kitchens, 176

South Carolina, 97

southern Democrats: opposition to food stamps, 83; in passage of Food Stamp Act, 84–86; in Senate Select Committee on Nutrition, 95–96; views on civil rights, 83; views on surpluses, 54–55

southern states: exploitation in agriculture of, 29; Food Stamp Plan in, 34; malnutrition in, 49; migration to northern cities from, 90–91

Soviet Union, 68

soybeans, 5

Special Milk Program, 53, 72

spending. *See* budget

states, US: allocation of House seats by, 79; block grants to (*See* block grants); costs of SNAP paid by, 14,

urban Democrats: in coalition with rural Democrats, 104, 108–109, 120, 125; in House Committee on Agriculture, 60; in passage of Food Stamp Act, 84–87; postwar demographic shift and, 79; in postwar revival of food stamps, 56–62

US Department of Agriculture (USDA): food insecurity defined by, 11; integration of FSCC into, 42; mission of, 11, 157; views on food restrictions in, 157–158. *See also specific programs*

US Department of Health, Education, and Welfare, 58, 83, 98, 108

USFoods, 172

Vermont, 55
Vietnam War, 93
Virgin Islands, US, 102, 193n35
voters, Black, 87, 97
Voting Rights Act of 1965, 79

Walk for Hunger, 167
Wallace, Henry A.: on distribution of surplus foods, 21, 24–25; in Food Stamp Plan, 31–33; on paradox of want amidst plenty, 190n15; on pork surplus, 22; on two-price system, 28–29, 31, 35, 176
Walmart, 20
War on Poverty, 84, 88
Washington (state), 14
Washington, DC, 38, 193n35
waste, in surplus-commodity distribution, 27–28
Waugh, Fred, 31, 50, 70

Weill, Jim, 3–4
welfare: corporate, 15; for farmers, 126; fraud and abuse in, 115; public opinion on, 113; SNAP enrollees receiving, 13
welfare, food stamps as, 18–19, 112–146; Chamber of Commerce on, 88; under Reagan, 113–124; welfare "reform" and, 113, 125–134. *See also* farm bills, attempts to remove food stamps from
"welfare queens," 115
West Virginia: Food Stamp Plan in, 38; hunger in, 66, 67; in Kennedy's election, 70, 78; Needy Families in, 71; pilot food stamp program in, 72, 74, 76
wheat: distribution under Hoover, 28, 170; and passage of Food Stamp Act, 85–87; postwar government purchases of, 53; prices during Great Depression, 23
wheat-cotton bill, 85–87
White House Conference on Food, Nutrition, and Health (1969), 99, 101, 165
White House Conference on Hunger, Nutrition, and Health (2022), 165–166
Whitten, Jamie: duration of service in Congress, 87; after elections of 1974, 105–106; on Food Stamp Program, 95, 100; in passage of Food Stamp Act, 81, 87; and poverty, 92; in USDA spending, 81; views on food stamps, 81, 87
WIC, 153–157, 224n19
Wisconsin, 55

work, incentives for/against, 15, 20,
163–165
working poor, 101, 118, 134–135, 161
work requirements: in 1970s, 102; in
1980s, 125; in 2010s, 4; analysis of
effects of, 163–165; lack of enforce-
ment of, 102; state requests for
waivers of, 164–165
Works Progress Administration, 30
World War II: agricultural policies

after, 47, 53–54; food prices in,
42, 49; food stamps after (*See*
food stamps, postwar revival
of); malnutrition during, 30,
49, 50
Wyoming, 14

Yang, Crystal, 163

Ziliak, James, 161

Founded in 1893,
UNIVERSITY OF CALIFORNIA PRESS
publishes bold, progressive books and journals
on topics in the arts, humanities, social sciences,
and natural sciences—with a focus on social
justice issues—that inspire thought and action
among readers worldwide.

The UC PRESS FOUNDATION
raises funds to uphold the press's vital role
as an independent, nonprofit publisher, and
receives philanthropic support from a wide
range of individuals and institutions—and from
committed readers like you. To learn more, visit
ucpress.edu/supportus.